NEGOTIATING NORMALITY

NEGOTIATING NORMALITY

Everyday Lives in Socialist Institutions

DANIELA KOLEVA

editor

Transaction Publishers
New Brunswick (U.S.A.) and London (U.K.)

First paperback printing, 2015

Copyright © 2012 by Transaction Publishers, New Brunswick, New Jersey.

This book is printed on acid-free paper that meets the American National Standard for Permanence of Paper for Printed Library Materials.

Library of Congress Catalog Number: 2011042482
ISBN: 978-1-4128- 4601-1 (cloth); 978-1-4128-5583-9 (paper)
Printed in the United States of America

Library of Congress Cataloging-in-Publication Data

Negotiating normality: everyday lives in socialist institutions / Daniela Koleva, editor.
    p. cm.
Includes index.
ISBN 978-1-4128-4601-1
1. Communist countries—Social conditions. 2. Communist countries—Economic conditions. 3. Socialism—Communist countries. 4. Communism. I. Koleva, Daniela.
  HN960.N44 2012
  306.0947—dc23

2011042482

Contents

Introduction
Socialist Normality: Euphemization of Power or Profanation of Power?

Daniela Koleva

There is nothing to tell, really. My life's been just . . . normal.
Opening of a Life Story (2000)
We've had a normal life—a good one, that is.
Conclusion of a Life Story (2008)

This book[1] does not ask what socialism is; it asks what it is to have lived through it. In foregrounding everyday experience, it offers a perspective on socialism not as a political system but rather as a kind of "ecosystem," a dense fabric of dynamic, though unbalanced, interactions between institutional regulations and people regulated. The case studies from several former socialist countries focus on the translation of socialism's major ideological principles into motives guiding people's lives. They are grouped around three common elements—socialist labor, the new socialist man, the socialist way of life—employing micro-perspectives to interpret sites of heterogeneity and ambivalence. Based on firsthand accounts, they look for minute deviations from the norms that have eventually led to renegotiation of the norms themselves. Focusing on routines, rather than extremes, they seek to understand socialism in its "normal state."

But What Does "Normal" Mean?

Of course, none of the persons cited above was asked this question. Normal people do not do so. At least, not in normal situations. They know the answer. Perhaps they cannot easily spell it out, but they can definitely—albeit intuitively—tell any deviations from the normal. And this is just enough. It is not their task to translate intuitions into concepts.

I however need to start with a concept. A concept is a word differing from most other words in that it is related to an institutional order (in the broad sense, including research paradigms). I shall start with the concept of norm and will then try to relate it to a specific institutional order (in the strict sense) and cultural code, that of state socialism.

"Norm" seems to be a key concept to think about culture, for culture has often been conceived of in terms of norms and normativity. This is where intricacies start, for the concept of norm has a certain spell. It means different things, which eventually turn out to be not so different. According to the dictionary, the first meaning of "norm" is "standard, model, pattern, type" (The Concise Oxford Dictionary—7th ed.). The derivatives are "normal," that is, compliant with the norm, corresponding to the standard, customary, regular (of a person—mentally and physically healthy), and "normative," that is, defining/imposing norms and standards. On the one hand, the word "norm" and its derivatives have a neutral descriptive connotation referring to statistical averages, to what is widespread and usual. On the other hand, norm is a criterion, a standard to measure up to, something to be achieved or preserved. This idea of correspondence/compliance with standards imports another connotation, that of correctness. Thus it turns out that the apparently neutral description contains a trace of judgment as well.

This ambiguity can be detected in the very etymology of the concept and in its various uses.[2] The Latin word *norma* meant a carpenter's square, so "normal" meant (and still does, in geometry) standing at right angle, orthogonal. As a geometry concept, it just describes a position. However, the word "right" and the root "ortho-" (its Greek equivalent) connote that this position is somehow also correct. Thus judgment seems to sneak into the description.[3] This is the spell of the words "norm" and "normal"—that they not only describe the actual state of things but also tacitly refer to a desirable state. They point not only to how things are, but also to how they should be. Even more, this correspondence/compliance in its turn also has a double meaning: on the one hand, it can be a "technical" correspondence, that is, correspondence to standards. On the other hand, it also contains the notion of ethical compliance, of moral correctness and righteousness. Thus it refers implicitly to the idea of justice. As a result, "normal" (as common, average, habitual) turns out to be at the same time "normative" (i.e., socially desirable). Although the distinction between fact and value, between the actual and the due, should be evident and indisputable, the concept of norm seems to elude such a logic.

As philosopher Ian Hacking has observed, contemporary ideas of normality as the statistical average excluding both positive and negative extremes were generated by the erosion of determinist conceptions during the last two centuries. Hacking sees a connection between the rise of statistical laws in lieu of determinism, on the one hand, and the rise of the idea of normality and deviation, on the other. No longer signaling a deficit of knowledge, indeterminism has become a kind of law—the law of chance—creating order out of chaos, as any law does. Thus the idea of normality, stemming from the nineteenth-century cultural and intellectual climate, has come to replace the earlier idea of "the nature of man."

Initially, normality was institutionalized through medical texts and practices. The contemporary meaning of the word was derived from the semantic pair "pathological–normal" as used in medicine. Pathology, which drew physicians' attention at the turn of the nineteenth century, dealt not with the sick organism as a whole but with the sick organ, subject to study and treatment. One of the first physicians to promote this approach was F.-J.-V. Broussais (1772–1838) in France. According to Broussais, illness was caused by the pathological state of an organ, which differed from its normal state not in kind but in intensity. That is why it was necessary to study the pathologies of the organs and to find ways to bring them back to their normal state. Thus "normal" was the secondary notion, while the primary one was that of pathology. Much ridiculed by Balzac (who thereby perhaps paved the way for the term "normal state" into common language), Broussais was respected by another contemporary, positivist philosopher Auguste Comte (1798–1857), who adapted his principle to the study of the "collective organism." With this extrapolation, the relation was reversed: The notion of normality became the leading one, from which all characteristics of the "object" had to be derived, and pathology was conceived as a deviation from the normal state. This implied that the normal was the center from which all deviations started. Therefore, paradoxically, although "pathology" was the opposite of "norm," they turned out eventually *not* to be radically different from one another. The normal started to appear as the minimum and the optimum, the limit and the center at the same time. The idea of the smooth transition from normal to pathological state and back lent a quasi-natural character to the process and screened out the issue of responsibility for it, no matter whether the "object" belonged to the realm of medicine or to that of sociology.

Normality as Euphemization of Power

As the idea of normality was transferred to the social and political sphere, a shift of meaning occurred: "the normal" was no longer identified just as an ordinary (non-pathological) state but rather as a desirable one, one that had to be achieved and preserved. As Hacking has observed, Comte's positivism did not point "to an existing norm and certainly not to an average. It was the only politically viable road to the 'true normal state.'"[4] The fact-value ambiguity of the term "normal" generated the tension between description and prescription inherent in the idea of normality. "That is why—Hacking concludes— the benign and sterile-sounding word 'normal' has become one of the most powerful ideological tools of the twentieth century."[5] Moreover, it has also turned out to be one of the most effective ethical reference points in modern culture.[6]

Hacking has demonstrated the dependence of this idea of normality, expressed in the notions of normal individual, normal society, normal life, normal crime rate, and so on, on what might be called a politics of measurement applied by statistics. Individuals (or life, or society) are normal if they are in line with statistically established tendencies. That is, statistical laws seem to slip from mere description into the position of moral indicators. They not only measure the "quantum of happiness" or "quantum of sickness" but also seem to establish by this very procedure what happiness or sickness is. Furthermore, because of the constitutive correlation "norm–deviation," data on deviations acquire crucial importance for both theory (to articulate what normality is) and practice (to impose it on deviant populations). Thus, the idea of normality, originating from the legitimization of indeterminacy and chance, generates in its turn the necessity for control and a new technology of social engineering in response to it.

These consequences have been elucidated by Michel Foucault. He has highlighted "the power of the Norm" as a "new law" in modern society where, in addition to surveillance, normalization has become a major instrument of power. In his analysis of the genealogy of power/knowledge relations in the field of juridical medicine, Foucault has demonstrated how this logic works: the psychiatric expertise substitutes the medical issue of identifying and diagnosing pathology for the legal issue of establishing guilt and responsibility. In this way, the legally responsible individual is replaced by the "correlative element of a normalizing method."[7] The psychiatric discourse sets apart illness and responsibility, treatment and punishment, but subsumes them under the same normalizing power (acting through different institutions—the clinic or the prison). At the same time, both jurisprudence and psychiatry seem to deal with the category of the "abnormal" conceptualized as a gradation from norm to pathology/deviation rather than as an opposition between them. Thus, the "normal" is again correlative with the abnormal/deviant, standing in opposition to it (as good to evil) and at the same time merging into it (through the distribution of all behavior between the poles of the normal/good and the abnormal/bad).[8] This "technology of anomaly," that is, of applying norms as a means of exercising power, makes this power opaque:[9] it looks as if it is "objective," as if it has no possessor, no agent, no direction, no privileged place. As a result, the whole "indefinite domain of the non-conforming is punishable"[10] by default, automatically.

The emergence of this new technology of power to replace and/or complement direct coercion can be also described using Bourdieu's concept of *euphemization*, as applied in a more general context by James Scott,[11] to refer to subtle ways of exercising power, which are unrecognizable as such and consequently—socially recognized.[12] "Normality" adds a patina of conformity and "natural-ness" to socially constructed phenomena. The knowledge about the normal is *doxa*, that is, one that rests on taken-for-grantedness, not on argumentation. The technologies of euphemized institutional power rely not only on the internalization and habitualization of ideological guidelines but also on counting, measuring, and classification. The regularities expressed by numbers are based on "new technologies for classifying and enumerating and new bureaucracies with the authority and continuity to deploy the technology."[13] That is, euphemization of power through the idea of normality depends on the existence of categories for what is to be counted, measured, and classified and on the continuity of institutions to introduce and sustain them. The power to classify is the power to define what is normal and what is deviant. Modern state institutions have used it to control populations—primarily those that have been considered to be in need of control: the deviant, the marginal, the poor. Research has proved that techniques initially developed for surveillance of delinquents have tended to be applied, with time, to all citizens[14] to ensure what James Scott has termed the "legibility" of populations for the sake of caring and control: only when specific categories of people (such as schoolchildren or women or workers) and specific life situations (such as maternity or unemployment) are identified, it is possible to take differential care of them by establishing appropriate structures and training personnel to staff them.[15] This "bureaucratic rationality" based on "abstraction and routinization" (Douglas)[16] relies on aggregate and standardized facts, omitting the uniqueness of individual circumstances in favor of a synoptic view.[17] Thereby, the institutional thinking imports in actual life situations a clarity and a fixity they do not really possess. Institutional thinking operates with "thin" categories, which are to a significant extent arbitrary. Once adopted, however, they tend to "forget" their own fictionality and to operate as if the situations or individuals falling in a certain category were indeed homogeneous. What is even more important, people gradually accept the labels: they start to recognize themselves in the categories imposed on them, to develop ideas of what is normal for "their" category, and to try to live up to it. Thus the "stylized facts" (Scott) invented by institutions to a great extent actually *create* the reality they claim to only describe and measure. Labels invented by bureaucrats "can end up by becoming categories that organize people's daily experience precisely because they are embedded in state-created institutions that structure that experience. The economic plan, survey map, record of ownership, forest management plan, classification of ethnicity, passbook, arrest record, and map of political boundaries acquire their force from the fact that these synoptic data are the points of departure for reality as state officials apprehend and shape it."[18]

Euphemization means that power is redefined in quasi-therapeutic terms: instead of direct coercion, it operates through establishing what normality is and preventing deviations. It only draws the outer borders of the normal, where the "perpetual penalty" seems to function automatically: it "compares, differentiates, hierarchizes, homogenizes, excludes. In short, it normalizes."[19] This redefinition of power entails a reduction of politics to mere administration. Euphemized power looks like pure technology, not like ideology. But its "neutral," technical practices such as classification, measurement, and statistics turn out to function as "value-giving" and therefore normative. Thus, social normality (what most people do) turns out to be social normativity (guidance, standard of correctness). The normal takes on the character of the *due* (what we ought to do) and the *good* (what we imagine as a goal).

Communist Power and Socialist Normality

Turning to communist power, I am interested only in the management of people, not in politics or economy. Likewise, I am not interested in the ideology or the system, but in the dynamic relations of power, what has been called micro-politics or, perhaps better, infra-politics. However, to apply these lower-case concepts to grasp "lower-case" realities, one has to refer also to the (upper-case) notions of ideology, politics and norm—not in terms of their coherence of meaning, but rather in terms of their implementation.

To ensure control over society, communist regimes employed not only "stick-and-carrot" methods, that is, repressions for the opponents and privileges for the loyal, but also a more sophisticated mode of control based on ideological models (social welfare as the foremost duty of the state: "all in the name of man, all for the well-being of man"), moral imperatives (work "for the benefit of society," i.e., as a civic obligation), societal norms (e.g., related to the "socialist way of life"), and a vast symbolic production articulating them.[20] In addition to all these, a host of administrative practices were developed, which ensured effective surveillance: personal documents including extensive data on the individual's residence, workplace, and so on, residence permits, control on movement, categories of social identification, which were far from neutral ("worker," "peasant-worker," "collectivized peasant," "kulak," etc.).[21] This form of diffuse power, seemingly having no agent and no locus, is also a version of euphemized power (power of the norm). The normative control worked through the framing of all possible definitions of what one was and what one ought to do—definitions that could not be contested. It precluded alternative imaginings of social conditions thereby contributing to the legitimation of the existing ones. Thus the very existence of the regime over the years had the effect of stabilizing it by ruling out alternatives (even ideas of alternatives); as Raymond Aron has noted, "the established institution has a tremendous advantage—that it exists."[22]

The concept of normality seems to offer a way out of the dichotomy of ideological model and lived experiences. The margin where the norms generated by ideology (the "official" ones) meet those generated by practices, or turn into such, is what I call socialist normality. Thus, normality bridges the actual and the due, the practice and the project, the "is" and the "must." While "normalization" is a concept that captures the impact of the institutions on individuals, their lives and their thinking, the concept of normality attempts to grasp these processes from the point of view of the individuals and to capture the constraints of their space of action and their maneuverings in it. The focus on normality foregrounds the everyday, the informal and the private, keeping an eye at the same time on the forms of its public legitimation, that is, its social and moral significance. Thus it links not to the "grand narrative" of socialism as modernization but rather to the far less visible side of the historical drama: the aspect of control and (self-imposed) normalization.

What is the specificity of socialist normality compared with the "universal" scheme described above? First, perhaps its all-embracing grip and the lack of alternatives. Even if modern institutions may have "thought" in, largely, the same way everywhere, they have functioned in different settings. With no intermediary between state institutions and individuals, with the regime's full grasp over the social sphere, with the party-state's power unbalanced by a civil society, with the strong centralization of state power, the conditions were in place for the institutions' imaginary to be given a real social life. Socialism as a modernization project implies not only "catching-up" efforts[23] but also rationalization and disciplining inspired by an administrative utopianism. In socialist settings, there could hardly be a viable alternative to the institutionally designed normality. Both the scope and the nature of institutional control make the coercive aspect of modernization relevant for considering its manifestations in any sphere, including individual life courses and everyday lives. Citizens had to relate to the state in almost every role or activity of theirs. Furthermore, the state not merely set universal rules for its citizens to follow in the course of their actions; it undertook to define their needs (on a scientific basis, of course) and to satisfy them. As shown in the contributions to this volume, it expanded way beyond the political sphere proper interfering into production, consumption, employment, education, health, housing, leisure, and so on. This "socialist paternalism" (Verdery) brought about a total dependence of the individuals on the state. Socialist bureaucracy possessed a unique power stemming from the accumulation of resources to be redistributed and from the control on their redistribution. Like a benevolent father, it identified people's needs and took measures to both satisfy them and discourage individuals from taking the initiative and do so themselves. While this social contract ensured certain legitimacy to communist regimes,[24] its result was that the state actually robbed the social actors of their power to act. Thus the party-state ended up governing people and at the same time representing their interests. Any attempt at an alternative representation was a threat insofar as it called into question the claims of the party-state. Thus the margins of acceptable deviations from the institutionally established normality were extremely narrow. Every deviation, for that matter, was considered pathological.

Next, while modern institutions may have applied the same bureaucratic technologies everywhere, their rationale has been informed by different projects. Therefore, another specificity of socialist normality was that it was apparently borrowed from utopia. A utopia coming down from the European Enlightenment, but alternative to the liberal modernization of the West: ensuring a rapid economic development, yet retaining moral superiority. Like any utopia, it "acted" on behalf of universal ideas, giving one answer to all possible questions, and a categorical one. This resulted in a heavy disbalance in the direction of normativity. "Normal life" had to significantly, if not entirely, overlap with the ideologically informed project. The "normal state" of society had to be exemplary; it could not be left to emerge according to the laws of probability embodied in institutional practices. It could not be left to shape itself after statistical averages. Quite the other way round: this ideal normal state was a target to be reached by the statistical averages. Utopia was being translated into life too literally, too straightforwardly. Perhaps this utopian thrust was the reason to equate development with warfare requiring successive heroic mobilizations, which made everyday life appear not simply residual but almost pathological, not just politically irrelevant but politically incongruous.[25] The politicization of work, consumption, procreation, and so on—virtually all spheres of live—made it impossible to distinguish politics from nonpolitics. On the one hand, everything was politics insofar as everything could have a meaning that transcended its actuality (even a can of tomatoes could be a nail in the coffin of world capitalism, according to a slogan from the 1950s in a Bulgarian cannery). On the other hand, only depoliticized individual reactions to power were possible rather than collective actions; thus the suppression of participation—of which the Czechoslovak post-1968 "normalization" is perhaps the paradigmatic case—led to actual depoliticization.

The regimes' heavy-handed social engineering efforts did have serious repercussions but not always the ones that were intended.[26] (After all, citizens were not passive objects of the state's designs.) Nevertheless, intentionally and unintentionally, they did determine the possible kinds of actions people could take and the possible kinds of lives they could lead. Discrepancies between the sacred revolutionary truth and the profane daily experiences had to be somehow accommodated. The rules changed in the course of their implementation. After the excesses of Stalinism, a certain routine of living established itself in the socialist bloc, interpreted by scholars as a consequence of a consensus around the principles of the regime that ensured its stability for a couple of decades to come. The notion of normality suggests that this consensus had a doxic character: it was based on a lack of alternatives rather than a choice between alternatives. Marxist–Leninist ideology gradually lost its charisma: it became routinized, domesticated, purged of its abstract nature. The result was a "decorative communism" (Znepolski), a reaction of social mimicry whereby support was increasingly substituted by rituals of support and performances of conformity.[27] While this consensus was necessary for the regime, it was obviously also necessary for the individuals as a basis that made it possible for them to appropriate spaces of reduced or neglected control, and to navigate within and between them. Stephen Kotkin's[28] approach to Stalinism as *both* a project of the regime imposed on the citizens *and* a project of Soviet citizens themselves highlights precisely this: socialism, an imposed norm at the beginning, was turned into reality in the sense that individuals accepted the social identities and roles crafted for them and tailored the prospects of their own lives accordingly. However, as Ivaylo Znepolski has noted, "the result [was] an unpleasant surprise for the constructors—the atomised society in its communist version seemed to be easy to dominate but increasingly difficult to organise."[29] Socialist normality thus appeared an eternal immutable present, where "everything was forever," and equally far from both the heroic past and the utopian future. But since it was the only reality at hand, people had to deal with it: not fight against, not resist, not protest—just muddle through. And that they did.

Normality as Profanation of Power

While the ways in which the communist state created the fields of action for the individuals can be theorized as "crimes against everyday life" leading to its pathological mutations,[30] the interest here is in the interactions between normative regulations and people regulated. Since individual situations—to refer to Beck referring to Habermas—"lie *across* the distinction between system and life world,"[31] it is necessary to look for the socially valid normality as it has been shaped in the everyday lives and the life courses of persons who have had to live within the normative settings elaborated by communist ideology and socialist institutions. Such a perspective makes it possible to ask how institutionally scripted roles were acted out by concrete agents. It is not only that institutional thinking has the capacity of transforming life but that its categories can also to some extent be modified, subverted, or even blocked in everyday life. Individuals not only accept, interiorize, and try to live up to the models and the categories imposed on them but often renegotiate them and even overturn them, albeit perhaps unwittingly. (To deny this would mean accepting the communist regime's claims on its thorough social-transformative role, even if not necessarily accepting its rationale.)

People in everyday situations possess agency, which in most cases does not equate with resistance. The manifestations of this agency can perhaps best be captured by Michel de Certeau's concept of tactics:[32] small fortuitous arrangements with the rules rather than challenging them. As opposed to the strategies of institutions, the tactics of "users" are actions unrelated to a project but nevertheless constructive. They "parasitize" on institutions taking advantage of chances and trying to manipulate events into opportunities:

> The actual order of things is precisely what "popular" tactics turn to their own ends, without any illusion that it will change any time soon. Though elsewhere it is exploited by a dominant power or simply denied by an ideological discourse, here order is tricked by an art. Into the institution to be served are thus insinuated styles of social exchange, technical invention, and moral resistance, that is, an economy of the "gift" (generosities for which one expects a return), an esthetics of "tricks" (artists' operations) and an ethics of tenacity (countless ways of refusing to accord the established order the status of a law, a meaning, a fatality).[33]

These micro-freedoms of tactics introduce a "Brownian movement" making tactics invisible for statistics since the latter is designed to capture only the "lexical" units, while the practices are analogous to the "phrasing" of these units: "What is counted is what is used, not the ways of using."[34] Insisting on the homology between rhetorical moves and practical moves, Certeau has developed what he has called a "rhetorics of practice" suited to capture core aspects of the socialist everyday as well. Like the colonized Indians he has referred to, socialist citizens used to passively resist in their everyday practices, not by opposition to the rules but by making uses of these same rules other than the ones envisaged by those in power. They used to navigate ingeniously between diverging rules and opposing principles, using one against the other.[35] As a result, they "metaphorized the dominant order: they made it function in another register";[36] thus they "escaped it without leaving it."[37]

The flexibility of tactics has a logic of its own, allowing a reappropriation of norms by those who try to (more or less) not abuse them. They import contingency and ambivalence in the norms by a range of improvisations—a kind of practical knowledge, which is limited, fragmentary, and contextual but at the same time dynamic and flexible. Such knowledgeable actions on behalf of the social agents imply another level of euphemization. It suggests not only the impossibility of direct determination of individuals' behavior but the possibility that social agents can also use it to their own ends:

> *What is required is not that one do absolutely everything that one should, but rather that one at least give indications of trying to do so. Social agents are not expected to be perfectly in order, but rather to observe order, to give visible signs that, if they can, they will respect the rules (that is how I understand the formula: "hypocrisy is a homage that vice renders to virtue"). Practical euphemisms are a kind of homage rendered to the social order and to the values the social order exalts, all the while knowing that they are doomed to be violated.*[38]

These "double games," which can be seen in the most ordinary forms of behavior, do not turn into radical normative transgressions. Rather, they represent "breaking the rules according to the rules," or what might be called profanation of power—a subtle reaction to the power of normalization working through its microscopic deflections and appropriations, not necessarily resistances.

Viewed in this perspective, conforming behavior can be interpreted as adaptational and pragmatic, rather than as a result of symbolic hegemony or normative consensus engineered by the elites. It can be assumed that "most subordinates conform and obey *not* because they have internalized the norms of the dominant, but because a structure of surveillance, reward, and punishment makes it prudent for them to comply."[39] The tactical manipulation of chances and appearances for one's own ends can be an effective but informal and unacknowledged agency, which leads to a profanation of power rather than resistance to it, to a cynical distance from it but not to opposition. Thus, in the very same way, as a relatively closed elite culture is created (as Bourdieu has demonstrated), a subordinate culture can be elaborated that is opaque to those above it,[40] based on dense social interactions and on a recodification of ordinary activities. Thus, according to James Scott, an "unobtrusive realm of political struggle"[41] is created that does not have much in common with the open politics in Western democracies and therefore can be designated as "infrapolitics" of subordinate groups. Infrapolitics has a peculiar logic of its own: it makes no public claims, draws no visible lines. That is why it can be inferred only from practice. These "elementary forms of political life"—whose viability is perhaps due to their rudimentarity—provide the situations where everyday apolitical concerns tend to acquire a political relevance. Kitchen-table dissidence, much ironized after 1990, seems to have provided both the structure (if this term is applicable at all) and the camouflage of the infrapolitics under communist regimes. While Scott has defined infrapolitics as "resistance that avoids any open declaration of its intentions,"[42] profanation of power, as I understand it, implies that the practices, which have indeed had subversive effects, have not been intended in this way. Their subversiveness has been a "side effect" rather than an intention. Alexei Yurchak[43] has drawn the attention to the "crucial and paradoxical fact" that "great numbers of people living in socialism genuinely supported its fundamental values and ideals, although their everyday practices may appear 'duplicitous' because they indeed routinely transgressed many norms and rules represented in that system's official ideology."[44]

It can certainly be assumed—as some of the studies in this volume demonstrate—that people have not simply avoided symbolic confrontation with the regime, but that ideology has indeed been part of their everyday consciousness. What is beyond doubt, however, is that the institutionally designed socialist normality was far from becoming commonsensical and automatic. Even a cautious approach could therefore recognize the microscopic acts of what Certeau has called the "bush-like freedom of practices."

Slogans and Realities

The assumption behind this book is that socialism in its "normal state" can be understood perhaps not so much through its events history (events are threats and therefore abnormal) as by the major tropes whereby the regime theorized itself and its goals—universal employment and socialist labor, the new socialist man, the socialist way of life—and their translation into motives guiding people's actions. These translations are the loci of ideological intervention into everyday life.[45] The parameters of normality and the ways of its negotiation seem to exhibit not only the family resemblances but also the variations between countries (Yugoslavia being the most salient case in point).

Rather than taking a totalizing view, the case studies that follow crisscross various micro-perspectives and interpret sites of heterogeneity and ambivalence. They look at situations of everyday life probing for weaknesses in the system and exploiting small advantages, rather than surges of open dissent. They deal with instances of discrepancy between normative orders and with cases of bending norms to accommodate them to actions rather than challenging or trespassing them. Such a gazing at banality offers a look at socialist lives in their taken-for-grantedness. It draws the attention to the ordinary rather than the exceptional, to routines rather than events. Normality rests on unarticulated assumptions. It implies only the answer to the question "why like this," but not the question itself: the answer seems self-evident while the question is odd. Normality then is difficult to problematize: the ordinary "cannot be spoken," according to Certeau; the everyday is "anticatastrophic," "frustratingly or euphorically anticlimactic."[46] In other words, normality is the residue that cannot be captured by rigorous scientific procedures. Because of its residual nature, it is difficult to construct as a theme. It becomes "visible" only in deviations and innovations. Innovations are in fact deviations from the norms that eventually lead to a change of the norms themselves. It is such digressions—examples of self-help, "making do," various ways of redefining one's situation—that the authors of the volume aim to uncover and discuss to understand how trying to be normal can affect what "normal" actually is. While people's experiences, actions, resistances, and self-positionings were indeed consequences of the power relations, this feedback effect or "looping effect"[47] was what made negotiations of normality possible.

The first three chapters of the volume focus on *socialist labor and its heroes*. Ewelina Szpak, Eszter Zsófia Tóth, and Nina Vodopivec deal with the realm of work placing the accent on categories of workers central for the representations of the victorious working class: agricultural workers in state farms in Poland, and textile workers in Hungary and Slovenia. Together with miners and construction workers, these vocations were saturated with symbolic meaning to stand for "socialist labor": "a matter of honour, glory, courage and heroism in the years of people's power."[48] Socialist ideology regarded work not in terms of the "labor market" but as the central merit of the individuals defining their social identity, their position in society, and their existential condition.[49] Work was to be the basis of the whole social order. In the first decades after the communist takeover, work was identified by the propaganda primarily with manual vocations and was represented in terms of bodily efforts and physical strain. Such representations easily combined with the quasi-military rhetoric of "battles" and "victories" on the "labor front." Thus, in the early-socialist symbolic hierarchy, vocational work (in the "material production," meaning primarily industry but also agriculture) seemed to be symbolically more valued than intellectual work. This was however not the case in daily relations at workplaces where unofficial hierarchies depended on a range of other factors, as the authors of the three chapters have proved.[50] In spite of all efforts aiming at what might be called a "centralization of meaning," the gap between the ideology of work and everyday work practices grew ever deeper.

Ewelina Szpak follows a historical approach, but with an unusual focus on the building of the "new socialist village" in accordance with the postulate of the worker–peasant alliance and the social-engineering project designed to convert peasants into a "detachment" of the working class. Hence the author's interest is in how the new principles of socialist labor influenced human relations. She has found out that everyday interpersonal interactions were affected by the overlap of social hierarchies and professional ones, which in its turn was partly a result of the interpenetration of living and working spaces on the state-owned farms in Poland. That is why, while "cataloguing" the job positions in a state-owned farm, she is interested not only in their formal descriptions but much more in the informal relations with those higher and lower in the hierarchy, as well as with the members of the community. The text uncovers the new inequalities emerging in this situation. It tracks down the subtle and intricate relations of power, respect, publicly imposed models, and expectations where gender plays an important role, access to various kinds of resources, personal preferences, and informal alliances generating distinctions in a society that claimed equality to be its core value and in a newly designed establishment that was thought to epitomize the principles of communist ideology in rural settings.

Referring to both work ideology and the construction of gender, Eszter Zsófia Tóth has shown two opposing constructions of normality existing side by side during socialism. The official one, discussed in the first part of the chapter, portrayed women workers as emancipated women who possessed all the marvelous qualities of "the new socialist person." However, these same women did not recognize themselves in that exemplary image. They were not proud about having been workers and found it strange that they had got the State Prize back in the 1970s. Rather, when they told how they coped with their everyday lives, they tended to stick to a notion of normality that significantly diverged from the official one. The category of women workers coined by the regime was not interiorized by those who were supposed to be designated by it. They used it only when they referred to the episode of getting the State Prize, and they placed importance on other aspects of the past in their stories. Tóth however shows that the picture is more complicated. On the one hand, she observes the women's passive resistance to be squeezed into a category coined for them by the regime. On the other hand, she notes their ambivalent attitudes to the recognition by the former regime, which makes them feel in retrospect as complicit with it.

Nina Vodopivec explores the changes brought about by postsocialism in a spinning factory in Slovenia. Starting with the changes in the spatial relations on the shop floor, she traces the introduction of new managerial strategies, disciplinary measures, and reorganization of labor. On basis of this, she sets to explore the perspective of the individual as an active subject rather than a "receiver" of institutional change. Thereby, she draws on approaches viewing subjectivity as constituted through experience. Socialist experience seems to be important as a strategy of vindication of the workers' claims, dignity, or competences. On the one hand, referring to socialism "consolidates a feeling of collective marginality and thereby a degree of solidarity between workers" (p. 55), while on the other, the memory of shop-floor relations during socialism generates expectations among today's workers for greater commitment from the management and the administration. Thus, socialism is not referred to as a political regime but rather as a system of social relations and various modes of negotiations. Coming close to some themes of the previous chapters, Vodopivec brings forth socialist and contemporary notions of labor and how these intersect in the self-perceptions and worldviews of the workers. She concludes that everyday working practices produced their own norms and values, which cannot be attributed to the ideological rhetoric of the regime.

In the three following chapters, Nadezhda Galabova, Ana Hofman, and Tanja Petrović are interested in how *the new socialist person* was created. They focus on institutions for socialization such as school, army (two of the most effective normalization agents, according to Foucault), and local cultural institutions designed to mold the socialist citizens in compliance with the regime's ideological project. The institutions for socialization were to inculcate the system's ideologies in the minds of the individuals and thereby to neutralize local resistances. At the same time, they had to ensure the reproduction of the existing stratifications by their naturalization. As the three authors show, the efforts to cultivate an appropriate mentality befitting the "new socialist man" (or woman) echoed in the social world in often unexpected and unintended ways, such as the intertwining of traditional authorities and state authority (Hofman, Petrović), which existed side by side, overlapping and parasitizing on each other. On the one hand, gaps are revealed to have existed between normative orders that allowed for using one against the other or ingenuously adapting one to the other. On the other hand, the authors suggest that between the "private" goals and motives of the individuals and the "public" norms disciplining them, there existed a limited space of the solidarity of everyday interactions that made possible a certain renegotiation of the existing stratifications without a challenge to their universality. Going beyond a mere registration of the discrepancies between ideology and practice, the authors focus on ways of manipulating ideologies (education as implementation of the meritocracy principle, the army as an institution fostering and embodying Yugoslav unity, women's emancipation) by social agents for gaining social and symbolic capital.

Nadezhda Galabova explores the ambivalent position of the elite English language schools in the education system of socialist Bulgaria. The very idea of an elite school diverged from the proclaimed principles of equality and meritocracy and was a threat to the homogeneity of the socialist society. The English language school turned out to be an institution producing distinctions in a society that sought to overcome them. Galabova is interested in how the ambiguous position of this type of schools was experienced on a daily basis. In her attempt to focus on the "double meanings," she looks for minute everyday transgressions in a situation of strictly controlled public behavior. Conceptualizing the subtle power plays in the perspective of time use and the appropriation of the students' private time (etatization of time), she demonstrates how "parallel to the homogeneous normative time of learning and examinations there was a constant undertow of negotiations between students, teachers, political authorities, and parents" (p. 69). At the same time, however, Galabova shows how narrow the interstices were where the agents could take advantage of the contradictions within the regulations imposed on them and could adapt the rules to their own needs.

In the next chapter, Ana Hofman turns to the ambivalences of socialist women's emancipation where the tension was not only between ideology norms and everyday practices, but between different sets of norms as well. This led to an interplay of various, at times contradictory, normative ideas of femininity, most notably the traditional ones that never completely lost their influence in rural areas and those proclaimed by the regime, aptly designated as "state feminism." Rather than uncovering the contradictions inherent in state feminism, Hofman prefers to focus on the interstitial spaces where gender hierarchies could be questioned and female agency could develop. She argues that rural women could sometimes gain power in an officially recognized way turning propaganda slogans of emancipation into a kind of actual emancipation—though not necessarily the one that was targeted. Combining a phenomenological feminist perspective with the narrative approach in musical ethnography, Hofman shows how amateur singers became a kind of cultural VIPs in their villages gaining prestige in an unprecedented way, renegotiating their personal social positions, and establishing new female roles that coexisted with the traditional ones.

Gender socialization and socialist gender models are the topic of Tanja Petrović's chapter as well. She is interested in masculinity as constructed in relation to the service in the Yugoslav Army (JNA)—the institution that was supposed to mold the "new socialist man." The author argues however that, in practice, army service was harmonized with more traditional notions of masculinity fitting socialist ideology into a patriarchal context and reconciling institutional/ideological models and familial practices. Petrović is interested in how former Yugoslav men negotiate their identity of JNA soldiers referring to both institutionally set norms and subversive strategies that mock at these norms. She highlights the quasi-ludic character of the subversive practices in the army, a fact that makes identification with JNA possible as an important part of the assertion of one's masculinity. At the same time, Petrović explores the contestations of this socialist "normal masculinity" in the post-Yugoslav space and its renegotiations. The very act of sharing JNA stories has direct political relevance in post-Yugoslav contexts being considered as lack of patriotism and pejoratively labeled as Yugo-nostalgia. The author however interprets the persisting sharing of army stories as negotiation and justification of a certain kind of masculinity rather than nostalgia.

Simina Bădică, Valentina Gueorguieva, and Hana Pelikánová focus on important aspects of *the socialist way of life*. They examine practices of consumption as a terrain of interaction and negotiation between institutions and individuals/groups. What the state deemed achievable was not just the satisfaction of the populations' needs but much more—the definition and regulation of those needs. In their effort to reorganize the way of life of their citizens, however, the regimes had to balance between their own promises to raise the living standard and the constraints of the planned economy. Therefore, the establishment of the "socialist way of life" came across insurmountable difficulties. The economic logic of supply and demand was replaced by the shadowy one of gift exchange where reciprocity found various forms (but always symbolically laden) and had a moral, rather than economic nature. Because of its moral nature, this type of exchange led to obligations and dependence on the supplier, be it an individual, an institution, or the state. On the one hand, the distribution of goods in situations of chronic shortages was a lever in the social engineering programs of the regimes, as shown by Pelikánová and Bădică. On the other hand, as all three authors demonstrate, consumption was a space of individual creativity, although the consumers were hardly aware of it. The practices of everyday life thus contributed to a delegitimization of the state power. To the extent that rules were not made explicit, they created a margin of indeterminacy and play. This is the margin where unsolicited practices, or what Michel de Certeau has called tactics, create their own relevance by "poaching" (Certeau) in the established order.

Simina Bădică is interested in a peculiar phenomenon of everyday socialism, queuing. She starts with the hypothesis that the queue not only reflected the organization of society, but also exemplified a feeling of "queuing justice," that is, a certain instrumental solidarity among fellow queuers. Like Galabova, she sees queuing as a form of the "etatization of time": the waste of time waiting in a line is a demonstration, and an actual exercise, of power. But according to Bădică, it can also be interpreted as a condition for complex relations of solidarity based on personal interest and a "distributive justice." Discussing the influential view that any imposed collectivism resulted in apathy, isolation, and breaking down of solidarity ties, Bădică sides with Daniel Barbu's more sophisticated observations about the "dependent individualism born under totalitarianism" and claims the existence of a solidarity understood not as a moral principle but rather, "on a small scale," as a harmonization of interests toward a common goal. At the same time, like Tóth, Vodopivec, and Galabova, she stresses the aspects of the internalization of the official discourse, challenging the modes of thinking of socialism in dichotomies—in particular, Vaclav Havel's dichotomy of living within truth and living within a lie. She argues that the border between truth and lie is not as clear as Havel has suggested in his famous text. The picture emerging from people's memories is gray scale, rather than black and white.

Valentina Gueorguieva develops this theme further, focusing on the consumption practices of an average Bulgarian family. Her research is based on the archive of the head of the family, a schoolteacher, who kept detailed consumption diaries for the whole family for thirty-two years. The diaries have been supplemented by his autobiography. Following Michel de Certeau's theory of "creative consumption," Gueorguieva makes a deeper sense of everyday routines arguing for their inventiveness as "the secret weapon of the user" enabling them to appropriate and renegotiate the "order" imposed on them (to assimilate it in the sense of making it similar to themselves). Thus, exploring the consumption "tactics" of the family, she views the "microphysics of power" (Foucault) as a microphysics of resistance to power at the same time. However, Gueorguieva's micro-focus and scrupulous attention to details makes her cautious enough not to qualify certain tactics of everyday consumption (including cultural consumption) as forms of resistance to the system or of compliance with it. Giving up the bipolar model of conformity–opposition to the system, she points to the complexity of the situations in which the "negotiating agents" used to act and suggests that their ways of action maintained and perverted the system at the same time. Thus she comes close to Gerald Creed's idea of "domestication" of socialism.[51]

Hana Pelikánová discusses housing as the sector where state paternalism in Czechoslovakia was best observable. She combines macro- and micro-levels of analysis reconstructing first the legal and institutional arrangements for a just distribution of housing and then the actual practices that resulted in making housing a means of social and political control. Drawing on rich interview material, Pelikánová shows various dimensions and mechanisms of this control: on the one hand, a series of "social criteria" (such as family needs and living conditions) that generated a certain feeling of security under socialism and on the other, a series of tacit preferences (such as party membership and "clean biography") that led to various tactics of adaptation. The chapter reveals a range of such tactics, both those of individuals and families struggling for a satisfactory living standard and those of companies using housing arrangements to attract and retain their workers. The complexities and ambivalences of the practices described lead the author to a cautious conclusion. Highlighting the state paternalism of the "normalization" period (after 1968), she also notes some of its unintended consequences such as the individualism inherent in a host of do-it-yourself practices described by the interviewees. Thus, the case examined by Pelikánová seems to support the hypothesis of "dependent individualism" put forward in Bădică's chapter.

Finally, Sanja Potkonjak attempts to build bridges between (auto) biography and history relating her own family history to generation-specific experiences of socialism. She focuses on the stories of three generations of women trying to capture and juxtapose their personal insights into socialism and the way they are renegotiated in the context of their retrospective accounts. Socialism has become "a stigma," but there is still "a need for coherence, structure, and rules, which were provided by the system we lived in" (p. 198). Setting out to explore the tensions between the "personally meaningful" and the "historically corroborated," the author admits that historiography has failed to capture individual experience while the phenomenology of socialist everyday has been sheltered in fiction. But telling one's story is also a way of fictionalizing oneself. Thus, it seems to follow that biography is a dissident endeavor by definition since it privileges the individual over the collective, diversity over homogeneity and private truths over the ideologically mediated ones. Potkonjak draws on post-Yugoslav female writers who meticulously explore everyday lives of individuals in an attempt not only to understand the daily workings of the power exercised by the system over the population (Slavenka Drakulić) but also to expose the fundamentalist and totalizing postsocialist memory projects that exclude any other way of remembering one's life but in the register of shame or guilt (Dubravka Ugresić).

* * *

The authors are nationals and residents of postsocialist countries, and socialism is part of their family memory and even of their own life experiences. I believe this plays an important role for their motivations and intentions. Their positioning in relation to their topic is authentic and ironic at the same time. Authentic in the sense of being based on local knowledge and insider experience (even though in most chapters it is not reflected). Ironic because of the authors' distanced positions in relation to that experience, due to their methodologically informed perspectives.

The overall approach is phenomenological/ethnomethodological in the attempts to capture behavior and speech that are seldom reflected on, based on understandings that are not articulated and maybe not even conscious, and to attempt interpretations reaching beyond the commonsense knowledge of the speakers/actors. The interpretations are informed by various theoretical perspectives: theories of social memory (Vodopivec), Foucauldian ideas of surveillance (Vodopivec, Galabova), Bourdieu's concept of *habitus* (Galabova), Michel de Certeau's theory of creative consumption (Gueorguieva), Judith Butler's concept of gender as performativity (Petrović), feminist perspectives combined with a narrative ethnomusicological approach (Hofman), theorizations of socialism (Bădică), and of autobiographical reflection (Potkonjak). They complement, often relativize, but do not substitute the narrators' accounts, which are central for the approach shared by all contributors. All studies are based primarily on personal documents and/or in-depth interviewing. Some thematize extensively the nature of the retrospective accounts and their dependence on present situations, touching on the interrelations of personal recollections and public memory (Bădică, Petrović), on the micro-politics of the interview (Galabova), or the researcher's role in shaping the memories of her interviewees (Vodopivec).

While the contributions to this book share a host of assumptions, themes, and findings, there seems to be a major conceptual incongruity: both terms, "communism" and "socialism," are used interchangeably throughout the book to denote what seems to be the same reality. Each of them is linked to a context. "Communism" refers to the so-called totalitarian paradigm, dating back to Cold War Western theorizing, especially in political science. While the concept of totalitarianism has been largely abandoned in Western research (almost entirely in history but less so in political philosophy[52]), it has kept reappearing in professional and wider public discourses in the postsocialist world since the early 1990s[53]—a fact that is perhaps no less indicative of value positions than of theoretical approaches. The term "socialism" is associated with the more recent "revisionist" paradigm, which takes up the "indigenous" term reconceptualized in social anthropology and history of everyday life and with a focus on resistances to the regime rather than the regime itself. Both paradigms have been criticized for privileging some aspects and glossing over others, for being "demonizing" or "normalizing" in their approach. Furthermore, each term seems to refer to not only disciplinary and theoretical, but also to national contexts, with "communism" preferred in Romania and the Czech Republic, as well as in French-language research.[54] The benign anthropological principle to use concepts of "natives" does not really solve the issue for the latter as a rule have been coined by the regimes themselves. It remains to be seen if different regimes could have given rise to different memories and different conceptualizations. But this is another project. In the studies that follow, terminological coherence has been sacrificed in order to give an idea of the different national strategies of dealing with the past and to respect the authors' choices, which are presumably guided by more than simple terminological preferences. If a value-free science is possible, it is certainly not the one about socialism. No matter how objective and impartial studies of the socialist past may be, their messages tend to be more complex than predicated by their research findings. The insider perspective is further complicated insofar as it calls for a moral self-positioning, not only a theoretical and political one. As to my own choice of concept, I guess it follows from my "post-revisionist" interest in people's lives and experiences rather than in the political system. Perhaps, it is also a consequence from my choice not to see my own life too pathetically in retrospect.

Some authors[55] have expressed concerns that the attempts to theorize the actually existed socialism—no matter how critical the theorizations might be—could turn into its exoneration by the very act of its contextualization and historicization. Such concerns are obviously even more relevant for the studies of socialist everyday life and what has been called here socialist normality—even if they do not aspire to theorization. Indeed, a wealth of representations of socialist everyday in memories, images, museum exhibits have had a "normalizing" effect, often in spite of their authors' intentions. Perhaps, scholarly interest in the socialist everyday (as a rule not driven by normalizing agendas) could also have such an effect if it does not problematize the "normal." But it can focus exactly on such problematizations: what it is that we consider "only natural" and how it has come to appear so. In such cases, the interest in socialist banality signals a shift of the attention from the totalizing efforts of the regimes to their effects on the populations, from the ideologies and instruments of power to its legitimacy. To study normality is to gaze with intense curiosity at trivial matters and try to understand the limits they set not only on the implementation of individuals' life projects but also on their very inception. Finally, it means—at least in regard to this book—not to try to arrive at one truth about the nature of socialism but rather to explore the many actual ways of having lived through it.

Notes

1. I started working on socialist normality as an Andrew Mellon fellow at the Wissenschaftskolleg—Centre for Advanced Study, Berlin, in 2004. The fellows' responsiveness, encouragement, and challenges contributed a lot to shaping my ideas, and WiKo proved to be a supernormal (i.e., exceeding the normal in a positive way) place for work and discussions.

2. In the following paragraphs, I draw on Ian Hacking, *The Taming of Chance*. Cambridge University Press, 1990, esp. pp. 160–79. For a more detailed *Begriffsgeschichte* of "normal" and "normality" as well as a convincing argument for their relevance to postsocialist transformations, see Alexander Kiossev, "The oxymoron of normality," Changing places (What's normal, anyway?) 20th European Meeting of Cultural Journals (Sibiu, September 21–24, 2007), http://www.eurozine.com/articles/2008-01-04-kiossev-en. html, accessed on March 25, 2010.

3. This connotation is much more obvious in words like "orthography" (correct spelling), "orthodoxy" (right doctrine), etc.

4. Hacking, *The Taming of Chance*, 168.

5. Ibid., 169.

6. Michel Foucault has also noticed the confluence, in psychiatric and juridical discourse, of the "two realities of the norm": as a rule of behavior and as a

functional regularity. See Michel Foucault, *Anormalnite* [Les anormaux. Cours au Collège de France] Sofia: LiK, 2000, 187–88.

7. Michel Foucault, *Anormalnite*, 42.

8. The normalizing power functions through "a whole range of degrees of normality indicating membership of a homogeneous social body but also playing a part in classification, hierarchization, and the distribution of rank. In a sense, the power of normalization imposes homogeneity; but it individualizes by making it possible to measure gaps, to determine levels, to fix specialities, and to render the differences useful by fitting them one to another. It is easy to understand how the power of the norm functions within a system of formal equality, since within a homogeneity that is the rule, the norm introduces, as a useful imperative and as a result of measurement, all the shading of individual differences." (Michel Foucault, *Discipline & Punish: The Birth of the Prison*. New York: Vintage, 1995, 184).

9. Foucault, *Anormalnite*, 187–89.

10. Foucault, *Discipline*, 178–79.

11. James C. Scott, *Domination and the Arts of Resistance. Hidden Transcripts*. New Haven: Yale University Press, 1990, 52–55.

12. Pierre Bourdieu, *Outline of a Theory of Practice*. Cambridge: Cambridge University Press, 1977, 191.

13. Hacking, *The Taming of Chance*, 3. See also Foucault, *Anormalnite*, 157–89 on the administrative construction of insanity.

14. For a wealth of fascinating case studies, see Jane Caplan and John Torpey (eds.) *Documenting Individual Identity: The Development of State Practices in the Modern World*. Princeton: Princeton University Press, 2001.

15. For a discussion of this process in early- to mid-twentieth-century Bulgaria, see Daniela Koleva, *Biografia i normalnost* [Biography and Normality] Sofia: LiK, 2002.

16. Mary Douglas, *How Institutions Think*. Syracuse: Syracuse University Press, 1986.

17. James C. Scott, *Seeing Like a State: How Certain Schemes to Improve the Human Condition Have Failed*. New Haven and London: Yale University Press, 1998, 80.

18. Scott, *Seeing Like a State*, 83.

19. Foucault, *Discipline*, 183.

20. See Katherine Verdery, *National Ideology Under Socialism: Identity and Cultural Politics in Ceausescu's Romania*. Berkeley and Los Angelis: University of California Press, 1991, for the disproportionate importance of symbolic–ideological production for the legitimation of communist regimes.

21. See Sheila Fitzpatrick, "Ascribing Class: The Conception of Social Identity in Soviet Russia," *Journal of Modern History*, vol. 65, 1993, pp. 745–70, for the construction of "class" in Russia in the 1920s and the role of social statistics in it. Most importantly, the author concludes that Soviet "classes" were defined "in terms of their relationship to the state rather than, like Marxist classes, in terms of their relationship to each other" (Fitzpatrick, "Ascribing Class," 770).

22. Quoted in Ivaylo Znepolski, *Bulgarskiat komunizam: Sociokulturni cherti i vlastova traektoria* [*Bulgarian Communism: Sociocultural Traits and Power Trajectory*] Sofia: IIBM/Ciela, 2008, 227.

23. *Dognat' i peregnat'* (Catch up and overtake [the West]) was a major Soviet slogan, which successfully migrated to the satellite countries after WWII. For instance, in a much quoted speech, Bulgarian communist leader Georgi Dimitrov set the task to achieve "in 15–20 years what other nations under other circumstances have achieved in centuries."

24. Katherine Verdery, *What Was Socialism and What Comes Next?* Princeton: Princeton University Press, 1996, 24–26.

25. Cf. Svetlana Boym, *Common Places: Mythologies of Everyday Life in Russia*. Cambridge, MA: Harvard University Press, 1994.

26. See Ulf Brunnbauer, *"Die sozialistische Lebensweise": Ideologie, Gesellschaft, Familie und Politik in Bulgarien (1944–1989)*. Wien–Köln–Weimar: Böhlau Verlag 2007 for a comprehensive study of the introduction of the "socialist way of life" in Bulgaria, its unexpected results, and its significant "side effects."

27. Alexei Yurchak, "Soviet Hegemony of Form: Everything Was Forever Until It Was No More", *Comparative Studies in Society and History*, vol. 45 (3), 2003, 480–510; Alexei Yurchak, *Everything Was Forever, Until It Was No More: The Last Soviet Generation*. Princeton and Oxford: Princeton University Press, 2006.

28. Stephen Kotkin, *Magnetic Mountain: Stalinism as a Civilization*. Berkeley, LA: University of California Press, 1995.

29. Znepolski, *Bulgarskiat komunizam*, 301.

30. Alexander Kiossev, "Crimes Against Everyday Life, or on the Patho-Anthropology of Socialism", in *20 Years After the Collapse of Communism: Expectations, Achievements and Disillusions of 1989*, eds. Nicolas Hayoz, Leszek Jesien, and Daniela Koleva, Bern: Peter Lang, 2011.

31. Ulrich Beck, *Risk Society: Towards a New Modernity*. Thousand Oaks: Sage Publications, 1992, 136.

32. See also Gueorguieva, this volume.

33. Michel de Certeau, *The Practice of Everyday Life*. Berkeley: University of California Press, 1984, 26.

34. Ibid., 35.

35. See Hofman, Szpak, Galabova in this volume.

36. Certeau, *The Practice*, 32.

37. Ibid., xiii.

38. Pierre Bourdieu, *Practical Reason. On the Theory of Action*. Stanford: Stanford University Press, 1998, 98.

39. Scott, *Domination*, 193.

40. Ibid.

41. Ibid., 183.

42. Ibid., 220.

43. Yurchak, "Soviet Hegemony of Form", 484.

44. See Brunnbauer, *Die sozialistische Lebensweise*, for an elaboration of this thesis in the case of Bulgaria: "Most Bulgarian women and men were of the

opinion that progress and rising material standard of life were something good, shared the conviction of the party that women should have jobs, thought it was right to treat one's fellow-humans with respect and solidarity, accepted the special value of art and culture, were proud with the history and folklore of their country, judged education as important, wanted to have an interesting job and had nothing against social commitments. . . . but in this as well as in the other cases, a wide gap lay open between the acceptance of the values of the regime in principle and their concrete realisation in people's lives" (Ibid., 695). For the Soviet Union see also Karen Dawisha, "Communism as a Lived System of Ideas in Contemporary Russia," *East European Politics and Societies*, vol. 19 (3), 2005, 463–93.

45. In another project, "socialist spaces" are seen as such sites of intervention merging the official and the unofficial, sacred and profane, utopia and reality (David Crowley and Susan Reid (eds.), *Socialist Spaces: Sites of Everyday Life in the Eastern Bloc*. Oxford and New York: Berg, 2002).

46. Boym, *Common Places*, 21.

47. Ian Hacking, "The looping effects of human kinds," in: *Causal Cognition: A Multidisciplinary Debate*, eds. Dan Sperber, David Premack, and Ann James Premack, Oxford: Clarendon Press, 1995, 351–83;. Ian Hacking, "Between Michel Foucault and Erving Goffman: Between Discourse in the Abstract and Face-to-Face Interaction," *Economy and Society*, vol. 33 (3), 2004, 277–302.

48. *Rabotnichesko delo* (the official daily of the Bulgarian Communist Party), August 29, 1954, p. 1.

49. Cf. Klaus Roth (Hg.), *Arbeit im Sozialismus—Arbeit im Postsozialismus. Erkundungen zum Arbeitsleben im östlichen Europa*. Freiburger Sozialanthropologische Studien, Bd. 1. Münster: LIT Verlag, 2004.

50. For the divergent meanings of the mining vocation, see Daniela Koleva, "'My life has mostly been spent working': Notions and patterns of work in socialist Bulgaria," *Anthropological Notebooks*, XIV, no. 1, 2008, 27–48.

51. Gerald Creed, *Domesticating Revolution: From Socialist Reform to Ambivalent Transition in a Bulgarian Village*. University Park: Penn State University Press, 1998.

52. See, e.g., Claude Lefort, *Complications: Communism and the Dilemmas of Democracy*. New York: Columbia University Press, 2007.

53. A recent example is the introduction to the *History of the People's Republic of Bulgaria*, a major collective work encompassing all aspects of the regime from 1944 to 1989: Ivaylo Znepolski, "Totalitarizmat—iz istoriata na edin nezavarshen debat" [Totalitarianism—From the History of an Unfinished Debate], in: Znepolski (ed.) *Istoria na Narodna republika Bulgaria: Rezhimat i obshtestvoto*. [History of the People's Republic of Bulgaria: The Regime and the Society] Sofia: IIBM/Ciela, 2009, 29–87. See references for Russia in Sheila Fitzpatrick, "The Soviet Union in the Twenty-First Century," *Journal of European Studies*, vol. 37 (1), 2007, 51–71, and a more general discussion in the special issue of the journal *Divinatio* vol. 31 (2010) on *The Totalitarianisms of the 20th Century in Comparative Perspective*. The narratives constructed by museums, such as the House of Terror

in Budapest, the Museum of Genocide Victims in Vilnius, and others, testify to the presence of a "totalitarianist" position in wider postsocialist publicity. In some recent research, totalitarianism has been conceptualized as an "atmosphere," a social experience rather than as a political system (Ádám Takács, "Totalitarianism as an atmosphere. Morality and mentality in Hungary under the Kádár regime," *Divinatio*, vol. 31, spring-summer 2010, 113–23).

54. Nadege Ragaru et Antonella Capelle-Pogăcean, *Vie quotidienne et pouvoir sous le communisme: Consommer à l'Est*. Paris: Karthala, 2010.

55. For instance: Dimitri Ginev, "Teoretizatsiata na socializma" [The Theorisation of Socialism] *Kultura*, no. 26, June 18, 2004.

1

"Living and Working Together": Formal and Personal Relations Between Workers of the Polish State-Owned Farms

Ewelina Szpak

> *We have the most pioneering political system . . . Since the political system is pioneering, it requires pioneers. . . . We must pay particular attention to that, to the working class people, we must change, modernize, train and socialize them.*[1]

These were the words of one of the delegates to the agricultural workers' convention in 1948, where the decision to establish the institution of state farms, commonly referred to in Polish as PGRs (the abbreviation for *Państwowe Gospodarstwo Rolne*, literally a "state-owned farm"). Apart from the above-stated ideological purpose of reconstructing social consciousness, another task set for the PGRs at the time was "to develop nationwide reserves of agricultural products, as well as to improve the quality of farming culture and to set the example of model management for local individual farmers."[2]

Similar to production cooperatives, endorsed strongly by the socialist propaganda, the PGRs were intended as the main agents of building "the new socialist village," compliant with the idea of the worker–peasant alliance. The role of the employees of these state farms as "the most rural part of the working class"[3] was to put into everyday practice the principles of socialist labor. The questions as to what these principles actually were and whether their popularization proved successful are the main objectives of my deliberations presented in this chapter. The sphere of labor not only was an arena for developing and implementing new production methods or techniques, but also reflected a range of mechanisms present in the communist social and economic system. These mechanisms were particularly evident in the sphere of interpersonal relations that are analyzed in detail in the text below.

This chapter, based on an analysis of memoirs and oral sources, is part of my project realized in the years 2001–04; the outcome of the project was the publication entitled "Między osiedlem i zagrodą. Życie codzienne mieszkańców PGR" ("Between a housing estate and a homestead. Everyday life of the residents of PGRs (Polish socialist state farms)").

Obviously the form and character of relations between employees were connected strictly to their attitudes to work. The identity of the workplace and the place to live,[4] which was typical for the PGRs, and in which the social hierarchy (i.e., that in a housing estate) overlapped with the professional one (i.e., that in a work unit) had a profound effect on the character of interpersonal relations.

Interestingly enough, the system designed as such was also perfectly in line with the ideological policy of reconstructing the Polish village and forming the worker–peasant alliance. The ongoing surveillance of the staff, which was possible in this form of settlement, enhanced the control and surveillance of behaviors and attitudes presented outside their workplace and beyond the working hours. This could have been a source of strong mutual distance and distrust between people, recalled by one of former PGR employees.[5] His words are even more meaningful upon consideration of the fact that he became acquainted with the reality of the PGRs only by the end of the 1970s. One can therefore ask what this distrust must have been like in the 1950s, when intimidation and fear of being suspected of hostile actions was much more common.

The multidirectional and multilevel character of the relations between the employees and the residents of the PGRs is best revealed with reference to the particular positions in a farm, starting with the director and following the hierarchy downward to end with regular farmworkers, referred to in general as "the staff."

Director

From the first day in office, a director's authority and scope of duties covered a group of six to eight farms. During the period of the existence of state-owned landed estates (PNZ),[6] the director of a district and a group of farms at the same time was often a landowner or a man of higher agricultural and administrative education.[7] A more thorough account of the relations between the director and the staff cannot be presented due to the lack of adequate sources. However, based mainly on the memoirs by E. Kłoczowski, it can be concluded that by the end of 1948, the relations between the director (called "the administrator" at the time) and the staff, as well as the entire organization itself, were different than in the later period. Less pressure imposed by the central authorities and less infiltration by the party (though not by the secret police, known in Polish as the UB) provided an illusory sense of having more independence and offering more possibilities for directors to undertake their individual initiatives.

In the PGRs established in 1949, at least until 1956, every director was required to have a "correct" political biography, most preferably to be a member of the communist party. It was also the period of the emergence of the professional merry-go-round, that is, reshuffling of those in jobs, a phenomenon characteristic for professional personnel in all social spheres.[8] Such merry-go-rounds and reshuffling entailed changes and swings affecting entire teams of managers.[9] This phenomenon itself shows much about the relations between employees, predominated by seeking protection from friends in high places, forming favorable professional relations, and "having contacts."

In general, in the 1950s, the directors were physically distant from their subordinate farms due to the load of administrative duties, office work, organizational activities, and in many cases also obligations due to party membership. Still, their periodical visits and checks in the farming units were intended to provide them with general knowledge of the situation at the farms. Apart from imposing discipline and controlling the work of the subordinates, such visits were also aimed at developing appropriate distance and commanding respect for the "administrator."

Although the official propaganda promoted the image of the director as a "father" and a guardian, which had certain effect on the recollections contained in the memoirs, the actual image of the figure of the director seems to have been far from that ideal. A director usually had his "trusted" adherents who would inform him of possible problems. In official terms, this role was assigned to the manager, who was directly subordinate to the director.[10] Yet the former would not always manage to live up to the expectations of the latter. In such

3

cases, other mechanisms were used, typical for the period in question, such as denunciations and complaints, often addressed to the director. Memoirists also described examples of such practices:

> . . . the director liked those who would denounce to him, and those were usually top grade skivers who wanted to win his favour in order to get a good job in which they would not have to work a lot.[11]

There were also cases when the weapon of denunciations and complaints was turned against the director. Embittered with their working conditions, with the manager, the foreman, or the director himself, the workers would seek help and intervention from other sources.[12] Particularly, popular media in this respect at that time were *Robotnik Rolny*, a magazine for farmworkers, and the Polish Radio, as well as local newspapers, which would also encourage such practices in a number of ways. The reports and complaints against the director addressed to the editors, which provided the writers with the possibility to avoid the local network of power relations, had different effects for the accused. The consequences, if any, were in the form of condemnation in the press, official relocation, or penalty imposed by a court. Usually, however, the only result was another shake-up.[13]

Particularly intense rotation of directors took place as a result of the reshuffling after 1956,[14] which enabled promotion to that position of a number of former PGR workers who were not "infected with the period of mistakes and distortions." Similar to other branches of the economy, the changes in the system of relations brought about by this situation were merely ostensible.

In the second half of the 1960s, the PGRs saw the inflow of the young generation of graduates from secondary schools or universities who were able to take up the positions of specialists and directors without the necessity to undergo many years of practical training. This reshuffling, coinciding with the shift between generations, seems to have speeded up the directors' tendency to become distant from their subordinate teams of workers, which had emerged already in the late 1950s. The expansion and development of farms along with decentralization and the growing administration further impeded the directors' chances to become well acquainted with all workers employed in a single team or a conglomerate plant. At that time, the director would seemingly become engaged mainly in holding prestigious and representative functions as an honored figure during celebrations and official events. His duties also included making employment decisions, allotting flats, or opening newly built facilities for use. Although the director remained responsible to his superiors (such as the District Committee of the Polish United Workers' Party) for the condition and the production of his subordinate farms, his contacts with the workers would boil down to control visits or interventions. In an interview, a director in position since the 1970s declares that he constantly strove to have the widest possible knowledge on the matters regarding both professional and living standards of his subordinate workers.[15] Still, this does not change the fact that the attitude expressed by his employees (and respondents) was characterized by strong distance mixed with a grain of fear. The workers' fear of their director was partially due to the fact that the latter, especially when engaged actively in the party, represented the ruling authorities as opposed to the ruled masses, a dichotomy that prevailed in Polish society during the period of socialism. One of the former workers mentioned it in an indirect manner:

> . . . the director is two-faced—he shows one of his faces to the management, where he pretends to be a stalwart supporter of the public interest, while on the other hand he has "preferred" workers at the farm.[16]

That same employee reflected as follows on the director's malfeasances he had witnessed:

> I was afraid that they would have dealt with it on their own first [on the level of the inspecting authority—E. Sz.], and I would have been turned into a fool. Attempts would have been made to either have me resign willfully or give me notice for some alleged reason.[17]

The relations between the director and the manager of a farm require separate discussion. Although especially in the 1950s the director could freely select "appropriate" managers as his subordinates, they would still clash and come into conflict with each other. According to the reports by one of the memoirists, such tensions between the director and the manager used to have a considerable effect on the rest of the staff.[18] Depending on the willpower and the traits of the two antagonists, the approach of the majority of other employees was shaped.[19]

Manager

The manager was a permanent resident of his subordinate farm where he worked and lived with his fellow employees, with whom he therefore also had more manifold relations.

Obviously, taking the position of farm manager, especially in the early period of the functioning of such enterprises, implied developing a conviction of ruling (quasi-owning) the farm. Even when the manager himself did not entertain such a conviction, it may have been present among the employed workers, who interpreted the reality in terms of living in a prewar homestead, a manor farm. The evidences of this way of thinking can be encountered in the memoirs of the pioneers from the Regained Territories (the areas incorporated into Poland after WWII).[20]

Yet this conviction vanished rapidly in the face of intense reshuffling of managers. The previously ordered interdependency between the homestead and its owner was replaced by estate–common (state) property relations, brand new for some workers and farmers. This new way of thinking also resulted in a new attitude toward the "new manager," especially since the latter would change frequently. This trend obviously translated into mutual relations at work, as exemplified by the mentions in the memoirs about disrespect for the manager.[21]

However, the same memoirs often informed that the managers enjoyed certain prestige and esteem. It can be concluded from an analysis of sources and interviews with employees that the crucial determinant of that situation in the absolute majority of cases was the permanence of the superior, his fairness, and his involvement in the farming activities.

Looking through source materials unveils the image of the perfect model of the manager that emerged throughout the years. Such ideal presentations of the manager, often encountered in the memoirs written for the purposes of contests, could be seen as postulated visions of the reality. Whether or not these presentations corresponded to reality, their essence lay in pointing to the expectations toward the new superior. In general, an esteemed and respected manager was expected to be an effective administrator capable of keeping his staff disciplined. He should abstain from alcohol and remain resistant to any sympathies and antipathies toward the workers. The manager could also win the respect of the staff if he was actively engaged in solving their living problems and, in particular, the housing situation. With his wider contacts outside the PGR, the manager could offer help in arranging for a piece of furniture, a bed, or domestic appliances. Such concern and interest in the employees' private problems was the easiest way to win their liking. Also the manager should, at least theoretically, intervene in the conflicts and clashes between farms, which need not have been triggered by work.

In this perfect image, the manager was often described as the model of attitudes, behaviors, and habits, the one who developed and introduced technical novelties in the community's everyday life.[22] According to the memoirs and the interviews, it was also the manager's initiative to purchase the first TV set, tape recorder, or car in the village. The manager's wife was also an important figure in the farming community, put forth as the actual model of behavior and habits for other women.[23] Was it really the case? Did the wife of an effective and highly regarded manager enjoy equally respected status among the PGR women? Was the manager himself actually that highly esteemed by his subordinate workers? It seems that the answer to these questions may not be unambiguous. It was often the case that the memoirs and recollections of former farmworkers featured individual-biased experiences and judgments. The same manager was often described as an excellent man by one of his former employees, while another would see him in the opposite way. Such subjective judgments were obviously connected to the position held by the respondent. The manager was described differently by a foreman who had worked close with him and who had been his direct subordinate and by a manual worker who had been in conflict with that foreman (and therefore also with the manager himself).[24]

The same applied to manager's wife. The attitude toward the manager could have been extended to his wife as well. This mechanism was understandable for the farmworkers who lived and worked together. In the majority of cases, the manager's wife did not work on the farm; she was active within her household, the flat, and the allotment of land for "private" use. In this way, equivalently to the manager who could set the tone of the public and professional life, his spouse was to provide an example of the ideal housewife for other women.[25]

The above model is an interpretation of a vision or expectations emerging in the attitudes of farmworkers, constantly exposed to the propaganda and the ideology of the period. A similar ideal image was developed with regard to the foremen and their wives.

Yet the interesting question is how close were these images to the reality? Taking into consideration the purpose to create emotional ties between the PGR workers and their workplace, underlined by the ideologists and the propagandists, it can be concluded that the managers' protective attitude was not as much the expression of their personal approach as the completion of the tasks and obligations imposed on them.[26] It is also worth noting at this point that both of these approaches need not have been in complete opposition.

It could be the case that this attitude of farmworkers, consolidated by the appropriate press, which emphasized the protective character of the state and the workers who represented it, was the source of complaints and denunciations, still encountered in the 1960s, with respect to the managers who did not care about the living standards and cultural development of the PGR communities.[27] This aspect points to the core of the system introduced and developed in the 1950s; paradoxically, instead of strengthening the manifested sense of shared responsibility and cooperation, that system generated the feeling of one's weakness and hopelessness in the face of its high expectations toward the representatives of the protective authorities. Yet it seems that one should refrain from any simplified assessments and judgments of the relations between the manager and the staff. The system of expectations and attitudes (and therefore also of imagination) developed throughout the period of the People's Poland with particularly strong influence on the class of unskilled and uneducated workers (not only farmers) was reshaping the mentality of the society to some extent. The degree of such reshaping, susceptibility to it, and its sources were determined in much more diverse and merging spheres of social mentality, experiences, and conditions, which cannot be simplified into a clear-cut scheme.

There were also conflicts in the relations between the manager and the employees. The source of these conflicts was the sense of social inequality, expressed mainly in the form of accusing the manager of either actual or alleged use of his influences to promote selected workers and favor them.[28] In the 1940s and 1950s, the most popular form of protection was the shared background or kinship between the managers and the persons they appointed. Later the prevailing argument became the connections and "scams" that were not linked closely to social or cultural affinity.[29] A particularly troublesome situation was a clash between the manager and the foreman. In this case, the prevailing esteem for the manager could have destructive effect on the organization and the quality of work of a given team of workers. An important determinant of the power of either of the antagonists was the support from the director or from the staff. Still, staff's support was connected closely to the foreman's attitude to his subordinates and his social status, influenced mainly by the foreman's seniority and time spent with the staff and the housing community. A specific example of this type of conflict was described by one of the newly employed managers of a state farm in the district of Hrubieszów:

> *The central figure was Kazimierz. As the foreman, the secretary of the local Party organization, the head of the works committee, deputy director and a member of the plenum of the district board of farm workers' unions ... [he] was considered a man who could do literally anything, who had gotten rid of a bunch of managers ... who hated being supervised and having a superior.*[30]

Foreman

According to the rules of the relevant collective bargaining, the foreman as the manager of a team of workers,[31] was classified as a manual worker.[32] Yet considering their scope of competencies and authority (managing human resources), as well as the amounts of wages, foremen were qualified as members of the local circles of professional elite. The foreman's direct and ongoing contact with his subordinate team and the fact that foremen usually resided at the state farm where they worked implied developing an extensive network of relations with team members and other residents, similarly as in the case of a manager.

In the 1940s and 1950s, many workers found the social and professional status of the foreman questionable, because his background was often the environment of former farmworkers. In this situation, enforcing discipline and maintaining authority could have been problematic.

The contacts between the foreman and the workers were an arena of conflicts and tensions, transferred also to the sphere of nonprofessional relations. The most frequent accusations made by workers against their foreman included negligent completion of work record books and entering false numbers of man-hours. Obviously the latter malfeasance was connected to the frequently mentioned problem of connections, contacts, and backing one's preferred workers. In light of the reports by former PGR workers and archive data, it can be concluded that although such acts did take place in practice, their origins were in a range of grounds and attitudes. It could have been the case that providing false or incorrect numbers of man-hours either resulted from the foreman's preference for a given worker or reflected false impressions of a farmworker who felt wronged despite actually having spent the major part of the day lying or sleeping.[33]

This considerable power of foremen in terms of awarding or punishing their subordinates for their work could have far-reaching consequences in the situation of unfair conduct of either of the two groups, especially when a wronged worker took his revenge on his foreman. Extremely interesting and obviously specific for the character of the period was the record provided by one of the foremen working in the 1970s and 1980s. He recalled the necessity to turn a blind eye to workers' outright acts of dishonesty, such as taking home tools or products from the farm.[34] This "blindness," typical also for managers, was characteristic for Polish laborers (factory workers included). In the reality of the PGR, the respondent would explain this way of conduct as resulting from fear of the consequences and revenge by the group of workers involved in the malfeasance.[35]

Even if the manager or the director intervened in such cases, the outcome was rarely positive. Dismissals on disciplinary grounds were occasional, while an admonition, if any, could have turned against the "informer." A specific feature of the PGRs was the requirement to show consideration for workers due to permanently severe manning shortages. In this situation, the farmworker, aware of his indispensability, was in a much better position. There were also cases when such workers would use blackmail on the foreman or the manager, as in the following case:

> [Ms.] Wiśniewska would repeatedly hand in her notice when she wanted to blackmail her manager and win concessions from him ... she would always succeed, for there was no-one to fill in for her. Well, she won't make it this time. I wish she didn't leave—she's a good worker.[36]

The acting and communicating mechanism described here did not apply only to the relations between the foreman and the workers. It seems to have been a matrix, which fitted perfectly for employees of other enterprises (though this obviously did not involve all employees). This refers to the client–paternalistic system analyzed by B. Szklarski and J. Jastrzębska-Szklarska, which developed in the period of the People's Poland:

The residents of Owczary [a state farm] would confirm that remaining silent about the often illegal conduct is an exchangeable good. The director repeatedly turned a blind eye to using machines, fertilizers and tools for private purposes in return for the gratitude of his subordinates and their readiness to repay. Intentional silence ties the patron to the client. The PGRs were not an exception here.[37]

Although the phenomena described above are characteristic rather for the period of the 1970s and 1980s, their range in the 1950s, and in particular during the period of the socialist labor discipline, is worth considering as well. It seems that the discipline was not strictly observed in practice, also in numerous municipal enterprises at that time.[38] Yet the purpose for such legitimization and regular confirmation of the appearances of its functioning and effectiveness were the cases of malfeasance revealed every once in a while, followed by court trials and reviling press articles.[39]

Accountant

Since the 1960s, the position of accountant, usually held by women, was not particularly popular at the beginning, probably due to irregular working hours and substantial responsibility on the part of the employee. In the era of Stalinism, accountants were often put next to their managers to bear responsibility for making losses and economic sabotage.[40] In fact, holding the position of an accountant in a PGR or in any other enterprise undoubtedly offered special opportunities to misappropriate funds. Remunerating inexistent workers or creating deficits was not rare.

The position of an accountant was also the sphere of conflicts and fights between workers that peaked during payment time, when the amounts of wages paid were not compliant with some workers' expectations. Although such conflicts could stem from the popular conviction in People's Poland that "everyone is owed two grand even when their work's been bad," the reasons for bitterness toward the accountants might also have other sources. One of them recalled the situation in the first half of the 1950s as follows:

I calculated the wages for the workers who worked really hard, but the required workloads were practically unfeasible and these workers finally earned very little money. I remember the months when a worker who attended to porkers made 400 zlotys or less. It was not his fault; it was because of the shortages in feedstuff and insufficient gains in weight. Still he would often address his regrets and claims to me, since I was the one who calculated his wages.[41]

Feminization of the accounting profession, particularly evident in the 1960s, was an additional trigger for conflicts at work. Despite the propaganda of progress, the PGR community was usually characterized by a fairly conservative approach not so much to women as to their competences and independence. This attitude was typical mainly of the pre-war generation with rural backgrounds. Numerous situations described by women (not only accountants) evidenced that they were often treated with contempt by their coworkers in similar positions who would thus emphasize their superiority and dominance.

Tractor Drivers (and Machine Operators)

Since the origin of state farms, tractor drivers were a specific group of workers. Their elitism and prestige in the 1940s and 1950s resulted mainly from the limited availability of mechanic equipment at farms and its considerable function in improving farmworks.

Tractor drivers' sense of uniqueness, often declared in public, was determined mostly by the ideology and propaganda of the period, which showed them as the chosen and irreplaceable pioneers of progressive farming. The words of one of the workers are a typical example of such peculiar professional narcissism:

Tractor drivers are special people. They don't like it when someone butts in on their work, as they believe they are the only experts in tractors. Since there was a time when songs were sung about tractors and tractor drivers, when they were praised every step of the way, their conceit and reluctance to accept any remarks became stronger. Each tractor driver felt as if he had been the main character in Jasne łany [lit. fair cornfields], a propaganda movie considered a masterpiece of the period and hence very popular at the time. The response to any comment addressed to them was always the same: "If you don't like our work, comrade, we can go and leave you to reap the crop with a sickle."[42]

This special position of tractor drivers, enhanced by the propaganda, had an effect on their status beyond work as well. The memoirs concerned with the 1950s show that these young and dynamic boys were extremely popular with women pioneers and girl workers.

The question that obviously arises here is concerned with female tractor drivers working at state farms. Official sources provide information about trainings organized for the women who wished to become tractor drivers.[43] The picture is supplemented by propaganda posters and enthusiastically described portraits of female tractor drivers as heroines of socialist labor.[44] Yet in practice such cases were rare, while the oldest state farmworkers practically denied their existence.[45] Therefore, a woman driver was rather an element of the surface reality of Stalinism. This theory is also supported by the hermetic nature of the environment of tractor drivers who were unwilling to allow other workers, not to mention women, to their machines, which they treated as their own. This does not mean, however, that there were no occasional cases of "mechanized women." Their appearance was more likely in the 1960s and 1970s, when technical education for women offered wider possibilities to become trained in this field, particularly in the context of the progressing mechanization of state farms observable since the early 1970s.[46] Despite the high prestige of tractor drivers in the society, certain gradation was noticeable in their circles as well. Being transferred to operate better quality equipment was an equivalent of professional promotion, the peak of which in that category of workers was taking the position of driver, considered a representative of the environmental and professional elite.

The position of tractor drivers was no longer strong when contrasted with foremen. The relations between tractor drivers and their superiors were the major source of problems. One type of such problematic situations was the cases when a tractor driver appropriated the machine he operated and treated it as his private property, often using it to carry out works "on the side."[47] Still it should also be added at this point that making private use of state-owned equipment was a peculiar element of the reality of the period, known in Polish as *boki* (lit. "sides").[48]

The recurrent problem with tractor drivers throughout the discussed period was drunk-driving, often resulting in the acts of bravado and showing off, the cause of serious or even fatal accidents at work. According to memoirists, former foremen, and drivers, the accidents were also due to insufficient driving skills or making machines available to nondrivers.[49] Responsibility for these accidents was also borne by drivers.[50]

The Staff (Manual Workers)

The overlap of the places where farm laborers worked and lived resulted in the development of close correlation between interpersonal contacts at work and outside work. The way of living, the lifestyle, the customs, the views—factors that need not have met the approval of fellow-workers in a municipal enterprise—were harder to ignore within the spatial identity of the workplace and the housing estate.

The social and territorial diversity of farm communities along with the ongoing staff turnover before the 1970s did not favor the development of group integration. The constant "openness" of the working and dwelling community to the often short-lasting contacts with people "from the outside" originally required specific vigilance and control. In the 1960s and 1970s, that tension and sense of danger due to contacts with "strangers" seemed to have been giving way to the specific form of adjustment to the way of living organized as such. By that period, there had also developed the division of workers into the permanent ones, who gradually became integrated with each other, and the remaining ones, often residing at a given PGR for several months though not sharing any long-lasting experiences with the rest of the dwellers.[51] In the 1940s and 1950s, the character of the mutual relations was also determined by prejudice and stereotypes. This referred mainly to different nationalities (such as Germans, Ukrainians, Russians). The attitude to the new reality also played an important role here. According to the sources, membership in trade unions, a party organization, or a self-government was a pretext to emphasize one's sense of superiority, as well as authority and influences,[52] an attitude familiar to the workers in other types of enterprises as well.

Similarly, the sphere of state farms was also characterized by the element typical for the majority of Polish workers in the era of Stalinism, namely the dislike for, if not the hostility toward those of them who demonstrated an enthusiastic approach to labor. Their eagerness to raise the quotas of standard workload was not motivating for the rest of the group, and neither was it welcome in the relations after work. Yet in light of today's reports, it is difficult to state whether such leading actually resulted from the ideological principle of competition or whether its grounds were purely material, since working beyond the established quotas was an opportunity to earn a bonus, a worthy incentive in the situation of permanent shortages.[53] The PGRs, same as other centers of socialist labor, saw the "iron heroes," the lead workers nominated from behind the desk and awarded for their false achievements with bonuses typical for the given period.[54] The remaining workers often felt genuinely hostile and aggressive toward such "heroes," which was an expression of their sense of social injustice and their protest against "connections and contacts."[55]

The model image of harmonious coexistence at state farms, popularized in the press, was difficult to achieve in the reality of the PGRs. The farm's community, though not monolithic, as shown above, would neither accept any distinguishing and outstanding individuals. This was often due to the feeling of envy and competition. The reasons could also lie beyond the professional life; for instance, there was a case when farming women criticized a fellow-worker for her attempts at highlighting her femininity with attire.[56]

Overt resourcefulness or successes at work could also become a subject of gossip and comments. A farm manager in the 1950s described the situation of women working double shifts with the following words:

> . . . people complain about her greed, as she wants to make money both in the piggery and in the barn . . . I know that rumours start each time I stand up for her . . .[57]

Another memoirist from the 1960s put it as follows:

> . . . when someone is really hard up, they say that she cannot manage on her own, but when someone is doing very well, they call her mean.[58]

The necessity to adjust to the requirements of a given environment at the expense of one's individuality was instrumental for gaining approval and avoiding social exclusion. Yet in some cases, the latter was a deliberate choice:

> . . . many workers did not like him because he neither drank vodka nor smoke, and he did not sympathize with the abusing ones.[59]

The character of contacts between workers was also based on the similarity of their work tasks or the time they spent together at work. During their work, the women in the field team or in the breeding team could often talk about matters not related to the farm or the production. Sometimes long-lasting and genuine friendships were established in that situation, though staying permanently together (both at work and at the housing estate) also generated various conflicts, arguments, if not fights. Although the latter were primarily men's domain, there were cases of fisticuffs between women as well. Their grounds usually were particularly touchy private issues or affairs of the heart.[60] Mutual relations were also influenced to a large extent by informal interdependencies, described as connections and contacts, or "cliques." The formation of cliques generated a range of attitudes, with covering up for one another based on the peculiar understanding of solidarity (or self-seeking) at one extreme, and denunciating, filing complaints, more characteristic of the 1950s and commonly referred to as "writing"[61] at the other.

The lack of integration in the groups of workers was also reflected in the minutes from the workers' meetings in the 1950s and 1960s. During the AOB part of such meetings, the workers often filed in mutual accusations and charges concerning improper ways of working, negligence, and so on. Yet it is difficult to conclude whether such conduct was founded on their actual concern about the farm, or it simply resulted from human malice and envy.[62]

The principles governing farming communities would also become evident upon hiring a new worker. One of the respondents who started his work in the late 1970s recalled laconically the "baptism" he was to experience at that time. Unfortunately the details have not been provided, yet the very mention signals that after years of cooperation at least some of the teams developed a system of typical behaviors, including some form of an initiation ritual.[63]

The customary "incorporation of the new one" into a group of workers (such as tractor drivers) occasionally required showing one's abilities or passing a test of practical or adaptation skills. One of the memoirists recalled it in the following way:

> . . . after some time the ice broke; my advice was no longer cuttingly criticized and my orders were fulfilled without protesting. The tractor drivers assumed that I must have known something about tractors, which I proved to them when one of the machines wouldn't start.[64]

It seems that these customs, even if rare, became characteristic particularly for the period of the merging of generations in the late 1960s and at the beginning of the 1970s. Their grounds were partly in the conviction prevailing among the older generation of farmworkers, and stemming from the farming tradition, about the predominance of practical knowledge, based on long-standing experience, over theoretical knowledge brought along by the young workers who would take up executive positions from the very beginning of their careers.

According to the ideological assumptions, the PGRs were intended as model socialist farms, which would develop emotional ties between them and their workers by means of the identity of the workplace and the dwelling and the extensive system of loans, payments in kind, and subsidies. The permanent presence of the supervising personnel (the managers and the foremen), as well as the overlapping official and unofficial relations (e.g., based on neighborhood) were intended by the creators of the new reality as possibilities to maintain ongoing surveillance of, enable interventions in, and have influence on the form of interpersonal relations within a farm/a housing estate.

Because of heavy staff turnover, frequent changes of workplaces, as well as regional and social diversity, the functional mechanisms of state-owned farms described briefly above quickly got out of the control of central authorities.

The phenomena and pathologies observed in the analyzed sphere of interpersonal relations strongly reflect the weakness and the artificiality of the imposed system, which basically distorted the workers' understanding and value of labor (i.e., their attitude to work). Its characteristic expression was permanently "negotiating the relations of power" within the farm and the responsibility for the farm, which became muddied as a result of these "negotiations" and workers' mobility. The ownership of a farm, nationalized and therefore "common" in ideological terms, in practice often implied certain connotations in workers, which came down to the following scheme: "what belongs to the farm belongs to the state, and as such it belongs to no-one."[65] A simple reflection of this approach was the lack of respect for the nationalized equipment, and its consequent instances of "appropriating" tools, creating deficits, taking things away from the workplace, and so forth.

Notes

1. *Przegląd Rolniczy* [Agricultural Review] 1948, issue 1, p. 8.
2. Ibid.
3. About the role of the sovkhozes and the kolkhozes in shaping the new identity of the workers of Polish state farms see, A. Doskocz-Winiarski, "The Agriculture of the Soviet Union," *Przegląd Rolniczy* [Agricultural Review] issue 10, 1948, 289–92.
4. The space of PGRs was in many cases founded on the basis of pre-war farmworkers' premises. It was also a common practice, especially in the 1940s, to build them from scratch. Their space, created in this way, was in many respects unique and unusual. In accordance with the idea of the peasants–workers alliance, it combined two previously separated social orders (the village and the urban working-class one). Therefore, on the one hand, the space of the PGRs remained rural in character, with its typical

17

self-sufficiency and the characteristic rural duties and areas, such as fields, garden plots, enclosures, stables, barns, and so on. Yet on the other hand, it was also an area of state company with its workshop and administration buildings and housing estates. These two spaces, the living and the working one, interpenetrated.

5. [a manual worker—PGR W.]—tape no. 11.

6. PNZ—the abbreviation for Państwowe Nieruchomości Ziemskie—literally a state-owned landed estates were set in 1946. Until 1948 they created a base (and a space) for later PGRs.

7. E. Kłoczowski, *Moja praca w Państwowych Nieruchomościach Ziemskich w Poznaniu (1946–1949)* [My work at National Land Estate (1946–1949)] Poznań, 1996, 55, which obviously did not mean that such positions were not taken by completely unprepared individuals.

8. See, e.g., Z. Zblewski, *Leksykon PRL* [Polish People Republic's Lexicon] Kraków, 2000, 99–101.

9. *Młode pokolenie wsi Polski Ludowej. Gospodarstwo i rodzina* [The young generation of rural of the Polish People's Republic. Farm and family], vol. 5, Warsaw, 1964, 481–82.

10. The multilevel structure of management in a socialist enterprise implied the situation in which an informer and a worker in one could provide information about the staff's mood not necessarily to the director, but for instance to the manager. This situation in the context of the 1970s was reflected in *Spokój* [*The Calm*] a film by K. Kieślowski, in which the main character, Gralak, was placed in similar circumstances by his manager who asked, "What do people say? Well, what do they say? Any complaints? Who took you in, Gralak? You must have someone to side with." See *The Calm*, dir. K. Kieślowski, 1976.

11. *Blisko ziemi, blisko ludzi* [Close to the ground, close to the people], ed. B. Wojciechowska–Kołłątaj, Warszawa, 1975, 115.

12. *Młode pokolenie wsi Polski Ludowej. Tu jest mój dom. Pamiętniki z ziem zachodnich i północnych* [The young generation of rural of Polish People's Republic. Here is my home. The memories of western and northern lands], vol. 2, Warsaw, 1965, 635; APP, IGT, file no. 96, pp. 45–46. A specific pattern for such letters could have been the problems originated by the editors, who would also come up with the descriptions of the obviously successful interventions. Such control over the society, for example, by means of publishing detailed personal data of the condemned persons in the press, was one of the major means of surveillance and enslavement, and a rather effective one, since putting it into practice was confirmed by the archive data from both the western and the south-eastern territories of Poland.

13. For example, Płoty State Archive, the District Court in Kamień Pomorski, file no. 167, pp. 72–73.

14. "Polish October" or "October 1956" refers to a change in Polish internal political scene, which was often described as the end of Stalinist era in Poland. This year was a time of big transition. After the death of J. Stalin and the Polish communist leader B. Bierut, the hardliner Stalinist faction in Poland was weakened. In October 1956 (after the workers' protests in June in Poznań), the power was taken by the leader of the reformers'

faction—Wladyslaw Gomulka. He started the temporary (two years long) time of liberalization of life in Poland.

15. [the director—PGR W.]—tape no. 1, 2.

16. *Młode pokolenie wsi Polski Ludowej, Awans pokolenia* [The young generation of rural of the Polish People's Republic. Generation advancement], vol. I, Warszawa, 1964, 92–93.

17. Ibid.

18. *Blisko ziemi*, 115–16, 126.

19. A particularly interesting example here is the attitude of the staff of the PGR N., who protested against the transfer of their manager and submitted a letter to the director, signed by 32 workers, requesting "keeping Citizen F. in his managerial position with regard to his perception as a good manager," Płoty State Archive, Zbiór akt zespołów PGR z terenu działania Oddziału Archiwum Państwowego w Płotach z lat 1945–1958 [Reference Collection of PGRs from the area of National Archives Branch in 1945–1958 file no. 206, p. 9]. Yet there were cases where the determinant of the staff's "support" for either of the antagonists was the power of his backing.

20. J. Czuła, *Z pamiętnika pioniera* [from the memories of a pioneer], Warsaw, 1956, 276. "Recovered Territories" (Polish "Ziemie Odzyskane")—as an official term it was used by Polish authorities and the propaganda of the People's Republic of Poland to denote those former German territories that were in the past a part of the Polish state and over time were lost and Germanized and which were returned to Poland after World War II.

21. E. Kłoczowski, *Moja praca*, 34; *Młode pokolenie wsi Polski Ludowej. Gospodarstwo i rodzina*, 93.

22. This role was often taken over by other workers from the local "elite," that is, the foremen, the accountants, or the drivers.

23. For example, *Blisko ziemi*, 90.

24. This rule was reflected in the experiences conveyed in the discussions with other former workers of the same team (and later of the same conglomerate plant) in the PGR W., where the remarks about the same manager (or the director) and other workers testified to the specificity of relations that were rather private in character.

25. This is an evidence of the presence in the reality of state farms of two models of women, which did not tally with each other: the first model was a female worker compliant with the pattern promoted by the propaganda, equally engaged in her social and professional work as men, freed from her housing duties by kindergartens, canteens, and after-school clubs, while the other was that of a traditional rural woman as a resourceful and hardworking administrator, housewife, and mother.

26. As provided for in the demand made during the meeting of managers, the secretaries of basic Party organizations and the head of the Workers' Self-Government in 1960, which stated that "white-collar workers, farm managers, accountants and warehousemen should be interested not only in production issues, but also the occupational health and safety matters and social conditions concerning the workers." See Płoty State Archive, the Inspectorate of the PGR in Goleniów (IG), file no. 4, p. 209.

27. For example, Płoty State Archive, SRwKP, file no. 127.

28. For example, Płoty State Archive, ZAZ, file no. 41, p. 89, 197; APP, IGT, file no. 96, pp. 45–46.

29. [manual worker—PGR P.]—tape no. 7.

30. *Kamena* 1965, issue 4, p. 4.

31. The system of working in teams, patterned after the Soviet sovkhozes, was introduced in the late 1940s. It replaced the earlier system of landless farming practiced in the state-owned landed estates and the PGRs. Based on the factory work patterns, the system of gangs was intended as a practical realization of the objectives of the workers–peasants alliance in the area of state farms.

32. *Układ Zbiorowy Pracy* [The Collective Agreement of Work] 1951/1952, 20–21.

33. [field workers—PGR W.]—tape no. 11. There were also such opinions: "the foreman was wrong most of the time, and he would consider himself an expert though his knowledge was scarce. There were clashes like between him and me, when I knew one thing, and he claimed the opposite"—[manual worker—PGR P.]—tape no. 7.

34. An interview that was not taped.

35. The examples of such revenges are provided in court files, for example, [in 1975] the price paid by a warehouseman from the PGR Ł. for informing the manager about the fact that one of the women had not shown up at work was having the tires in his motorcycle cut by the woman's common-law husband; APP, SRwKP, file no. 265; it must be noted, however, that such feuding was an element of the reality of the period in general, as evidenced by such feature films as *The Calm* by K. Kieślowski referred to above.

36. J. Czuła, *Z pamiętnika*, 278.

37. Based on their own field studies, the authors exposed the attitude of the director as the patron positioned higher in the hierarchical structure of the organization. According to the author, the lower levels of the patronage, such as the positions of the manager or the foreman, were involved in the system as well; J. Jastrzębska-Szklarska, B. Szklarski, "Od klientelizmu do paternalizmu—biednej społeczności pegeerowskiej droga przez transformację" [From clientelism to patronalism. The road of transformation of the poor PGR communities], in *Lata tłuste, lata chude—spojrzenia na biedę w społecznościach lokalnych* [Years of fat, lean years . . . The insight into poverty in local communities], ed. E. Tarkowska, Warsaw, 2002, 114–115.

38. B. Brzostek, *Robotnicy Warszawy. Konflikty codzienne (1950–1954)* [The Workers of Warsaw. Everyday Conflicts], Warsaw, 2002, 49.

39. For example, *Blisko ziemi, blisko ludzi* [Close to the land, close to the people], ed. B. Wojciechowska-Kołłątaj, Warsaw, 1975, 29.

40. For example, Płoty State Archive, SRwKP, file no. 216.

41. *Tu jest mój dom*, 191.

42. *Blisko ziemi*, 67.

43. *Biuletyn Ministerstwa Państwowych Gospodarstw Rolnych* [The Bulletin of the Ministry of State Farms], issue 28, 1952, 1.

44. Such as *Robotnik Rolny* issue 3, 1951, 11.

45. A mention of the "lead woman tractor driver from Żuławy" appeared actually in one memoir. See *Nasze nowe życie. Pamiętniki z konkursu na wspomnienia mieszkańców ziem zachodnich i północnych* [Our new life. Memoirs of the competition for the memoirs of the inhabitants of the western and northern Poland] ed. Z. Bigorajska, E. Jabłoński, Warsaw, 1978, 198.

46. Quick mechanization in the 1970s was mentioned by one of the respondents. According to that former worker, it had to do with the order to eliminate the horses and send the "horsemen" to train as tractor drivers [the foreman, the manager—PGR W.]—tape no. 3.

47. About the "private" jobs approved by the director: Płoty State Archive, IGT, file no. 96, p. 59.

48. T. Toborek, "Ukraść czy skombinować," *Biuletyn Instytutu Pamięci Narodowej* [The bulletin of the Institute of National Remembrance] issue 2, 2003, 40–41.

49. Płoty State Archive, IGT, file no. 96, 115.

50. For example, [the foreman, the manager—the PGR W.]—tape no. 3. Drinking alcohol at work as a popular social custom was also discussed by Z. Zblewski: "The regular propaganda campaigns for sobriety at work and the number of accidents caused by drink-drivers, along with the famous '1 pm' as the hour before which alcoholic beverages could not have been sold, evidence that in People's Poland drinking alcohol at work was an actual problem, and it was often heavy drinking"; see "Życie codzienne w PRL. Rozmowa B. Polak z A. Dudkiem, Z. Zblewskim i M. Zarembą" [Everyday Life in PRL. Interview with A. Dudek, Z. Zblewski and M. Zaremba] *Biuletyn Instytutu Pamięci Narodowej* [The Bulletin of the Institute of National Remembrance], issue 2, 2003, 24.

51. It seems that this limited bond between the "old" dwellers of the housing estates was the basis for the closeness declared in the present relations between respondents, which need not have been as perfect as in today's descriptions provided by the former workers.

52. Płoty State Archive, ZAZ, file no. 38, p. 63.

53. [tractor driver—the PGR W.]—tape no. 4. This target of the competition at work in the factories in Warsaw was also described by B. Brzostek; see B. Brzostek, *Robotnicy Warszawy*, 64.

54. Płoty State Archive, ZAZ, file no. 37, p. 185.

55. Płoty State Archive, ZAZ, file no. 162, p. 47.

56. *Blisko ziemi*, 251.

57. J. Czuła, *Z pamiętnika*, pp. 285–86.

58. *Tu jest mój dom*, 291.

59. *Nasze nowe życie*, 123.

60. An example of such conflict between two women aged twenty-something was provided in the court files: the conflict was based in the accusation and slander of the emotional attitude toward one of the superiors and the "loose morals" on the part of one of them. An interesting element of the conflict was the fact that one of the tinderboxes was calling the defendant "an Ukrainian"; Płoty State Archive, SRwKP, file no. 205.

61. [field foreman—the PGR K.]—tape no. 10.
62. For example, *Tu jest mój dom*, 636.
63. [manual worker—the PGR K.]—the tape no. 6. One of the typical "initiation rituals" of the past period (though probably also practiced in other periods) concerning the adaptation of the new worker in the gang was the custom reflected also in the reality of the PGRs and presented in *The Calm* by Kieślowski, based on an evening meeting between the "new" worker and the rest of the gang over "a pork chop and a bottle of vodka."
64. *Blisko ziemi*, 67.
65. *Tu jest mój dom*, 294.

2

"Women Workers" in Hungary: Identities and Everyday Lives (Microhistorical Analysis of Life-Story Interviews)

Eszter Zsófia Tóth

On April 1, 1970, the members of the Liberation Brigade of the Budapest Hosiery Factory received the State Prize.[1] The award ceremony took place in the parliament. The award consisted of a medal and a cash prize for each worker. The brigade was featured in a lot of newspaper articles about women. This was probably the only occasion in the lives of these nine women when they felt that everyone in socialist Hungary was equal and enjoyed equal opportunities. By the time they got the prize, they had worked for many years as semiskilled workers in the molding workshop of the factory. The workshop was considered the lowest prestige department of the factory because of the fumes, the amount of steam in the air, and the unbearable heat that persisted through summer and winter alike. At the time they received the prize, all members of the brigade had reached middle age. They had moved to Budapest shortly after the end of World War II, at the age of sixteen or seventeen. Their migration from small villages and rural communities in the poorest parts of the country to the city was driven not only by a struggle to survive, but also by a desire for adventure, freedom, and change.

Despite lacking skills, they immediately found work in the city with the help of relatives and acquaintances from their home villages, who had already settled down in Budapest. Many of them started working as

23

domestic servants and went to work at the factories of the capital city as soon as jobs were made available in the 1950s. Some married before entering industrial employment, and others immediately afterward, mostly to skilled workers. In this period of their lives, however, the greatest struggle was not about finding a suitable husband but about finding a proper job. The place where they worked for several decades, often together with their skilled-worker husbands, was the Budapest Hosiery Factory, founded in 1951.[2] By the end of the 1950s, most of the brigade members had already given birth to their first children. According to the propaganda of the time, they were enjoying privileges both as industrial workers and as women. The reality, however, was quite different. Many of them were not allocated a state-owned flat, as was the common practice at the time, and if they did not want to pay for a rented flat, or to live in unheated and damp flats, they had to solve their housing issues by themselves. Therefore, after the suppression of the revolution in 1956, many of them squatted in abandoned flats. As a consequence of their unhealthy working conditions, they suffered from illness and premature aging much more than their direct superiors who did not perform manual work in the shop. By the time they received the award, some of them were already either divorced or widowed. The eldest of the State Prize laureates retired soon afterward.

The members of the Liberation Brigade experienced the intervention of the state in their lives most strongly in their workplace: they had to participate in the "labor competition," to establish a "socialist brigade,"[3] and in order to advance at work, it proved helpful for them to join the party and for their husbands to join the Workers' Guard.[4]

This study sets to analyze the role of work and its official public recognition with the award of the State Prize in the formation of the brigade members' identities, set against other factors and events in their everyday lives. Personal identity is interpreted here as a construct that changes over the years depending on one's self-identification through belonging to different social groups in the course of one's life.[5] Recollected identities can therefore be interpreted as social constructs, whereby the groups to which the subject has belonged carry symbolic importance.[6] In this particular case, "recollected identities" are the narrator's self-presentations in the course of the interview, based on his or her personal history of belonging to certain social groups. Not only identity, but also the group, is dynamically evolving over time.[7] Likewise, the significance attached to a specific group changes over the life course. This is easily established in the life-story narratives: the narrators attach significance to their belonging to different groups at different periods of their lives. The processes of moving away from one group and joining another may coincide. Life-story narratives, however, are generally not very well suited to revealing such dynamic processes.[8]

The study is primarily based on multi-session life-story interviews with the nine brigade members, carried out on several occasions between 1999 and 2003. Furthermore, interviews were conducted with their husbands, colleagues, and superiors—a total of twenty-three people. In addition, I conducted one interview with each of the women from the brigade together with a family member who had not migrated to Budapest. Although many of them had worked temporarily in the capital city for some time in their lives, they had eventually decided not to settle there but to return to their hometowns. These nine respondents still live in the small towns of Túrkeve, Mezőtúr, and Zalaszentgrót today.

My interview partners belong to three age-groups. The two oldest brigade members were born in the early 1920s and came from a working-class background, one from Budapest and the other one from Abony; both had one older sibling. The members of the middle age-group were born between 1927 and 1934, and all came from large families who made their living from farming. They had moved to Budapest only after World War II. The members of the third and youngest age-group were born around 1940 and came from working-class families. These worked for the most part as the supervisors of the semiskilled workers in the factory. Therefore, the interviews with them were used only to shed light on the role of the workplace in shaping identities.

According to the official discourse of the time, the socialist brigade was a collective organized primarily around ideological norms. Its members presumably belonged to one and the same social group, in this case the industrial working class. Despite this assumption of homogeneity, the narratives of the brigade members diverged significantly: even when they were referring to the same events, they attributed different meanings and importance to them. Furthermore, they gave emphasis to different factors that determined the course of their lives and thus constructed their identities in very different ways. A common history of the brigade as a collective could be constructed only at the expense of the uniqueness and the particularity of their individual life stories.

To make the picture even more complicated, there is a temporal dynamic to be taken into account as well: various anchors of identity, related to the interviewees belonging to certain social groups, acquire different significance for them at different periods of their lives. Emotional ties to the workplace, experiences pertaining to the award of the State Prize, as well as household-related activities and consumption practices, which were less emphasized, or completely absent, in the female role models disseminated by the propaganda, can be recognized as identity-forming factors in the narrative structure of the interviews. The interviewees found it important to talk not only about their fellow prize-winning brigade members, about the "collective," and about the factory (which had been closed down by the time of the research), but also about their homes and about the Trabant car they bought with the money, which accompanied the award (see Figure 1). In 1970, the sum amounting to twenty thousand forints was a huge amount of money for people of their social status: one of them bought a car, another one bought a sewing machine, and so forth. The interviewees oftentimes accounted for their relation to the material objects and elaborated on how they came in possession of their flat, or of particular consumer

Figure 1 The First Woman Car Owner in the Factory, 1970

Interviewee's archive. Reproduced with premission.

goods. The emphasis put on such facts offered the author a better understanding of the values shared by these working women in the postwar decades.

Women Workers in the Socialist Brigade

First, I will look into the narratives of the workplace and of the award as the one and only occasion in the lives of my interview partners when they were given official recognition as semiskilled women workers.

The importance ascribed to labor competition in the narratives of the brigade members was not as unambiguous as Padraic Kenney described it with reference to the Polish workers in the early years of socialism: "Labor competition was nothing less than a wager on the enthusiasm of new workers because it offered them a chance to earn more money, gain advance in the factory, and see their names in the newspaper."[9] For Mária, the leader of the brigade, taking part in the labor competition was a way to present herself as an independent, successful woman. As a leader of a socialist brigade, she could meet high-ranking politicians, among whom János Kádár, the first secretary of the Hungarian Communist Party (MSZMP). As a leader of a prize-winning brigade, she delivered lectures at party congresses. When she talks about it now, her statements still bear traces of the propaganda clichés of the time, suggestive of the strong influence the state ideological discourse had exerted on my interviewees.

By contrast, Erzsébet, a member of the brigade, recalls her involvement in the socialist brigade above all in terms of the tasks she was assigned in addition to her factory work. After fulfilling her daily quotas in the workshop, she had to carry out a lot of additional compulsory work: she helped old people with their laundry, with ironing, and so on. This charity work, although said to be voluntary, was required by the rules of the labor competition. The socialist brigades were entrusted with three major tasks: achieving above-average work results, increasing their professional, political, and general education, and living in "the socialist way," implying an exemplary private life, good cooperation with the comrades, and active participation in social work and public affairs. To this end, the leader of the brigade had signed an agreement with the local council for volunteer work, providing assistance to the elderly. The brigade members were not being paid for these activities since they were an essential part of the brigade movement. Erzsébet told me a story about her experience with caring for an old lady as part of the labor competition:

One day Marika [the brigade leader] came and told us that we were assigned a new task in the labor competition: we had to help old women who were living alone. Every week I had to wash her [the old woman's] hair, to clean up her flat. I had to go to her place after I finished my work in the factory. One time, as I got there, I heard noises from behind. I glanced back . . . I thought someone was following me. I saw that a man came by to the old woman. I started cleaning up, but I also kept an eye on him. I listened to the noises. I think he was the lover of this old woman. Afterwards, I told this story to my co-workers in the factory. I told them that a woman who is having a lover should be able to clean up herself. I didn't go there anymore . . . [10]

This episode suggests the existence of quite complex relations within the brigade. On the one hand, Erzsébet explains that she was obliged to help this old woman, because the assignment was part and parcel of the labor competition. On the other hand, she emphasizes her independence in the brigade, as she had the option to drop this activity. In her story, her decision appears to be self-made and not influenced by the leader of the brigade.

While their husbands proudly described themselves as "skilled workers" or "shift machine shop supervisors," my female interview partners hardly ever referred to themselves as "women workers." They did it only when pointing to the fact that they had won the State Prize in 1970. Some of them still refer to this achievement with pride today,[11] even though they find it strange now that they had won an award that usually went to actors. When speaking in this context, they use the kind of phrases that the official press of the time used to describe them in the reports covering the story. Then why were they so reluctant to describe themselves as "women workers" in the interviews?

It seems that belonging to the category of "women workers" plays a less important role in shaping the personal identities of the interviewees than their loyalty to the factory or the award they won together as a brigade—an achievement that they experience today both as a form of recognition and as a stigma, because the recognition came from a regime now proven to have been corrupt.[12] Over the course of their lives, being a "working woman" has meant to them nothing but a means of hanging on to urban life.

In 1968 and 1969, the magazine *Nők Lapja (Magazine of Women)* ran a series of articles that discussed whether "being a working woman was a mark of status." In the first article in the series, the journalist admitted that she "wrote the phrase only with difficulty."[13] From the numerous contributions to the debate, it became clear that many young women did not want to take up appointments in the shop floor of the factory anymore, but yearned for the cleaner and more comfortable office jobs instead.[14] The readers were presented with the full range of popular stereotypes about factory work. A year later, my respondents received the State Prize as manual workers and as a socialist brigade.

"They Called Me a Movie Star": Gender and Work in the Life Stories

The state ideology in socialist Hungary used gender as a symbolic construction tailored to the achievement of its own goals. In the language of propaganda, the emancipation of women was a metaphor for gender equality on the labor market and in everyday life. The life-story narratives of the nine brigade members alerted me to the impact state propaganda has had on the ways of presenting gendered experiences in everyday life. These stories are documents particularly pertinent to the analysis of several aspects of the gender relations. When discussing gender and everyday socialism, I should point out that gender discrimination on the labor market was common in socialist Hungary, as supported by a large body of research on the place of work in women's lives during the socialist period, undertaken after the fall of the regime.[15] Contemporary literatures on female employment have promoted the idea that the increased number of working women and the drastic changes in the everyday life of the families after World War II reshaped the public and private spheres of the working-class life. At the same time, sociologists have observed changes in the notions of masculinity and femininity, as well as in the expectations of domesticity and marriage.[16] Such studies have suggested the development of an increasingly complex communist gender ideology. This complexity is also reflected in the life-story narratives of the working women I have interviewed.

Migration appears to be an important topic in the narratives of the brigade members and a topic closely related to their gendered self-presentations. All nine women were born and grown up in extended families in small towns and villages. They moved to Budapest after World War II as young girls. In their life stories, they tend to elaborate on this event and explain their motivations. The decision to migrate was not an easy decision for them to make, as it was related not only to their economic situation. Erzsébet told in detail about her migration experience, at the same time revealing other aspects of the process.

At first she presented herself as an obedient girl: her mother had advised her to find work in the city to earn more money than she could in the village and so she did. Next, she emphasized the influence of her female migrant relatives who depicted the city as a place of attractions and entertainment.[17] They did not admit, however, that one of the reasons behind their decision to migrate to the city was their desire to escape from the patriarchal way of life in the villages and/or from their dependence on their male relatives. My interviewee's brother strongly argued for the traditional notions of gender roles. To sustain this argument, he used the well-known "tale" about the decline of the traditional family under socialism. He emphasized that the main reason for the decline of the family was that many women went to work in the industry.[18]

My female interviewees used both individualist and group-oriented strategies in the process of migration. Their adaptive strategies had to be individualistic, for migrants depended primarily on their own resources and initiative. At the same time, they had to be group-oriented too, for marginalized migrants from the rural areas used to rely upon others as well, usually relatives or fellow villagers, as revealed in much of the anthropological literature.[19]

The brigade members claimed that the need to start working at a young age—either in the family, or as a domestic servant, had shaped their attitude toward work. They all regard work as a necessary investment of time and energy for the purpose of making a living and, if possible, for deriving more pleasure from life outside the job.[20] For these women, who used to do unskilled and semiskilled jobs, work was an unquestionable part of their lives after migrating to Budapest.

Teréz emphasized that as a young girl she was expected to work in the extended rural household she belonged to, because she was the eldest daughter in the family. She described her duties as traditional women's work that she disliked: it was her duty to do the housework and to look after the younger children. According to her life-story narrative, the traditional women's work appeared to be the most important push factor for emigration from the village. That is why, after moving to Budapest, she did not want to work as a domestic servant, and she found a job as a semiskilled worker in construction instead. Later, she lost her job and went back to her village for a short period of time when she worked as a seamstress. After her marriage, she settled in Budapest and gave birth to two sons in the early 1950s. She emphasized in the interview that her husband was very reluctant to let her work. She expanded on her situation:

I told my husband that I wanted to work in a factory because we had
no money for buying a coat. He let me go to work, but only for a short
time. We bought the coat. After that I told my husband we had to buy
coats for the children too.[21]

Teréz presented her situation as fairly uncertain. She had had a hard
time persuading her husband to let her get a job, and then she had to
negotiate with him about keeping the job on a temporary basis, every
time trying to come up with the right reasons:

The children were born, they had grown up a bit, and they needed
winter coats. I told my husband that I would work only until I made
enough money to pay for four winter coats. Then I told my husband
I would keep working while they were still growing up. And I went on
from there. I can't stand being without a job.[22]

Throughout her story, Teréz made it clear that her goal in life was not
to run the household, but to take up a job in the labor market. It was
not only income that mattered to her: she described her workplace
as a symbol of her independence. She was a trade unionist and a keen
member of the communist party. Party membership seemed a natural
obligation to her since her father had been the first member of the communist party in her village. After the change of the system, Teréz never
wanted to become a member of a party again. In her story, however,
she described herself as a woman who spoke out her mind in front
of everybody at work, including the director of the factory whom she
came to know very well in the course of her union activities.

In some of these narratives, we can again discern the influence of the
official public rhetoric of the time. The pressure of the "double burden,"
depicted as a "second shift," was a metaphor for women's duties in the
household in addition to their paid work in the public sphere and a
recurring topic in the newspapers. My interviewees never used this
expression. Manci, however, did underline the pressure of the double
burden. She depicted her life as a hard one: she had to be a good mother
and a good worker at the same time. She presented herself as a good
cook and mentioned that she had to do the washing and the ironing
not only for her husband and sons, but also for her brother. Nowadays,
she washes and irons the clothes of her tenant.

Sometimes, the stories bring out aspects of the traditional social
lifestyle of women, such as passing down skills and knowledge from
mother to daughter, for instance. Mária, the leader of the brigade,

points out the traditional lifestyle of women as an ideal. One could hypothesize that these stereotypes, featured in the stories of the interviewees, appear both as a self-image and as a tradition inherited from the past generations.

Finally, gender stereotypes coming from the popular culture of the time can be found in the interviewees' self-presentations as well. For Anna, the oldest member of the brigade, cinema seems to have played a central role.[23] She enthusiastically compares her husband to the contemporary movie star Pál Jávor, when recalling the time they were courting. According to her account, he sent her flowers and serenaded her with gypsy music. Speaking of herself, she seems to have taken great pride in her appearance. She stressed the fact that as a young woman, she was thought to be so attractive that she was nicknamed "the movie star":

> I am very proud of it, that I was called a movie star by my brother's friends and by the projectionist in the cinema. I was so pretty and I loved cinema so much.[24]

The identities of these formerly working women, as constructed in the interviews, seem to be anchored in their belonging to certain groups. One of them is the group of the industrial workers. Their identity as women workers, however, is not a very pronounced one, and it relates only to the fact that they spent most of their lives as industrial workers. In this relation, the award of the State Prize does not seem to be of particular importance to them. Albeit expressed and referred to in a variety of ways, gender is one of the few stable identity categories that I established in the life narratives of my interviewees. The narratives pertaining to their consumption practices, however, appear to be much more conspicuous.

The Role of Consumption

It should be pointed out that the interviewees—men and women alike—spoke a lot about consumption, coping with their everyday life and their homes.

In the socialist period, it was prohibited to bypass the official distribution channels of the centrally planned economy. The "Profiteering" section of Act V of 1961 on the Penal Code prescribed a maximum sentence of three years of imprisonment for those "engaging in commercial activity or maintaining a business without the requisite permit, or b) conducting economically unjustified intermediary trade in goods, or speculating in other ways conducive to profiteering."[25] The interviewees told of a case of proceedings started against a female coworker at the Budapest Hosiery Factory who sold clothing items (pullovers and cardigans) in the factory. The incident can be found in the archives as well, classified along with the larceny cases in the factory. The woman was reported on suspicion of "profiteering":

> *The profiteering that occurred in the boarding shop of the Folyamőr utca [factory] in March this year [1968] was carried out by Mrs György H[26] and the requisite official measures are in progress.*[27]

The same report includes cases of selling three cardigans, worth 520 forints each, stolen in 1967. The sale of goods on the premises of the factory was criminalized, and those who wrote the report treated it as if it were a case of stealing "public property," such as tights produced at the factory, or stealing "private property" such as clothes or valuables of other workers. Nonetheless, vendors were prepared to take the risk of being prosecuted by the police. There was a big demand for cheap products, which were in short supply in the shops, and this activity provided the vendors with an extra income for work performed at least partly outside working hours.

Several respondents recalled this particular case. This was not just because they had bought goods from the vendor, for they had done it before on several occasions, but because they had been called upon to report directly to the representatives of a law enforcement agency how they got hold of products that were out of stock in the shops.

> *György: Well, the wife was involved in a case where the police . . .*
> *Erzsébet (laughing): Hunch-Buffet.*
> *György: Hunch-Buffet was what we called the security officer.*
> *Erzsébet: He came over to us . . . He said, nothing's going to happen to you, just tell me whether you sometimes buy stuff from Mrs—.*
> *György: Who brought in the raincoats.*
> *Erzsébet: Yes, she used to bring in stuff to sell at the factory. She worked in the shop, just as me, and a neighbor said to her, sell these clothes, as many as you can, and the money will be yours. Well, they were made out of some material—we didn't know much about quality— when we put them on, they stretched terribly. (We laugh.) It was all right when I tried it on. Then you had to dry it flat because you were not supposed to spin dry it. Our names were all in her ledger if we*

had bought from her, because we would pay for the goods in instal-
ments when the pay-checks came in. We couldn't have bought them
any other way. With our hands on the cross in court, we had to say
we were telling the truth.[28]

The above exchange illustrates very well a common pattern observed
in storytelling. First, the interviewees recalled the situation with the
security officer holding them up for making a purchase, and then they
described the events that had led to it. The excitement and the fear
they felt at the time were still present in the story, even if rendered
jokingly. The woman prosecuted for illegal trade was a coworker
and she was not the only one selling things. Others might have faced
prosecution too. The nickname of the security officer *(Pupkredenc)*
suggested that he was someone in power, ridiculed as a hunchback,
but no less threatening for that. Malvin, when telling the same story,
specifically pointed to the fact that she was lucky because the policeman knew very well her village.

That's what Zs. was hawking around. There were three sizes. I took
one home and tried it on, and took it back the next day because it was
too tight for me. Meanwhile she had not crossed my name off her list.
Well, some time later, they caught her and found my name there. And
where the Parliament is, in that part of the town, I don't know where,
on what street it was, we had to go to the police station. There was a
good many of us and they had us in one by one, not all at once. And
then they asked if I'd bought stuff too. I didn't buy anything, I said. And
he says, well, why's my name down? And I said it was because it was
no good and I'd taken it back. And then they said something to me,
that policeman did, why I'd wanted to buy. I said, look, you couldn't
buy them in the shops. And we knew that perfectly well. And he says,
did we know? We didn't. They brought them in, how would we know?
We said we didn't know. He asked where I was born and everything,
and I said I was born in Mezőhegyes. Then he looks at me: "You were
born in Mezőhegyes? Tell me where." And I say, Homestead 43, etc.
And then he changed his tone of voice.[29]

He did not raise his voice and he talked to Malvin nicely afterward,
because as it turned out, he also knew that place. When telling about
this particular episode, Malvin behaved as if she were still at the police
station, stressing that she had not done anything illegal. Nor did she
say outright that retailing on the premises of the factory was considered a crime at that time, leaving her sentence half said (*And he says,*

did we know? We didn't). She would rather underline that they knew nothing, and they just wanted to buy goods that were in short supply. The theme of self-justification recurs in other narratives as well: they wanted to buy something, but the size was not right, and their name remained written down in the ledger.

Informal trade, as represented in the stories, could be interpreted as a case of "outwitting" the system. The attitudes of the interview partners toward the women and the men who sold things illegally at the factory were quite sympathetic for a number of reasons. On the one hand, they knew that the goods offered were not available in the shops, and on the other, they considered this way of trading a good opportunity to make some extra cash off the record. The appeal of the "black market" is rendered visible in the details about it found in the narratives, sometimes embellished with fantastic elements. For instance, the woman who was prosecuted is said to have brought in the goods she was selling in the factory by ship. (Of course, she might as well have had a relative working on a seagoing vessel.)

> *Apparently, they brought it in by ship and sold it duty-free . . . Those, proved to have bought stuff from her, had to pay twice—once when they bought it, and then again at the police station. The second payment was their punishment. So the goods turned very expensive for them in the end, although she sold things that you couldn't get at the time.*[30]

From the narratives about the woman who sold goods illegally, it can be gathered that she was dismissed from the factory and her coworkers lost touch with her. Exploring further on this topic, I asked the interviewees if they themselves had ever sold anything in the factory and, if so, what it was. The responses were sometimes detailed, sometimes brief. László's laconic account was as follows:

> *I sold to the women nice pullovers and cardigans that you couldn't get in the shops. A friend of mine and I went to Poland by train.*[31]

Later, I asked the others whether they remembered buying anything from him.

> *Laci*[32] *used to peddle stuff. When we saw Laci, we knew he had something. We'd always ask what he'd brought. I bought this bracelet from him, for instance. And this ring. It's magnetic and has a healing effect. You keep it here for your blood pressure. (She demonstrates.) And here,*

> *when you are sleeping. (She demonstrates again.) He always came by*
> *the shop and always sold the things cheap.*[33]

László's activities are favorably presented in the narratives as a way of helping the working women, by supplying them with cheap consumer goods that were difficult to find. He had a reputation as a reliable trader, someone you could count on. Another informal trader, Teréz, had to resign from the responsible position she occupied in the factory's trade union because she had sold rings with the portrait of the assassinated American president J. F. Kennedy. She was reported for this, and the authorities thought it was unbecoming for a party member to sell Kennedy rings, and not Khrushchev rings, for instance. (The Soviet leader had been ousted by then, and in any case, she would have been hardly able to sell such rings for two hundred forints a piece.)[34] Teréz told me at length about the goods she sold and how she got her merchandise, which earned her some extra income:

> *There was an old lady at the boarding shop; she had an American*
> *relative who sent her rings. And this old lady asked me to help her*
> *sell these rings. I said, why not. Some extra money. And X. Y., too,*
> *bought a ring from me and wore it for two months . . . It was a Ken-*
> *nedy signet ring, a gold ring, I think, selling for two hundred Forints.*
> *It wasn't expensive. She wore the ring for two months and then she*
> *told them in the party committee that I was selling rings with Ken-*
> *nedy on them.*[35]

The same storytelling pattern is observed in many other narratives in which the women explain why they took jobs as domestic servants when they were young. "Lending a hand" as the main motive for a woman to take a job outside the home is a recurring narrative element, as if the respondents were ashamed to bring up need as a motive in the interview situation.

Mária, the leader of the brigade, sold pullovers in the workshop and for that reason got herself into trouble with the party committee and with the factory's security officer. She recounted that the security officer employed the official parlance when trying to make her ashamed for her illegal trading activities. He said that retailing was a petty bourgeois thing, incompatible with holding a public office or membership in the party committee, and unworthy of the "socialist man." Mária recalled this event when I asked her about the case of police prosecution, mentioned earlier:

I did some selling as well, you know. And I was reported. That place where we lived, next door, you know, there was a lady who had relatives in Czechoslovakia, and she . . . brought knickers, bra, and other things over from there, and she asked me if I wanted to try and sell them. Well, of course, I took them in the factory and sold them, but the security officer noticed. I was reported . . . The security officer told me he knew I was selling something. I said, prove it then. Then he said I was a member of the district party committee, and this, and that, how could I do that? . . . But he couldn't prove it. (She laughed.) Nothing ever came out of it.[36]

In this instance, Mária presented herself as a daring and successful woman, since she could make a career for herself in the party and have success as an informal "businesswoman" at the same time.

Another common form of informal trade was selling homemade food. There was a contingent of workers commuting to the factory from the villages around Budapest, particularly from Csév (Piliscsév, Esztergom County), who would bring homegrown and homemade produce, unavailable at the city's markets, on a regular basis. They would leave "offerings" in the fridge for the managers and workshop supervisors in the hope of career advancement—some accepted the gifts and some did not—ordinary workmates, however, had to pay for their sausages and black pudding.

The Csév people brought disznótoros [blood sausages] for sale. Every year they'd ask me if I wanted some. I'd say yes. They made black pudding differently from us at home, with a lot of white breadcrumbs, but it was delicious.[37]

Judging by the stories, informal trade at the workplace had reached considerable proportions and had resulted in thick networks within and outside the factory. Interviewees reported that the furnace workers used to buy liquor in working hours from the vendors of homemade *pálinka* (brandy). The janitors were also involved in this trade and would inform the furnace workers whenever a new shipment arrived.[38]

* * *

In conclusion, a variety of identity aspects seem to be interwoven in the life stories of the women workers. My intention was to single out only a couple of them in order to illustrate the complexity of the narratives of these women, viewed from the perspective of their "normal" lives as workers, consumers, family members and community members. Understanding how working people came to be storytellers in the interview situations is only the first step toward achieving a better understanding of how and why they structured their life accounts the way they did.

One can draw the conclusion that belonging to the category of "women workers" does not play a significant role in shaping the personal identities of the brigade members. Despite the fact that they spent most of their lives as industrial workers, their identity as workers is not a central one. Much more important to them is the issue of their emotional ties and loyalty to the factory, or the award they won together, experienced today as both a form of recognition and a stigma. At present, the identities of the former members of the brigade as workers have been overshadowed by other group identities and personal roles, which tie them to other consumer groups and other workplaces, to the family, and the home. After she left the factory, Mária, the former brigade leader, worked in a theater for around twenty years. Today, she talks more readily about actors and performances; in her glass cabinet, I saw an autographed photo of an actor displayed, not her State Prize medal.

Notes

1. Copying the Soviet practice, the State Prize was established in 1963 in Hungary as the most prestigious award in the country. Eligible for the State Prize were individuals and teams who "conducted research, or were engaged in research and development; those who have made a substantial contribution to the construction of socialism; innovators; those who have introduced new methods of work; those who were recognised for their role in production management; those who have achieved exceptional individual performance in production, in the curing of patients, or in the development of public health, childcare and education." The State Prize was for the first time awarded to a socialist brigade in 1965. By 1985, 44 brigades had received the award, accounting for 4.7 percent of all the awards given. MOL XIX-A-92. 13. d. Állami Díj bizottság. Jelölőlapok. 1970. Darvas Pálné, Klement Tamás, Terjék József (eds.) *Kossuth-díjasok és Állami Díjasok almanachja* [Almanach of State Prize Winners] 1948–1985. Budapest, 1988, 449, TVRGY. 1963/36. számú törvényerejű rendelet.

2. Imre Czeglédi, *A Gyulai Harisnyagyár 75 éve. 1900–1975* [The History of Hosiery Factory in Gyula] A Budapesti Harisnyagyár Gyulai Gyára, Gyula, 1975, 121.

3. The movement was started in 1959, using the Soviet Communist Brigades as a model. It was essentially a specific form of labor competition that

went beyond the purely economic goals pursued. It not only aimed at achieving outstanding work results by the brigade members, but also at contributing for the formation of the new self-conscious socialist man. The slogan of the movement was "Working in the socialist way, Living in the socialist way." http://www.osaarchivum.org/files/holdings/300/8/3/text_da/32-1-124.shtml

4. Workers' Guard (or Workers' Defender Guard, as it was initially called) was a paramilitary organization founded in 1957. See Germuska Pál-Murányi Gábor, *A látható légió* [Visible Legion], HVG, 2001, február 3. 7377.

5. A thorough summary of research on identity up to date found in Györgyi Bindorffer, *Kettős identitás. Etnikai és nemzeti azonosságtudat Dunabogdányban* [Dual identity. Ethnic and national sense of identity in Dunabogdány], Budapest: Új Mandátum Könyvkiadó/MTA Kisebbségkutató Intézet, 2001, 18–34; Ferenc Pataki, *Élettörténet és identitás* [Life story and identity], Budapest: Osiris Kiadó, 2001.

6. Willem Doise, "Social representations in personal identity," in *Social Identity*, eds. Stephen Worchel et al., London, Thousand Oaks and New Delhi: Sage Publications, 1998, 23.

7. Stephen Worchel, "A developmental view of the search for group identity," in *Social Identity*, 73.

8. On the distinction between individualism and collectivism, see Darío Páez, et al., "Constructing social identity: the role of status, collective values, collective self-esteem, perception and social behaviour," in *Social Identity*, 213.

9. Padraic Kenney, *Rebuilding Poland: Workers and Communists, 1945–1950*. Ithaca: Cornell University Press, 1997, 238.

10. Interview with K. Györgyné and her husband, K. György, March 16, 2000, 8. Interviewed by the author.

11. Interview with S. Vilmosné, October 25, 1999.

12. On the different meanings the members of the brigade attach to the award, see Eszter Zsófia Tóth, "Én nem istenítem Kádárt, de olyan ember volt." Egy Állami Díj emlékezete munkásnők életútelbeszéléseiben" ["I don't Adore János Kádár, but He Was Such a Man." The remembrance of State Prize in Women Workers' Narratives], in *Múlt századi hétköznapok*, ed. János M. Rainer, Budapest, 2003, 211–30.

13. "Rang-e munkásnőnek lenni?" [Is it good to be a woman worker?], *Nők Lapja*, November 9, 1968.

14. This was certainly the case in the 1950s as well, but it was featured less frequently in the official press. On the model gender roles in the period, see Sándor Horváth, "Párkapcsolatok Sztálinvárosban: 'Itt nálunk Sztálin felé fúj a szél'" [Relationships in Sztálinváros: "By us, the wind blows to Sztalin"], *Mozgó Világ*, (5) 2001, 69–87.

15. Annegret Schüle, *"Die Spinne." Die Erfahrungsgeschichte weiblicher Industriearbeit im VEB Leipziger Baumwollspinnerei*. Leipziger Universitätsverlag GmbH, Lepizig, 2001; Joan Wallach Scott, *Gender and the Politics of History*. New York: Columbia University Press, 1999. Joan Swan, "Ways of Speaking," in *Imagining Women. Cultural Representations and Gender*. Cambridge: Polity Press-Open University, 1992, 56–67.

16. See, e.g., Naomi Wolf, *Misconceptions. Truth, Lies and the Unexpected Journey of Motherhood*. London: Vintage, 2002; Magdalena J. Zaborowska, *How We Found America. Reading Gender Through East European Immigrant Narrative*. Chapel Hill and London: The University of North Carolina Press, 1995.

17. Interview with K. Györgyné and K. György, March 16, 2000, 15; July 7, 2001, 44. Interviewed by the author.

18. Interview with F. József. Túrkeve, October 10, 2002, 6. Interviewed by the author.

19. George Gmelch, "Migration and Adaptation to City Life," in *Urban Life. Readings in Urban Anthropology*, eds. George Gmelch and Walter P. Zenner. Long Grove, IL: Waveland Press, 1996, 191.

20. Same patterns: Herbert J. Gans, *The Urban Villagers*. New York: Free Press, 1962, 122.

21. Interview with T. Károlyné, April 13, 2000, 33. Interviewed by the author.

22. Interview, September 2, 2002.

23. On the role of cinema in the working-class families, see Anna Valachi, *József Jolán, az édes mostoha. Egy önérvényesítő nő a XX. század első felében* [Jolán József, the Sweet Stepmother. The Selfmade Woman in the First Half of the 20th Century], Budapest, 1998, 19–22.

24. Interview with E. Pálné, July 11, 2000; July 13, 2001. Interviewed by the author.

25. Act IV of 1978 on the Penal Code, which came into force on July 1, 1979, classified "speculation" as a misdemeanor, subject to up to two years of imprisonment. The phrase "engaging in commercial activity . . . without the requisite permit" was replaced with "pursuing unauthorised commercial activity." This wording remained in force until January 1, 1988. Afterward, an amendment to the Penal Code, in force until May 15, 1993, read: "§ 299 (1) Anyone who continuously a) trades or maintains a business in an unauthorised way, or b) conducts economically unjustified intermediary trade in goods, or speculates in other ways conducive to profiteering, is to be punished by imprisonment for up to two years, severe corrective/educative labor, or a fine . . . § 299 (4) If the behavior constituting the crime defined under Point a) of Paragraph 1) consists of unauthorised conduct of activity requiring an official permit and the perpetrator receives such a permit from before a substantive ruling is made by the court of first instance, the sentence may be reduced without limit or wholly laid aside in cases deserving special consideration." Speculation as a crime was abolished after May 15, 1993, and the law recognizes only "influence peddling" as such today.

26. She does not play a significant role here; therefore, I am using this form of her name.

27. BFL BB Fond 8 XXXV (8) C, Budapesti Harisnyagyár iratai. Report on the situation with the social [i.e., public] property in the two Óbuda hosiery factories, April 11, 1968. The case was also on the agenda of the factory's party executive committee meeting on April 16: "16. In the boarding shop, police proceedings for profiteering against Mrs H. are underway. She

has made substantial transactions, selling in instalments, amounting to 4000–5000 Forints a month. It is necessary to mobilise several people for the social court proceedings; the trade union has requested assistance."

28. Interview with K. Györgyné and K. György K., November 30, 2002, 69–70. Interviewed by the author.

29. Interview with F. Józsefné and S. Józsefné, November 19, 2002, 53–4. Interviewed by the author.

30. Interview with S. Balázsné, January 10, 2003, 20. Interviewed by the author.

31. Interview with Cs. László, October 25, 2001, 14. Interviewed by the author.

32. Laci is a nickname for László.

33. Interview with F. Józsefné and S. Józsefné, November 19, 2002, 53–4. Interviewed by the author.

34. The author of the handbook for socialist brigade leaders did not advise naming brigades after Kennedy either, regardless of the fact that he had been assassinated. Tibor Fábri, *A szocialista brigádvezetők feladatai és munkamódszerei* [Tasks and working methods of socialist brigade leaders], Budapest: Táncsics Kiadó, 1972. On the removal of T. Károlyné, see BFL BB Fond 8 XXXV (8) C, Budapesti Harisnyagyár iratai. Meeting of Branch I, October 4, 1970.

35. Interview with T. Károlyné, October 3, 2001, 41. Interviewed by the author.

36. Interview with S. Vilmosné, January 14, 2003, 65–66. Interviewed by the author.

37. Interview with F. Józsefné and S. Józsefné, November 19, 2002, 52–53. Interviewed by the author.

38. Interview with T. Károlyné, October 6, 2003, 55. Interviewed by the author.

3

Yesterday's Heroes: Spinning Webs of Memory in a Postsocialist Textile Factory in Slovenia

Nina Vodopivec

In people's memory, as well as in the discourse of Slovenian historiography, the period of socialism is represented as a repressive regime. Nevertheless, narrations of textile workers in Slovenia show that their memory is redefined by the textile industry's current situation, everyday practice, and a presentiment of what the future might bring, as well as the way in which various social groups perceive the past.

In this chapter, I deal with interpretations of different people regarding the transformation of a socialist factory into a postsocialist enterprise by addressing the following questions: how textile workers construct their memories when confronting postsocialist redefinitions of work, and what meanings they attribute to work while facing new management strategies and reorganizations of labor.

The case of the textile industry perfectly exemplifies the transformation processes. During the post-WWII period, industrialization occupied a central place in the socialist concept of modernization. However, the story of the textile industry goes further back. Namely, industrialization was literally initiated in the textiles, whereas at present, in addition to being an arena of the strongest deindustrialization, it is also a common subject in discussions on globalization.

The analysis of the fieldwork at the shop floor of *Predilnica Litija* spinning factory (Litija is a small town in central Slovenia)—where I worked as a blue-collar worker for two months in 2004—is based on the interviews and conversations I had with retired and employed workers, managers, directors, and trade unionists in textile factories across Slovenia. One of the reasons I chose this spinning factory was that it is one of the few textile enterprises in Slovenia still operating. Before Slovenia's independence in 1991, the number of employees in the Slovene textile industry amounted to 74,845 people; by 2009, their number dropped to 12,533. As to the *Predilnica Litija*, the number fell from 1200 in 1980s, to 385 in 2005. The company managed to find a niche market by specializing in the production of yarns and threads for medicine, furniture, and the automobile industry, as well as decorative and technical textiles.

The interviews conducted with former and current employees of the company, established back in 1886, show the importance that people attribute to the factory's long existence. Most of the workers I talked to had mothers, aunts, and grandmothers, sometimes even fathers, uncles, and husbands employed in the same factory.[1] Recollections of the factory thus overlap with those of their families; in people's minds, the local "spinning tradition" is strongly intertwined with their "family traditions."

In 1994, *Predilnica Litija* was registered as a joint-stock company and in 2005 as a limited liability company. Congruent with the dominant privatization pattern in Slovenia, the factory's managers and workers became the majority shareholders. As argued by some Slovenian economists, by using such a model, Slovenia fostered the continuance of self-management. However, further restructuring brought about major changes, and the mere fact that a number of retired and employed workers still hold company's shares does not say much. The question to be addressed is who are the majority shareholders and the pertaining implications in the context of power.[2] The research of economists conducted between 1996 and 1998 on 150 medium-sized and large companies showed that as a result of privatization, the number of managers holding shares increased, whereas the respective number of workers decreased.[3] In this respect, we can therefore talk about *managerial capitalism.*[4]

Following these changes, the *Predilnica* redefined its entrepreneurial orientation and production, reorganized its division of labor, spatial relations, and, by way of that, social relations between its employees as well. However, their managerial staff encompasses almost the same people as prior to 1990/91, which is relevant for detecting and mapping various modes of negotiations between new forms of management and practices of the past.

After Slovene independence in 1991, new business techniques and managerial strategies were developed under the influence of international standards. International standards, such as ISO standards or Total Quality Management, were designed by engineers of modern management strategies to ensure reliability and quality of products. Yet these standards were also aimed at authoritatively homogenizing internal organizations of various enterprises in different countries.[5] Thus, these standards did not only change workplaces and organizations of labor, but also workers, their bodies, and minds. Many such strategies and techniques (standardization, quality control, participatory management, as well as ideas of private property or joint-stock companies) strive to transform the employees into flexible, *self-regulating* and *self-monitoring workers.*[6]

New business strategies and discipline techniques are supposed to achieve a higher level of worker independence. "Our objective," explained the head at the shop floor in Litija, "is not to keep warning the workers, make them work out of fear or only under constant surveillance."[7] The idea was, he continued, for the workers to internalize the requirements of the company and realize them independently. Yet this organization of work implies its own control too.[8] It is achieved by systems of greater responsibility and powers of decision.[9]

Spatial Discipline in a Factory

The construction of work within the context of contemporary economic politics, neo-conservative or neo-liberal views with rhetoric on self-regulated free market dictates higher mobility and flexibility for the worker. Such changes are not only specific to postsocialist countries; the Fordist production in Western Europe or the USA has witnessed significant changes, too.

A main feature of the socialist organization of labor was division into small units—assembly lines (similar to the Fordist organization of labor)[10]—where workers routinely operated only one part of the process. Nowadays, it is quite the opposite; employees are mobile and qualified to perform various jobs. The emphasis is placed on small and flexible companies with workers qualified to perform various jobs responding to quickly changing market demands. New techniques point out individual responsibility;[11] the emphasis in production has shifted from a product's quantity to quality with every worker being responsible for her/his product.

Based on rationalization and flexibility, the *Predilnica Litija* spinning factory workers operate not one, but two or three machines of the same line in a process. One line is composed of various phases aimed at treating a certain material, that is cotton, linen, or a mixture. In the year 2000, managers and foremen started introducing the so-called 3-plus-3 strategy, according to which workers were supposed to be trained to operate three different machines on the same line. However, while working on the shop floor in 2004, I did not notice all workers operating three machines nor that all of them were engaged in such training process.

These management reorganizations significantly affected both the division of labor and the spatial choreography of workers on the shop floor. New systems of spatial relations were developed in order to achieve discipline, order, and efficiency. Spatial relations do encompass not only spatial disciplining of bodies, but also disciplining of mind.[12] It is precisely determined, measured, and marked on the floor where a worker should stand. As a part of spatial disciplining, each worker is to stand at a set interval from the next one, with the distance being determined by systems of lines. The system encompasses lines drawn on the floor, which mark individual working places, positions of machines, pots, directions of carts, and precisely determine positions of workers and their moves outlining their physical actions. Spatial distance and noise make communication between workers impossible. Interacting would demand leaving their place, thus they are in no position to communicate.

Discipline on the shop floor is thus not only provided by meters. The architectural structure of the factory allows everyone to be visible at all times. As suggested by Foucault's concept of Panopticon, spatial relations shape subjectivities and have the power to discipline. Factory architecture is characterized by hierarchical, ongoing, functional, and independent surveillance, a gaze that is ever vigilant. The result is that workers are responsible for their own self-discipline. Rather than being repressive, the power created through such factory architecture is anonymous and productive.[13]

In their locker rooms, the workers constantly discuss the issue of increased surveillance in comparison with the socialist past.[14] Once I asked a worker in Litija about devices on the shop floor ceiling, and she replied she had heard they were aimed at video monitoring. "Of whom?" I asked, surprised, and her answer was "Us." Whether this is true and whether managers actually have installed video cameras on the shop floor ceiling is less relevant than the fact that such are the interpretations produced by the workers. By the way, I did come across a newspaper article about a video surveillance system in a factory: in 2002, a director had installed cameras in one of the textile factories in Slovenia.[15]

An assistant who had started working in the spinning factory only recently and heard his colleagues' stories about the relations in the socialist past told me thus:

> *During the period of socialism, the relations between workers were a lot better. After the 1990s everything has changed. When you go around, workers look at you as if you were spying on them or controlling them; nowadays they all keep to themselves.*[16]

In this case, the memory of the past has been internalized through mediation, which points to specific power relations at present.

Despite factory discipline (Foucault, 1984), which exercises control over workers and dictates spatial choreography, everyday life on the shop floor still remains a place of various negotiations. A coworker told me that when her machine or yarn really drove her crazy, she would say out loud, "Oh, what the hell, I'll have a cigarette." When she had calmed down, she could get back to work. "This is the best way to avoid kicking the machine," she said and added that now going to the locker rooms is only allowed during breaks: "Elderly workers say that in the past they could take more breaks and had more liberty in going to locker rooms." Yet according to her, the foreman on the shop floor turns a blind eye and sometimes even comforts them. "Don't you worry. Just wait. You'll see, it will get better."

The question thus remains how new visions and strategies are implemented by the management, and how they are accepted and transformed by the workers. New strategies clearly do not develop in isolation, but within the framework of past practices and memories of them.[17] Workers directly or indirectly question and contest new authorities of efficiency implied in international standards through their memories of previous relations and systems. For example, on the shop floor, among the workers and foremen—in spite of the new systems of evaluation—experience remains the constituent of power, which is more important than formal knowledge. Workers evaluate each other according to their experience. Skill in operating machines and long working hours are thus the most important factors even though the new system tries to establish new hierarchies of evaluation. When characterized as inflexible, workers use their experience and memories to legitimize their place in the factory.

At this point, I would like to address the issue of flexibility on the shop floor. On the one hand, the position and the place of a worker are precisely determined. There is a board at each shop floor's department displaying which machines are operated by each and every worker. These boards make each individual's place perfectly clear. Workers can't leave their places to walk around the floor. On the other hand, based on the premises of flexibility and changing demands, workers are supposed to be mobile and qualified to function in various jobs. Workers themselves, however, are not happy when it comes to changing their working places, in particular when this involves leaving their group or department. Such attitudes can not only be attributed to their losing the sense of belonging as they are often referred to as "the borrowed ones"; they also feel they can't demonstrate or prove their skills and experience. A worker on the shop floor explained this by saying as follows:

> You are trying to prove what you are capable of. And you say to yourself, I will make it. And the others who don't work as hard as you do, they stay. When you show what you can do, they send you away. And you think, why bother and work hard, they will just push you around as they please anyway.[18]

Among workers, mobility[19] is often perceived as a punishment. In addition, it makes work more difficult, because it involves working behind different machines that demand different skills and movements—that is, a great flexibility of the body is necessary.

From Socialist Workers to Flexible Subjects

According to a human resource manager in Litija, "only people who managed to switch from socialism in their mind-set are happy." Managers in general, as well as those in the spinning factory, point out the importance of getting over the "socialist tradition." In the name of improved efficiency, the state bureaucrats and managers in Slovenia promote different forms of worker and employee disciplining, and define individual responsibilities by way of a strong hierarchization. Attitudes not compliant with these categorizations are labeled as remnants of past socialist times, both in the factory and by the general public. Factory managers define present strategies through the critique of the past socialist system, which they portray as incompetent and inefficient. They refer to it as "democracy" in quotation marks, in which workers were far too free and protected.[20] In comparison with current free market rationalism, socialism is considered an "emotional" system. "The factory is an economic enterprise, not a social welfare institution," a human resource manager in *Predilnica Litija* explained and added that when she first heard others talking like that, she was upset, but now she understands that this is how it is supposed to be.[21] In such views, a socialist enterprise is displayed as a social valve that prevents conflicts between people without providing profits or meeting market demands. The head of the shop floor explained: "This is how selection is made now, whereas socialism encouraged laziness."[22]

Whereas in socialism the emphasis was put on a collective and social responsibility, today it is placed on individual and self-responsibility. The *Predilnica Litija* managers constantly remind the employees of things they used to take for granted in the past, but which are now definitely gone. This can also apply to the employment itself, although on the shop floor I heard only once how hard one had to fight to keep one's job. Compared with the "capitalist West," the managers attribute to Slovenia a higher degree of social security. But such security is no longer taken for granted. "I tried to explain at a meeting today. We have social security and other benefits, but if we abuse them, we'll have to enforce a different system," said the head of a department in a conversation. Based on such opinion, individuals nowadays are obliged to earn and justify their social security or other benefits, such as health insurance, provided by the administrative system. Any misuse or instances of fraud may result in their abolition.

The management instructs the employees on the contemporary meaning of self-responsibility, because in their words, "these days money is all that matters." At a seminar organized in the factory for all shop floor workers, the head of the shop floor tried to illustrate his thesis on responsibility with a story about his aunt from America, who had to cover her medical expenses "yet a while ago."[0] The story about self-responsibility in the US health-care system was interrupted by a listener who said he was "once"[23] told "that America was here." We all laughed, and I found it interesting that nobody further discussed the topic. In this case, America was used in a symbolic sense, as a promised land. By not saying a word and laughing at the commentary, the head agreed that "time ago" America—meaning "the promised land"—was actually the socialist Slovenia. On the other hand, we might as well say that the listener confirmed what the head was trying to point out, namely that the so-called old socialist benefits, long taken for granted, are gone for good.

In the view of managers, economic and political elites, as well as this factory's management, workers are related to socialism. Their socialist experience is supposed to have made them socialist subjects and, as such, less adaptable to changes. As a result, the factory managers refer to socialism much more often than shop floor workers do. In such a discourse, managers tend to be portrayed as rational subjects, those who—by adapting to changes—are capable of educating workers on changes brought about by the postsocialist transformations. At the same time, however, even though the management introduces new strategies as opposite to the principles and practices of socialism, it often presents them in a manner that highlights historical continuity.

The flexibility demanded by managers and emphasized by modern transnational economic discourse differs, however, from workers' interpretations of it. Workers argue that the experience of socialist constraints and shortages made them a flexible labor force and thus more appropriate for a capitalist enterprise. In particular, they draw attention to their prompt adaptability to batch production as well as their experience in working long hours, not to mention tough conditions and using old, worn-out machines. In such cases, workers do not claim that the socialist organization of work and production was better, but that their experience from socialist times legitimize their contemporary status of better workers in the capitalist enterprise.

On the other hand, managers, too, use their experience of the past when referring to various strategies of survival. Such experiences are supposed to help them at present. The former director of a textile factory compared the Yugoslav economy with the EU. The very memories of past experience in socialist Yugoslavia and various past management strategies are supposed to play an important role in promoting the economic position of Slovene enterprises as well as the state in relation to the EU.

Using the *economy of shortage* concept, socialism is presented as a system of various modes of negotiations between administrative politics and a factory.[24] Despite differences between the Yugoslav economy of workers' management and planned economies in other Eastern European communist countries, the concept can be applied to Yugoslavia too. Tax policies, increasing import prices, loans, duty taxes, and other administrative measures constantly restrained socialist factories in their operations. In spite of workers' management, the Communist Party remained the top executing agent in power.

According to economists and historians, the socialist economy in Yugoslavia functioned according to internal policies of enterprises that were—contrary to general declarations—silently backed by certain communal and republic authorities. The enterprises found their own ways to identify gaps in regulations, thereby producing half-hidden stocks.[25] In conversation, a former director from Litija stated that the party policy had dictated development of the economy by quotas. Everything was determined by the plan. Yet directors searched for alternative options. "We knew how to handle the state administration. Although it was complicated and hard, it was worth it. That is why I went to Belgrade once or twice a week." In an interview I had with the former director of the spinning factory, the strategic inquiry for solutions was labeled as "handling the state administration," as well as some sort of smuggling (*Šverc*).[26] Similar stories told by former directors of other textile factories across Slovenia are also corroborated by the analyses of other communist countries; a director's political function or activity proved efficient in economic terms.[27]

All this "bargaining" between the state and directors resulted in a particular internal discipline on the shop floor, which allowed workers to shape their creativity and inventiveness. There were also a great number of shop floor workers who helped the socialist managers overcome the technology drawbacks, as well as the shortage of stocks or materials. They relied on workers to make adjustments in time. The result was a very particular relation between the shop floor managers and workers—Burawoy and Lukacs referred to it as a special social contract[28]—by way of which workers received, in return, security and employment stability, as well as financial, material, or symbolic rewards for their hard work and extra hours. This particular "mutual dependence" allowed shop floor management and workers some autonomy and flexibility in organizing the production. Aging machines constantly broke down; therefore, workers had to improvise by employing their skills, knowledge, and experience.

Shop floor interpretations of mobility during socialism among elder retired workers differ from those of their younger colleagues now. "I know everything. I've worked everywhere," said a retired worker proudly and went on: "He (a foreman) told me he was short of a worker and asked if I could take over."[29] Such a switch of working place was interpreted by the worker in the context of a tacit confidentiality pact between herself and her supervisor; in such cases it was the superior who asked the worker for help.

On the one hand, such memories reveal mechanisms of socialist economy, especially the already mentioned bargaining established between workers, directors, and the state. On the other hand, retired and current workers still employ these remembrances in establishing their expectations and demands in the contemporary transformed social space. As already mentioned above, workers manipulate with their experiences when management treats them as inflexible. However, workers too can, to a certain extent, adopt management's explanations.[30]

The European Worker

Flexibility is one of the main features of the *new* worker portrayed by European Commission documents. According to the commission, in addition to being flexible, workers should also be multiskilled and mobile. Social anthropologist Angela Procoli studied the commission's standards for this new "European worker." She identified trainings for a multiskilled, flexible, and mobile labor force, which are congruent with the standards of modern economy, as places of institutional violence against workers, as well as a place where individuals shape their identities.[31]

At present, a worker is not only replaceable, in actual practice, but also in the discourse of economic politics and contemporary strategies of managing enterprises.[32] Nowadays, the political documents and newspaper coverage is all about managers. The postindustrial discourse makes no mention of industrial workers, and the subject as such has become anonymous. In postsocialist countries, the public discourse on industrial workers, former subjects of the socialist ideology, has changed dramatically; exhausted victims of the socialist economy have replaced the images of revolutionary and self-sacrificing textile workers, and yesterday's heroes have become social anachronisms. The power relations in these two public discourses prove to be very different.

However, diligence and dedication to work are values that have remained important in the contemporary factory environment, despite the fact that today these values no longer translate into financial remuneration and social affirmation. Workers were proud of working as many as twenty or thirty years in the factory and hardly ever taking a sick leave. Such is also the criterion by which they value their colleagues. Made redundant in 1990, a female worker believed that losing her job was her own fault. She could not understand that she had been laid off, even though she presumably never went on a sick leave and had always been a hard worker.

Another worker, who has been employed in the spinning factory since 1991, took over the dominant discourse of the *new European standards* used by the economic elite and factory management.

> *Now you have European worker standards, and this is why the relations have changed. There's less freedom. Further to this, you are only valuable to the management and factory as long as you're healthy. But workers who are on a sick leave have serious health problems. All of a sudden you have become a sort of a second-grade worker. It's ok as long as you're fit, but if you're not, they sort of think you're a write-off, somehow less wanted.*

Yet like many other workers, she wondered about the form in which the results of "hard work" have materialized.

> *If you're a good and hard worker, you are supposed to be getting some reward. And when profit is gained, you should benefit from it, too.*[33]

People still consider work a value for which they expect to receive social affirmation and which should, as in the past, result in a payment or reward (financial or otherwise).

Instead of a "lifetime job," the current trend toward a flexible, partial, and dynamic (worker) identity changes the relations between labor, workplace, and the broader community, resulting in the dissolution of many local, formal, and informal social networks.

The socialist ideology, which interpreted labor as production in the literal sense of the word, created a symbolic and political hierarchy: physical work had greater moral and symbolic value than intellectual work, and industrial work had a greater value than agricultural work. This was not merely an ideological construction. In people's everyday life, factory work played an important and constructive role. The life of an individual was defined by the work he/she performed on a daily basis, in terms of both time and space. A job in the factory meant financial recognition (according to the workers, overtime was particularly well-paid) and workplace provided stability. By way of lifetime employment, one's existence was anchored in a single social and cultural environment. Employment in a factory provided additional benefits (such as health and social insurance, pensions), as well as lunch or brunch in the canteen, holidays in summer retreats owned by companies, housing in the apartment buildings, or loans for building their own houses. Everyday working practices, which during the socialist epoch also related to local social contexts, produced their own norms and hierarchies that cannot be considered equal to the ideological rhetoric of the regime.

"People were not dedicated to socialism, but to work," said the former director of a textile factory in the suburbs of Ljubljana.[34] The socialist discourse on the significance of factory labor and the working-class community reinforced and co-shaped the sense of belonging to the factory. An informant working in the *Predilnica Litija* spinning factory (her grandmother and mother had been employed there as well) said thus:

> *The factory was a myth in Litija. It enjoyed an enormous reputation, and those who got a job there considered it their first priority. But not today, not at all. The myth has changed considerably.*[35]

"It is better now, the organization is much better," told me a worker in a conversation and after a while added, "It is just that we have to work a lot more. Before there were 1,100 people, whereas now . . ." The sentence I frequently heard on the shop floor often remained unfinished. In the locker rooms or on excursion I could hear workers complaining about the lack of people per shift. "Fewer people working and more work," were the most frequent replies to my question about what has changed.

Narratives about the factory's past are filled with contradictions and relate to various current discourses on the working class, as well as remembrances of the factory and work in the past. In addition to being nostalgia driven, present discords can also foster memories of the past disputes.

The construction of labor is closely related to time breaks—that is, "before" and "now." The term "now" can apply to yesterday, two weeks ago, or sometime following 1991, which obviously presents an important date in people's memories. An event that divides time into "before" and "now" is not clear; it can be either the year 1990 (dismissals of workers by the factory and not the multiparty political elections), 1991 (loss of the Yugoslav market or the war in Slovenia), or the break remains undetermined in time.

The break in narrators' interpretations between the past and the present changes their relation to the past and, by way of that, also their various identities. However, the breaks do not only encompass total ruptures. Present narrations on strategies of survival show that people's relation to the past does not imply dramatic changes. People perceive it as a break because they expect continuity. "It is hard to change this socialist mentality we grew up with," said a foreman at the shop floor, "that we have to take care of ourselves and not to expect others to take care of us." However, it is not only about following changes, as stated by the foreman. People at present also shape the memory of the socialist past, which legitimizes their specific expectations.

On the one hand, memory consolidates a feeling of collective marginality and thereby a degree of solidarity between workers as opposed to the "state" and its politics, while on the other, it is exactly because of this memory that workers expect greater commitment from the administrative system. Workers share a common idea that their subjective positions have been rejected, and it was their desire to be socially recognized that made them recollect the historical significance of their role in the factory.

Social Memory

The construction of the past is a process emerging in the present. When addressing the issue of social memory and socialism,[36] it is important to understand the current postsocialist transformation in Slovenia and the role of the industrial workers within it. In the common communication space, people construct their own experience and images of the past. Based on the concept of performativity,[37] I argue that rather than being carriers of our memories and experience, we live them by acting. I have a similar view of identity, memory, and experiences: not as "something within us," but something that we constantly keep constructing.

A number of researchers apply "general" notions of experience and memories as something that we simply have. Feminist researchers Teresa de Lauretis[38] and Joan Scott[39] pointed out a discursive construction of experience. Joan Scott problematized naturalizations of workers' experiences in the work of Paul Thompson. Thompson argued that working-class experience is an ontological basis for its identity, politics, and history.[40] Scott pointed out that subjectivity is constituted through experience. Due to the social construction of discourse, the experience is both collective and individual. Thus discourse is not a medium that allows experience to be expressed, but it is of key importance in shaping both form and content of experience.[41]

In addressing the social memory of textile workers, one should bear in mind that such memory is fluid and situation based. Memory in a singular form can be discussed only if considered to be based on social relations. Thus the dichotomy between "the governed" and "the marginal" or between "political memory" and "lived memory"[42] may be problematic.[43] Instead of pointing to interactions and correlations, the analytical separation of political memory on a macro level and private memory on a micro level artificially reproduces and consolidates such separations. The relevant question is not which memory is more authentic or spontaneous. Thus I do not perceive workers' "lived memory" as opposed to the "political" one. In my view, such dilemmas present themselves because of another analytical separation, that is, the one of representations and social relations. I firmly believe in the importance of pointing to the articulation of connections between the social and the political levels, as well as between representation and social experience. It is not about memory *per se*, but about how memory actively organizes social relations. Another question raised at this point is about the protagonists involved in memory shaping. I argue that there are a number of actors involved in memory shaping. Namely, in addition to workers themselves, there are also various management and human resource management strategies, present and past policies in Slovenia, different international institutions, imaginaries of factory's retired and employed people, as well as researchers with their own academic traditions. Memory is a subject that requires an analytical, relation-based approach. And above all, it needs to be dealt with in the context of power relations.

Michel Foucault drew attention to the power of discourse. By way of his *counter-memory* concept, he created a space of a new type of history—the genealogy.[44] At first, Foucault defined the counter-memories as "liberating divergence and marginal elements."[45] Later on, upon analyzing the concept of power, he approached such romanticizing of the marginal in the sense of inherently liberating in a more critical manner. Counter-memories cannot be constructed outside the hegemonic field of remembering. Although the counter-memories oppose the hegemonic ones, they do take shape within the dominant heterogeneous cultural memories. As the prefix implies, they draw on mainstream currents to redirect their flow.[46]

The memories and interactions between people take place in the context of relations of power. In the past, anthropology did not deal with the issue of memory construction. As reporters of memories, the ethnologists and anthropologists complemented the folklore collections and rescued silent groups or ordinary people from oblivion.[47] By illustrating the life *from below*, the researchers tried to allow marginalized groups to tell *their* stories. Anthropology deals with the representation of the *other*, and although not addressed explicitly, the question remains for whom or in whose name it speaks. This raises the issue of political and ethical responsibilities.[48] Due to the fact that research was intertwined with political implications and aimed at raising awareness and promoting political action of *suppressed groups*, feminist critical theory addressed this question even more explicitly.[49]

By pointing out the embodied hierarchies between the researcher and the narrator, the authors drew attention to the fact that no such thing as a neutral or objective way of writing and researching—the representation—exists.[50] My writing is placed in the context of these discussions. Memories are shaped by actions, practices, and events, as well as by the researcher. Memory-shaping takes place in conversations, in my case also in conversations between workers and me. During the time I spent at *Predilnica Litija*, some people began talking about the past because they knew I was interested in the subject. Eventually they started to discuss the socialist past with their coworkers, their parents, and grandparents who had also been employed in the factory. In our conversations, I did not merely reveal their memory but also co-shaped it.

Conclusion

In *Predilnica Litija*, there are a number of factors that provoke tensions and constitute new modes of memory: changes in spatial relations on the shop floor promoted by new managerial strategies, disciplinary measures and reorganization of labor, various modes of negotiations regulating relations between state administration, international organizations (World Trade Organisation, International Monetary Fund, World Bank, etc.), and local enterprises.

Although narratives of the past feature various contradictions, I argue that the meaning of the factory as a socialist project constructed in the memory of people is significant because it defines and legitimizes their present positions in various ways. People refer to the socialist past when interpreting the capitalist present and legitimizing workers' subjectivities or the position of the enterprise.

Finally, I would like to point out that socialism does not exist in people's memory as a political regime, but as a system of social relations and various modes of negotiations. In everyday life, institutional changes cannot be considered without reference to people. Processes of social transformation can thus not be reduced to the transition from socialism to neo-liberal capitalism.

Through analyses of everyday strategies and negotiations between various attributions of meaning, I draw attention to the perspective from which an individual speaks. In doing so, the industrial worker is not merely a passive "receiver" of institutional change, but rather an active subject. In my research, I paid particular attention to the shop floor workers, because I find their changed position in the contemporary political context an extremely significant issue.

Notes

1. Workers who managed the machines were, and remain to this day, mostly women, which is rather typical for other factories in Slovenia.
2. It is also important to consider the participation as well as the number of workers' representatives on the supervisory boards.
3. Janez Prašnikar (ed.), *Poprivatizacijsko Obnašanje Slovenskih Podjetij* [Post-privatisation behavior of Slovene enterprises], Ljubljana: Gospodarski Vestnik, 1999.
4. Cf. Ivan Szelenyi, *The Rise of Managerialism: The New Class after Fall of Communism*. Collegium Budapest/Institute fro advanced study, discussion paper 16, 1995.
5. Steven Casper and Bob Hancke, "Global quality norms within national production regimes: ISO 9000 norm implementation in the French and German car industries," *Organization Studies*, vol. 20 (6), 1999, 961–85. See also Elizabeth C. Dunn, *Privatizing Poland, Baby Food, Big Business, and the Remaking of Labor*. London and Ithaca: Cornell University, 2004.
6. Emily Martin, *Flexible Bodies*. Boston: Beacon Press, 1994; Chris Shore and Susan Wright, "Coercive Accountability: The Rise of Audit Culture in Higher Education" in *Audit Cultures*, ed. Marilyn Strathern, London: Routledge, 2000, 57–89; Dunn, *Privatizing Poland*, 20.
7. Conversation in *Predilnica Litija*, April 2004.
8. Michel Foucault, *Nadzorovanje In Kaznovanje: Nastanek Zapora* [Discipline and Punish: The Birth of the Prison], Ljubljana: Delavska Enotnost, 1984, 176–77.
9. Instead of direct control, alternative forms, for example, responsible autonomy developed (Andrew L. Friedman, *Industry and Labour: Class Struggle at Work and Monopoly Capitalism*. London: Macmillan, 1977, 43–57).

10. Despite many similarities, socialist and Fordist productions were not identical. In the socialist case, the planning authority was centralized at the level of the state and not the company (Kate Brown, "Gridded Lives: Why Kazakhstan and Montana are Nearly the Same Place," *American Historical Review*, vol. 6 (1), 2001, 42; cf. Dunn, *Privatizing Poland*, 14).

11. Susan Wright, *Anthropology of Organizations*. London and New York: Routledge, 1994, 5.

12. Lisa Rofel, "Rethinking Modernity: Space and Factory Discipline in China," in: *Culture, Power, Place: Explorations in Critical Anthropology*, eds. Akhil Gupta and James Ferguson, Durham, London: Duke University Press, 2001, 155–78.

13. Foucault, *Nadzorovanje In Kaznovanje* [Discipline and Punish], 171–77.

14. This surely does not imply that there was a lack of surveillance in the past. The idea of Panoptikon is that every factory architecture delivers its own *disciplinary regime*. I would like to point out that the current tensions and conflicts contribute to a more intense feeling of being under surveillance.

15. Brane Piano, "Na Monitorju Opazujejo Delavke V Spodnjem Perilu," *Delo*, 25. 01. 2002, str. 6. ["Women workers in their underwear are being watched on monitors," Delo daily, January 25, 2002, p. 6].

16. Conversation I had with the assistant on my first visit to *Predilnica Litija* in 2001.

17. We should, however, take into consideration that the company's director is a local who lives not far from the factory. In addition, his father had worked on the shop floor, and he was the factory's fellowship holder during his studies.

18. Conversation with a worker in May 2004.

19. In this case, the mobility encompasses changing workplaces, not hierarchies.

20. Workers themselves, congruent with the idea of market economy, often agree with such interpretations, especially when speaking in general about the success of the factory. However, we have to remember that we are dealing with a factory that is still in operation. This is a significant issue, together with the aforementioned workers' support of the management—members of the local community, who in many cases had their parents working at the shop floor.

21. Interview in February 2004.

22. Ibid.

23. He referred to the period prior to 1990/91 changes.

24. Janós Kornai, *Economics of Shortage*, Amsterdam: North Holland Publishing, 1980. See also Katherine Verdery, "Theorising Socialism: A Prologue to the 'Transition'," *American Ethnologist*, vol. 18, 1991, 419–39.

25. Jože Prinčič, *V Začaranem Krogu: Slovensko Gospodarstvo Od Obnove Ekonomske Politike Do Velike Reforme: 1955—1970* [In a vicious circle: the Slovene economy from reconstitution of economic policy to the great reform: 1955—1970], Ljubljana: Cankarjeva založba, 1999.

26. Interview in August 2004.

27. Cf. Katherine Verdery, *What Was Socialism and What Comes Next?* Princeton: Princeton University Press, 1996, 22.

28. Michael Burawoy and János Lukacs, *The Radiant Past: Ideology and Reality in Hungary's Road to Capitalism.* Chicago: University of Chicago, 1992.

29. Interview in February 2003.

30. Dunn, *Privatizing Poland*, 82.

31. Angela Procoli, "Manufacturing the New Man: Professional Training in France—Life Stories and the Reshaping of Identities," in: *Workers and Narratives of Survival in Europe, The Management of Precariousness at the End of the Twentieth Century*, ed. Angela Procoli, New York: New York State University Press, 2004, 84.

32. Dunn, *Privatizing Poland*; Birgit Müller, "Productivity and the Person: From Socialist Competition to the Capitalist Mission in Eastern Europe" in: *Workers and Narratives*, 149–72; Procoli, "Manufacturing the New Man."

33. Interview in April 2004.

34. Interview in April 2000.

35. Interview in February 2001.

36. J. Jacob Climo and Maria G. Catell (eds.), *Social Memory and History.* Walnut Creek: Altamira Press, 2002; Paul Connerton, *How Societies Remember.* Cambridge: Cambridge University Press, 1989; James Fentress and Chris Wickham, *Social Memory.* Cambridge: Blackwell Publishers, 1992; Maurice Halbwachs, *Les cadres sociaux de la mémoire* [The Social Frames of Memory], Paris: Albin Michel, 1994; Maurice Halbwachs, *Kolektivni Spomin* [Collective Memory], Ljubljana: Studia Humanitatis, 2001 [1950].

37. Paul Connerton argued for performativity when analyzing rituals and ceremonial practices (Connerton, *How Societies Remember*, 58–59).

38. Teresa De Lauretis, *Alice Doesn't.* Bloomington: Indiana University Press, 1984, 159.

39. Joan Scott, "Experience," in: *Feminists Theorize the Political*, eds. Judith Butler and Joan Scott, New York: Routledge, 1992, 22–40.

40. Scott, "Experience," 30.

41. Ibid., 37.

42. Marie-Claire Lavabre, *For a Sociology of Collective Memory*, 2005, http://www.cnrs.fr/cw/en/pres/compress/memoire/lavabre.htm.

43. Luisa Passerini pointed that out at an oral history conference in 1982 (Marianne Debouzy, "In search of working-class memory: some questions and a tentative assessment," *History and Anthropology* vol. 2, 1986, 266).

44. By way of this, Foucault separates history and memory; he ascribes memory continuity and identity that recognizes only Self in the Other, whereas the historical narrations focus on blood relations, heritage, and class transfer of ongoing tradition from the past to today (Michel Foucault, *Language, Counter-Memory, Practice, Selected Essays and Interviews by Michael Foucault.* Ithaca: Cornell University Press, 1977).

45. Foucault, *Language, Counter-Memory, Practice*, 51.

46. Ann Burlein, "Countermemory on the Right: The Case of Focus on the Family," in: *Acts of Memory. Cultural Recall in the Present*, eds. Mieke Bal, Jonathan Crewe and Leo Spitzer, Hanover: University Press New England, 1999, 208–17.

47. Borut Brumen, "Umišljena Tradicija *Dobrih Starih Časov*" [Invented tradition of the good old times], in: *Zemljevidi časa: zbornik ob 60-letnici Oddelka za etnologijo in kulturno antropologijo*, eds. Zmago Šmitek and Borut Brumen, Ljubljana: Oddelek za etnologijo in kulturno antropologijo, Filozofska fakulteta, 2001, 193.

48. Gayatri Spivak, "Can the Subaltern Speak?," in: *Colonial Discourse and Postcolonial Theory*, eds. Patrick Williams and Laura Chrisman, Harvester: Wheatsheaf, 1993, 66–111.

49. Rosi Braidotti, *Nomadic Subjects*. New York: Columbia University Press, 1994.

50. Clifford Geertz, *The Interpretation of Cultures*. New York: Basic Books, 1973; George Marcus and Michael J.M. Fischer, eds., *Anthropology as a Cultural Critique: An Experimental Moment in the Human Sciences*. Chicago: University of Chicago Press, 1986.

4

Negotiating Spare Time: Magic at Work in the Everyday Life of a Bulgarian Socialist School

Nadezhda Galabova

While working on a project about the everyday life in the first English language school in socialist Bulgaria,[1] I interviewed some graduates of this school and two of the stories I recorded struck me as extremely interesting and deserving a special analysis. Like all the other narratives, talking about assiduous studying, examinations, and strict grading, these two also represented the intense learning daily routine the students of the school were submitted to. At the same time, however, both stories described two situations in which the hard-and-fast rhythm of learning and testing was disrupted and the narrators were magically exempted from examination.

In order to outline the broader context, within which these stories appeared, I will first expand on the history of the English Language Schools in socialist Bulgaria and then will continue with the topic that the current chapter sets to discuss.

After removing its coalition partners from power in 1948 and establishing itself as the sole political subject that claimed to represent and defend the interests and aspirations of the people of Bulgaria, the Bulgarian Communist Party closed all schools funded or supported by private and foreign organizations. With Decree 1445 from August 2, 1948, the state discontinued the activities of these schools. Thus, many schools where Western languages were taught disappeared from the educational map of Bulgaria. This initiative was part of the state's efforts to homogenize and integrate the educational system of the country. Having proclaimed the establishment of a completely new society where equality and emancipation regulated the social order, the state had to make sure that steps in that direction were taken. The purging of the schooling system from past residues, foreign influences, and unsupervised channels of education was part of the efforts to provide equal opportunities for everybody. The state could guarantee this through unified, centralized rules aiming to bring up reliable and efficient young citizens.

Along with this, however, the political authorities were aware of the fact that the lack of cadres who could adequately use foreign languages and communicate with the West might lead to an isolation of Bulgaria and damage its international image. Therefore, they not only closed down the private schools but also initiated the foundation of a similar type of school—this time state-controlled. It had to provide excellent education in all school subjects from the mass school curriculum, as well as intensive foreign language training. The task assigned to the school was to educate such model citizens who, in spite of being constantly exposed to Western influences, would keep their loyalty to the communist creeds and promote the achievements of socialist Bulgaria in the West. Thus the first state school for foreign language learning appeared in 1950 (Secondary School for Learning of Foreign Languages—SSLFL). It was housed in the buildings of the closed American college in Lovech (a regional center in North Bulgaria) and had to, literally, take its place. The SSLFL had to transform the illegitimate cultural capital the college used to produce, to invisibly incorporate it in the new social order, and make it function for the benefit of the socialist state. By its very establishment, the school acquired a dubious publicity. Although it was supposed to alter the goals of foreign language learning and adapt them to the new situation, the school was still considered an heir of bourgeois traditions and treated with a lot of suspicion by the general public and the authorities alike. Furthermore, the fact that the students of the school were incessantly exposed to cultural influences coming from the West turned them into a potential threat for the homogeneity and uniformity of Bulgaria's socialist society. As a result, the admission to this school had to be closely supervised. In order to make sure that the students admitted to this extraordinary space were reliable indeed, the authorities kept under a strict control the selection procedures. The ones let in the school had to demonstrate not only excellent academic results but also (this was even more important) a trustworthy family background: children and grandchildren of ex-partisans and of current members of the party *nomenclatura* and the bureaucratic state apparatus were much favored since the family background was seen as a guarantee for ideological loyalty.

The selection at the entrance, however, did not facilitate the school's incorporation in the educational field of socialist Bulgaria. In fact, this caused further problems, because it acquired an image of an elite place, a place producing distinctions in a society that revered equality and collectivism. Over the years, the access to this type of schools was liberalized due to the fact that their number increased.[2] Nevertheless, the pressure at the entrance was great and the admission to these schools was considerably stricter than that to mass secondary schools. Language schools were considered to provide a better education (not only in terms of foreign language acquisition). More importantly, they offered better career opportunities and prospects for upward social mobility in a society where most people had very limited choices for professional and social development.

When I focused my research on the English Language School in Sofia,[3] I was mainly interested in studying how the ambiguous position of this type of schools was experienced on a daily basis. I wanted to see how the everyday school life was organized and how the complicated relations between the political authorities, the school, the parents, and the students were enacted in the territory of a particular educational institution. In my attempts to get a better insight into the interconnections between the various sides that actually built up the history of this school, I examined not only its archive, but also recorded some reminiscences of former students of this school. My preliminary hypothesis was that the stories I would hear would give me an idea of the "underlife" in the school. I expected that they would talk about youth rebellion and subcultures, misrule, and disobedience to the imposed order. I supposed this would be their way of distancing from today's problematic perception and presentation of the socialist past.

Contrary to my initial expectations, however, the narratives did not in the least focus on this aspect of school life. The interviewees' stories were not small pieces of a counter-history. What they emphasized was the extreme work/study load they were subject to. The unquestionable knowledge and competences they had acquired in this school was the common topic in all the interviews. Being recorded long after the socialist symbolic world had ceased to exert its complete control over the agents' actions and thoughts, these stories had to find a safe ground to talk about their past while at the same time presenting it in a form that would be acceptable today. In a moment when coming to terms with Bulgaria's socialist past was liable to numerous, many of them contradicting, interpretations, the interviewees had to find an unquestionable point of view to look back at the years spent in 114th ELS. For them, it was precisely the intensity of learning and the comprehensiveness of the knowledge the school had provided, which secured them against the conventionalities of time. The rationality of the school qualifications went far beyond the misconceptions of the socialist state; it transcended time and measured up with universality. Such a point of view could not only account for the past upward biographical trajectory of these graduates, but also ensure their present-day acceptable public identity. That is why their narratives were full of stories about painstaking studying, exceeding (supernormal) academic standards and relentless examinations. Concentrating on the hard work and the time devoted to learning, the interviewees showed that their admission to the school was neither a stroke of luck, nor a benevolence/gift on behalf of the party. It was something they had struggled to get to—their excellent academic (and later on in life, social) performance was not a consequence of a privileged position, but of personal merits demonstrated through passing every exam with an A-grade. This "A" raised them above the contingences of time; in their eyes it was a reference to the past, which, because of its universality and rationality, could not be denounced by the present.

> We didn't feel privileged at all. On the contrary, we studied far more than in the other schools. And I still believe in this, till this very day I haven't changed my mind. Some people might have had the idea of elitism but it actually didn't exist. We were simply children devoted to, how shall I put it, to our love—the language. That was the only thing that distinguished us ... So I can say—judging from the career path of my classmates—that we were given an excellent preparation. Everybody, till the last person, went to university. The better part graduated in English philology; later on they became professors, journalists ...
>
> This school taught me how to think independently. This is where I first got acquainted with Shakespeare works, Jack London, the Russian classics. So I can't say that my life has been wasted—my love for the language, my thirst for knowledge was reared there.[4]
>
> The ELS was a very good school. There we studied a lot! A lot! A lot! Now when I come to think about it—in Chemistry we studied from university textbooks ... You see, we studied something like English

literature, Chaucer, we studied about some pilgrims (she laughs), Hamlet! We had to write papers . . . and I look at my old textbooks— no pictures, nothing like today's textbooks. Here, look, that's it— underlining and taking notes (she flicks through the pages)—these are extracts from Martin Eden. We studied something like English literature . . . well, it wasn't probably like English philology at university, but . . . That's it. I'm not quite sure what the students of the English language school learn these days! And there are no pictures! . . . You see, the average score of my class was A–,[5] you can imagine the hard work this involved. You see, there were no privileges as far as testing was concerned. Nobody from our class managed to graduate with first-class honours (only "A"s) although we were the class with the highest results in the school.[6]

There was no nepotism when we talk about examining. Studying in this school was really hard. The teachers "pursued" us like mad.[7]

This somewhat self-congratulatory discourse (the recurring theme of the hard school days and the supernormal standards the ELS students had to meet) appears against the background of the widespread public opinion about the present decline of the educational system in Bulgaria. Even if they do not overtly mention it in their stories, all interviewees implicitly judge and criticize the contemporary situation. The (latent) comparison between the past and the present of Bulgaria's educational system stays as a backdrop of this discourse. It, actually, becomes a narrative strategy through which the interviewees can legitimize their claims for authentic academic and professional achievements. Their accomplishments are valuable and worthy of consideration because, unlike the present-day educational practices, they are not lacking in stability and gravitas; they measure up with universality. Now students are not involved in the learning process, and they are not interested in what school can give them. The knowledge they acquire is skin-deep, partial, and lacking in authority. The interviewees juxtapose this contemporary condition with the academia-like atmosphere of their school days, the university textbooks they used as (unquestionable) sources of information, and the seriousness of their studies. Nowadays' studying is "light and unserious"[8] whereas in the past it was with "no pictures"; it was with underlining and taking notes. Nowadays' students are interested only in having fun whereas in the past the interviewees had to meet supernormal/university/universal standards. This line of thought is continued by another interviewee (currently a lecturer at university) who laments as follows:

> *You know how it's these days. The skills you need today are different—*
> *tests, multiple choices, you need immediate reactions, flexibility, while*
> *it was different with us. We had to study things in depth, in details,*
> *our knowledge was exhaustive.*[9]

Thus, the interviewees assert the significance of their education (and as a matter of fact, the meaningfulness of their whole biographical trajectory) by stressing the fact that it is not a result of a party affiliation or appropriate networking. Playing on the fact that the school was treated with suspicion by the political authorities and constantly referring to some world classics (Jack London, the Russian classics, Chaucer, etc), the interviewees point out that the knowledge they had access to and the skills they acquired there go far beyond the limitations and arbitrariness of the socialist state. Essentially, they have nothing to do with the socialist past; they actually supersede the past (and even the present) and align with universality. They can tell you "other things."

> *She (a teacher from the school) was so inspiring, her teaching ignited*
> *our love for the language, a kind of curiosity that the language can*
> *tell you other things.*[10]

Bearing in mind this broad context within which the narratives were generated, two of the recorded interviews attracted my attention as odd examples, because they showed a slight diversion from the general pattern of narration. Of course, they also talked about extreme workload and excellent grades, obtained as a result of great strain. Interestingly enough, they also talked about moments when the poor grade was avoided because the narrators were magically exempted from examination.

This magic at work in the everyday life of a socialist school is the focal point of my discussion here. The main aim is to study how the examination situation—a situation which Foucault points out as exemplary for the interventions of the modern state in the public and private lives of individuals—is enacted or, shall I say "underacted," in a Bulgarian socialist context.

Many researchers of Bulgarian state socialism will doubt whether the concept "modern" can inarguably be used to describe the economic and political development of the country in the period in question. Here I will not detail the existing positions in the discussion on "socialist modernity," but I will simply state mine.

Along with Foucault, on whose findings I will extensively rely later in the chapter, the methodological framework of my text is largely influenced by the point of view of current cultural anthropology,[11] which refuses to accept the existence of a fixed number of universal "modern" criteria, apply them to the analyzed object, and record the degrees of adherence to/deviation from them. Instead, it is interested in the spaces of overlap, intersection, and coexistence of different patterns of lifestyles, diverse temporal structures, and intermingling territories.

What gives texture and savor to historical research is not outlining clear-cut, neat, and homogeneous units of analysis, but interpreting those places of heterogeneity, mixture, and double meanings where standard methodological tools do not work.

It is exactly because of their oddness and resistance to being assigned to a specific category that the two narratives attracted my attention. By diverting from the common pattern,[12] the two stories help us see a somewhat different and peculiar aspect of the daily routines in a social-ist classroom. They shed light on moments that would have otherwise passed unnnoticed; they show how the rational progressive rhythm of public living was doubled by magical and seemingly inexplicable events that allowed the students to "steal" some time for themselves while preserving the required image of model youths.

I will develop this argument by referring to Foucault's analysis of the situation of examination. Then, drawing on the two interviews, I will see how this situation is enacted in a Bulgarian classroom. Fi-nally, I will try to "thicken" the description of these events by adding information from the archive of 114th ELS—minutes from teachers' meetings and head teacher's reports. By the end of the chapter, I hope, I will have shown how parallel to the homogeneous normative time of learning and examinations, there was a constant undertow of negotia-tions between students, teachers, political authorities, and parents. These negotiations restructured the imposed rhythm of living and studying and intermingled the school time of total public exposure and striving to meet the required normality with "magical" moments of "irrationality."

Etatization of Time: Examinations and Grading

Foucault's observations about the intricate connection between the examination situation and the formation of individuality are essential for the further unfolding of this chapter. Therefore, I will here point out some of his most important conclusions and then discuss the extent to which they can be applied in the interpretation of socialist Bulgaria's schooling practices.

In *Discipline and Punish*,[13] he states that unlike premodern times, when the status of individuals was related to how visible and outstanding they were, the modern state recognizes people as citizens to the extent to which they adhere to some general prescriptions for "normality." The more they fail to meet these norms, the less publicly reliable they are and, accordingly, they have to be submitted to a series of disciplinary measures, which will help them achieve normative and rational standards.

The main technique, which the state authorities use to homogenize individuals and inculcate the proper conduct, is surveillance. The feeling of a complete exposure, public accountability of every gesture, movement, and activity generates in the mind of the individual an "uneasy conscience." It becomes the supervisor inside that will always see to it that the rules are followed. Knowing that they are constantly observed, the individuals take upon themselves the enforcements of power, they inscribe in themselves the attitude of the authority, and role-playing the two parts—the one of the supervised and the one of the supervisor—they become the principle of their own submission. Thus, the panoptic tower—the symbol of the state's total surveillance— becomes unnecessary. It is invisibly incorporated in the mind of the individuals. What they have to do from now on is strive to come up to the public rules of normality as well as bear the disciplinary punishments whenever they fail to do that.

The process of examination represents the essence of state control over the individuals; it is the proper realization of the act of surveillance and inculcation of normative/normal civil behavior. In the examination situation, we can see how the hierarchical supervision and the normative sanction unite.[14] The gaze of the examiner objectifies the examined. The individual is exposed within a field of an absolute visibility where every move, every activity is supervised and evaluated as meeting or violating the rules of normality. Respectively, the extent of conformity with the norm is graded and this grade demonstrates not only the degree of normality, but also the pedagogical/disciplinary steps that need to be taken to transform the "abnormal" individual into a healthy, sane, reliable, and publicly acceptable adult.

It seems to me that an important observation on the connection between the modern state and schooling is Deyan Deyanov's analysis of the examination situation. In an article studying the role of schooling in the production and reproduction of the social order, he expands on Foucault's arguments by adding new details.[15] He points out that the act of examination is not only a means the state (through the school institution) uses to collect data about the public conduct of students, but also an instrument to invade private lives. The examination, respectively the grade, testifies how the student's unsupervised private time has been spent, how much of it has been devoted to acquiring the prescribed public norms.[16]

Thus, nothing of the individuals' privacy is left to them. The time stored in the bodies is extracted, made publicly available, and subjected to use for the public good. Every single moment, every temporal slice is taken over by the state—the ultimate goal is to transform the individual's private time into effective work, into a practical contribution to the welfare state. Drawing on Verdery,[17] I call this "etatization of time." The prospects for privacy, for spare time, available for personal pursuits, are annihilated. Time is thoroughly occupied by the state, which makes allowance for no disposable moments, no vacancies, and no vacations.

The organization of time under Bulgarian state socialism is not in the least different from the one described in Foucault's and Deaynov's theoretical observations. Since the country aspires not only to catch up with the West, but also to become its "other" counterpart, temporality there is structured around the appeal for constant acceleration, for an ongoing effort to compensate for the lost time. Socialist living means incessant work to make communist utopia come true. The time of the socialist citizen is work time, time of the worker. Every moment spent on privacy, every minute spared for personal matters is branded as a "waste" and an act of sabotage against the progress of the state. Therefore, these lapses distance the individual from the prescribed normality and might result in the individual's dropping out of public recognition.

Even though schools are not manufacturing institutions, their main task is to instill in the youth—the future builders of the country—such working habits and inculcate such work ethic that will lead to their formation as model citizens.

The organization of social living around the terms of excessive temporality, of mobilization of the individuals' time for the sake of the state, is reproduced and even intensified in 114th ELS. As I pointed out earlier, the government founded this school with the special assignment to educate and rear outstanding young citizens who would be able to adequately communicate with the West without losing their loyalty to the communist creeds. They had to represent to the capitalist world (and to Bulgaria itself) the perfect face of communism—the fulfilled communist utopia. This automatically imposed a set of supernormative requirements upon the school. Its students were to acquire knowledge and skills measuring up to the utopian future. They were supposed to show "now and here" those qualities and abilities that would be inherent in the communist citizen "then and there"—in the bright communist future. These exceeding norms, prescribed to the students, meant an even further acceleration of time and a deeper penetration of the state-imposed rules within their bodies and minds. In order to meet the requirements, they had to devote an immense amount of time to achieving the impeccable image of versatile and model citizens.

Evidences for this temporal excess, this school time of hard learning, and merciless examinations, of no spare time and striving for the highest academic standards can be not only found in the archival documents of 114th ELS, but also heard in the recorded recollections of the alumni. Nevertheless, the reminiscences expressed no regrets concerning the time spent in the school. The interviewees did not feel deprived of their private moments or devoid of the opportunity to construct, on their own terms, their identity. In the narratives, the school time was not in the least negatively marked, since in the eyes of the narrators it was seen as devoted not to acquiring the regulations and norms of the socialist state, but the eternal, universal truth. What they were at the moment of narrating, what they had made of themselves, had nothing to do with the socialist state. It was the absolute knowledge they had made efforts to acquire, which gave them the confidence to proudly refer to their school past. In their stories, the striving for A-grades was not a result of the imposed need to meet the state's prescriptions, but a very personalized and conscious labor of love.

That is why the two interviews describing instances when students tried to avoid examination and their wish "magically" came true give us a slightly different perspective on the daily life in the school and deserve a detailed interpretation. They shake the otherwise stable image of the students from this school as the ones who never failed to meet the norms for excellence and self-righteously sacrificed their private time for the sake of knowledge.

Magical Happenings

What I will continue with are two longish quotations from the interviews in question, which represent the stories I have been building this text around.

Story one:

In Chemistry now I remember we had a teacher—Kapka was her name, but now I can't remember her family name. I recall a very interesting happening. The whole class wants to be excused (i.e. not to be examined, N.G.) because the previous lesson we had a kind of cultural activity.[18] *And I was "framed" to talk to the teacher because I was in charge of the self-governance*[19] *of the class. And she comes in, and I tell her: "Can we be excused for today?"*[20] *She looks at me and answers: "No!" and opens the register. And she says: "Student number 8, come to the blackboard!," or number 9, I can't remember, but this was me. And I go to the blackboard but until I reach it, I am shaky on my legs. She says: "Write down this and that!" Those were some horrific formulae and we would write them from one end of the board to the other. I don't remember anything now. I then tell her: "But there's no chalk." You see, we've hidden the chalk. And she tells me: "Well, fetch some!" What can I do—I go to take some chalk and bring it to her. And she says: "Thank you for the chalk, sit down!" She didn't examine me, she just wanted to make me sweat.*[21]

Story two:

The teacher in Chemistry was the one who pursued us madly. Rumour had it that she had been a partisan. Well, I don't know, but these are some of the legends that go around in a school. And she used to speak horrible English, horrible! Extremely bad! I mean, her pronunciation was awful, the grammar was OK. And she used to write 4 blackboards with formulae and we had to know them for the next time. This was a nightmare. Everybody would play truant. I was one of the 5–6 people who wouldn't. And every lesson she'd say: "Student number 1—to the blackboard! Well, student number 1 is absent, then student number 2—to the blackboard! Well, student number 2 is absent, then student number 3 . . . If number 3 is also absent, well, then—those who are here, they'll be examined!"

And I remember this very well. We used to sit in numbers in pairs. And I remember that the girl who sat next to me and I, the two of us, we'd say: "If only it wasn't this time! If only it wasn't this time! If only she wouldn't examine us!" It was something like an incantation. We'd hold our hands and repeat: "If only it wasn't this time!" You know,

73

there was such a system of examinations—once you were examined, they wouldn't touch you for 3–4 weeks, they'd examine the others. But the fact that the others played truant made things terrible.

You see, this teacher was rather rude. She'd tap us with the pointer, lightly, of course, on the head. She'd shout: "Stop chewing that gum!" Actually, she was a very kind woman but nobody could understand that. If you could pluck up courage to tell her: "Excuse me, I am not ready to be examined today!," she'd say: "It's all right. Take your seat!" The other teachers would give you a poor mark without even thinking. We just didn't know that such an approach could work with her. I mean, she gave the impression of being a real Cerberus. In fact, her heart was in the right place."[22]

At first sight, it seems a pure coincidence that both stories involve Chemistry teachers. There is a considerable time gap between the two events and the teacher cannot have been the same. On the other hand, it is not surprising that a natural science subject caused so many problems to the students of this school. They experienced a lot of difficulties trying to master the contents of the subject, as well as the English language it was taught in. This shows once again that the high academic standards, which the school imposed on its students, included not only the Humanities, and the English language in particular—after all, it was a school for intensive English language learning—but also all the other subjects the curriculum comprised. Since this was an institution that aspired for excellence, none of the subjects could be ignored because this would impair the perfect image imposed on these students. They had to exteriorize their personal temporality, transform it in a versatility that would contribute to the welfare of the country.

Against this background of hard studying and strict exams, the two events become even more intriguing. They enable us to see two exceptions to the rule—two instances when particular students were able to, literally, take their time and spare it for themselves. They did not have to demonstrate how much of it they had devoted to mastering the state prescriptions; a few moments of their private time were left unheeded.

The narrators did not have any explanations as why this might have happened.[23] For them the stories represented strokes of luck—the curious happenings were ascribed to the teachers' momentary whim, which disrupted for a while the otherwise rational and lucid order of the school temporality.

Fortunately, the archive of 114th ELS can help us "thicken" the description of these stories by giving us insights into some aspects of the school life, which the narrators did not know or preferred to be silent about.[24] I cannot say that the archival documents reveal the real reasons of the teachers to act in this particular way. They, however, can give us an idea of the inner life of the school. They can broaden our understanding of the relations between teachers, political authorities, parents, and students. It was these relations that gave reality to the school and made allowance for certain ways of conduct that did not quite match up to the norms.

The detail from the first story that is worth paying attention to is the excuse of the narrator—she mentioned that the whole class was not prepared to be examined because they had participated in a Komsomol activity. This seems to be an important clue because the minutes from the teachers' meetings are full of comments on Komsomol activities—how they are used by the students as excuses for not being prepared for a lesson and even playing truant.

At a pedagogical meeting, a music teacher—they were the ones deeply involved in these activities because they were responsible for the proper musical support of the events—complains: "The students tend to excuse their absences from the choir rehearsals with attending some other activities and vice versa."[25]

Three years later another teacher is infuriated by similar student tricks:

> We mustn't allow our students to miss classes before a preparation for a concert or another activity. Our comrades from the Komsomol mustn't call the students when they are supposed to be in the class-room. Students mustn't be exempted from classes because they have to write some slogans or attend a Komsomol meeting. Our students talk about self-governance, but behind it they hide their bad performance at school. They slip into bad ways of showiness.[26]

Later on in the years this is still a repetitive complaint on behalf of the teachers:

> Last but not least, we must look into the problem of absenteeism as common for the whole school. There are cases when a lot of absences are registered because the better part of the students are late for classes—for example when there is a Komsomol conference held . . .[27]

Although these extracts do not coincide with the exact happening the interviewee talked about, I still think that they can help us with the interpretation of the story. They show us that the "false" pretence of the Komsomol activities was very often the students' excuse for not being ready for examination or even for not attending the class. Despite the fact that the narrator represented this experience as something really strange and rare, it turns out that similar practices were not uncommon. On the other hand, the teachers could never be sure whether these students' claims were not actually real.

In addition to the incessant time rush for a better academic performance and higher test results, the students of this school had also to undergo another type of examination. The public manifestations, the demonstrations before the gaze of the authorities were yet another of the state's techniques, directed at extracting personal time from the students for the sake of the public good. The goal of these public, mass activities was to confirm the affiliation of the school to the united state organism, which celebrated its perfect condition, to annihilate all chances for unsupervised spare moments and to consolidate the private temporalities into one synchronized rhythm of living that prospered under the benevolent look of the political authorities.

At the time the first interviewee was a student in 114th ELS, the activity, which focused the time and energy of many young Sofia citizens, was the Ninth International Youth Festival in 1968.[28] A letter sent by SGNS (*Sofiiski Gradski Naroden Savet*—Sofia City People's Council) to all schools in Sofia can give us an idea of the importance of this event and the amounts of time and efforts invested in its organization:

> An extreme tension was created due to the pressing tasks about the preparation of Sofia students for the participation in the Ninth World Youth Festival and the ambition to accomplish all the other traditional activities (anniversary celebrations, ceremonies, concerts, commemorations, and initiatives of various public organizations).
>
> In order to eradicate some defects and eliminate the current workload of teachers and students:
>
> I decree that under no circumstances shall teachers and students be diverted from their classes or from the preparation for the Festival"[29] (emphasis mine).

We can see that participation in mass activities was as important for the students as their academic performance. This shortage of time for both academic examinations and manifestations (of loyalty) before the gaze of the authorities was used by the students to spare some moments without being supervised. They maneuvered between these equally strenuous temporalities and managed to hide from the surveillance of the authorities, while at the same time keeping up with the imposed norms. This is, it seems to me, what happened to my interviewee. The examiner could not be absolutely certain whether the excuse was authentic or not, so her little revenge was to "make the student sweat" just to show her that they could not easily fool her. As the students played serious and preoccupied youths, she played a strict and relentless teacher. That is how, while following, as if perfectly, the social roles prescribed to them, the teacher and the students alike, managed to negotiate the normative rhythm of school life and to outwit the public temporality they had been submerged into. It is important to underline here that it was not only the students who tried to restructure the school life rules. The teachers, being involved in this interaction, also had to adapt their behavior to the sometimes paradoxical reality—they had to be strict executives of the authorities' requirements and at the same time turn a blind eye when these requirements caused obvious contradictions.

Now, after proceeding with the second story I will discuss the narrators' decision to leave their experiences without an explanation/interpretation.

The second story was definitely more expressive in creating an air of mystery and magic about the event. The interviewee mentioned that together with her classmate they would use a kind of incantation, a kind of spell, begging an invisible power to divert the examining teacher's look away from them. It was, however, the teacher's kindness that eventually exempted them from an examination. Cerberus herself (as the Chemistry teacher was nicknamed) excused the student (or an anonymous classmate—the story leaves it unclear whether the interviewee was talking about herself) for not having spent enough time studying. This happy ending was put down to the eccentricities of the examiner's character but is still difficult to understand against the background of the teacher's, generally, formal and overdemanding attitude to the students.

A suitable direction for the interpretation of this story can be sought in the high truancy rates the interviewee mentioned. About the time the narrator was a student at 114th ELS comments on similar cases regularly appeared in the head teacher's reports on the educational (under)achievements of the school:

Students miss Maths and Chemistry classes of teachers who we deeply respect. The students respect them too. But the students are so frightened by these teachers that even the slightest sign of the teacher's attention to them is interpreted as a threat. This is an issue we have to handle. We must do away with the practice of the pedagogue of fear. We must give way to a lively, optimistic mood of real creative work... Well, of course, we mustn't spoil the children ...[30]

It is necessary that all teachers from our school critically evaluate the criteria they use to grade the skills and abilities of our students, basing these criteria not on the extremely high level of performance of two or three excellent students from a class, but on the requirements of the curriculum for all secondary schools in the country. This, of course, doesn't mean that we should lower our demands, because that might demobilize our students. We should, however, change their conviction that their preparation is unfairly graded.[31]

The comments of the head teacher were a result of the regular inspections the school was submitted to, inspections assigned by the Ministry of Education and the Regional Inspectorate. The conclusions of these inspections were that "the students are overworked, they are given a lot of homework assignments."[32]

It was no secret either for the head teacher or for the teachers that influential parents, who had personal connections with the higher authorities, initiated some of the inspections. Clues for this can be found throughout the archival documents.[33]

At the beginning of this chapter, while discussing Deyanov's article about the examination situation, I underlined that it gives an interesting direction for analysis. Now it is time to return to this point[34] and to repeat some of Deyanov's observations. He emphasizes that the examination situation is not only a means for collecting information/knowledge about the individual, but also a tool the publicly-disciplinary power uses to completely invade the individual's privacy, to check on how adequately the individual spends his/her private time achieving the norms, prescribed by the state. The authorities' insight into the "private" and "family" life of the student, however, might happen to be an advantageous one. There are certain "distinguished" "families," whose public acceptability, whose recognition by the state is higher than others. Due to their family's/private links, some students can be predisposed to meet the state norms with a greater ease than others. For them it is not necessary to dedicate their spare/private time to achieving distinction because it has already been assigned to them.

The conditions of exceeding grade have secretly been negotiated to suit them.

In reality, this is what happened when some teachers from this school for excellence were put under pressure to lower their unattainable requirements. The privacy, the family networking of some students secretly colonized the normative school temporality. The normative school rhythm was negotiated to fit the personal feeling of time of certain students while preserving the pretence for rationality and universal normality.

This is my interpretation of the second story. I am not implying that the interviewee directly influenced the Chemistry teacher. Rather, it seems to me that she fortunately benefited from the general change of the Chemistry teacher's attitude to the students. After being constantly reprimanded for causing truancy and frightening students with her too strict and formal methods of teaching, "Cerberus" had to reconsider her relations with the students and acquire a much more "individualistic" and personal approach to them. And this is how the interviewee (or, in fact, the anonymous student she was talking about) got away with a poor mark.

The final notes I want to finish this text with refer to both interviewees' reluctance to explain or interpret the strange happenings they talked about. They preferred to keep a certain air of irrationality and uniqueness around their stories. The narrators wanted to remember and recall these events as those rare moments of magical experiences when the chores of daily work/learning were disrupted by single moments of enjoyment and happiness, when the monotonous work rhythm was invaded by a spare moment of leisure. Yet it was important for them to represent these lucky exemptions from examination as something utterly different from the regular school life. These stories had to be left to themselves, to their magical aura. Any interpretation would have normalized and integrated them in the daily routine of the school. This, however, would have ruined the imposed and still preserved by the alumni of 114th ELS image of an academic brilliance achieved through hard work and assiduous learning rather than luck.

Nevertheless, listening to and interpreting stories like these can give us a better picture of the everyday life in socialist schools. Perhaps they can even enhance our awareness of the specific Bulgarian socialist modernity that causes so many terminological misunderstandings. They can help us substitute the macro-level of analysis with a microscopic one and see that it was not only the authorities that intervened in individuals' lives, imposed norms, and prescribed identities. The agents also had their chances to subtly influence the regulations and, taking an advantage of the paradoxicality of the system, adapt the rules so that they could suit their needs and desires.

This takes me back to the beginning of this chapter where I stated that, while bearing in mind Foucault's description of the examination situation—the main tool of the state for instilling normality—I would also look for those spaces of overlapping and interactions where the direct imposition of clear-cut models did not work. This is exactly what the stories, though unwillingly, told us. They provided us with two microscopic everyday-level narratives, which showed that the prescribed normality, which the state strictly imposed, could be negotiated; there was much more to the life in this school than simply complying with the state regulations and meeting the supernormal targets. Its history consisted of constant shifts and adaptations of the rules, complex interactions between the groups, which made use of the system's inconsistencies to both preserve the image of model citizens, devoting their time to the state, and spare some moments for themselves. The magic at work in the everyday life of the school made it possible for the students "have their cake and eat it," to take their time and yet give it to the state.

Notes

1. Nadezhda Galabova, *Socialism and its foreign language: the English language schools in the cultural field of socialist Bulgaria (1950–1989)* (PhD dissertation, in Bulgarian).
2. The school in Lovech housed three departments—English, German, and French. In 1954, however, the number of students willing to study these languages increased so much that the departments had to be separated to form three different schools. The German stayed in Lovech, the French moved to Varna, and the English, in Sofia, became the first secondary school for English language. Later on, such schools appeared in all regional centers of Bulgaria, but this growth in number was still far away from turning these institutions into mass schools.
3. Hereafter I will refer to it as 114th ELS—the name used in most school documents.
4. The interview was recorded on June 12, 2005; the interviewee is a woman, graduation year 1955 (years spent at the school 1950–55), the English department of the school in Lovech.
5. According to the Bulgarian grading system 5.50 out of 6.
6. The interview was recorded on September 22, 2005; the interviewee is a woman, graduation year 1969 (years spent at the school 1964–69).

7. The interview was recorded on September 14, 2005; the interviewee is a man, graduation year 1981 (from 1976 to 1981).
8. The interview was recorded on September 22, 2005.
9. The interview was recorded on October 15, 2005; the interviewee is a woman, graduation year 1965 (from 1960 to 1965)
10. The interview was recorded on July 19, 2005; the interviewee is a woman, graduation year 1977 (from 1972 to 1977)
11. See, for example, Arjun Appadurai, *Modernity at Large. Cultural Dimensions of Globalization*. Minneapolis: University of Minnesota Press, 1996; Mike Featherstone, Scott Lash, Robert Robertson (eds.), *Global Modernities*. London: Sage Publications, 1995; Hommi Bhabha, "Culture's in between," in: *Multicultural States: Rethinking Difference and Identity*, ed. David Bennett, New York: Routledge, 1995. Concerning the aspects of modernity in a socialist context see N. Ssorin-Chaikov, "On Heterochrony: Birthday Gifts to Stalin, 1949," *Journal of Royal Anthropological Institute*, vol. 12, 2006, 355–75.
12. I assume that similar experiences were something typical of school life. None of the other interviewees, however, mentioned anything similar to the two stories in question. I can only speculate on the reasons why—perhaps in the course of the interview—this did not seem important to the other narrators. Or, perhaps, while being interviewed, they wanted to preserve the immaculate public image of a perfect student who never found excuses for avoiding examinations and were always ready to face difficulties.
13. In this chapter I use the Bulgarian translation: *Nadzor y Nakazanie*. Sofia: Universitetsko izdatelstvo Sv. Kliment Ohridski, 1996, 196–201.
14. See Foucault, *Nadzor y Nakazanie*, 198.
15. Deyan Deaynov, "Izpityt y Kritika na Modernoto Uchilishte" [The exam and a critique of the modern school], *Sociologicheski problemi* 3–4, 1994, 85–92.
16. Another aspect of Deaynov's article, which I need to mention here and will expand on later in my text, is the analysis how the school's outlook of the private life of the students might be beneficial for those whose "family history" and habitus are more publicly acceptable than others." Due to their family predispositions, some students can achieve a higher grading, a higher public recognition—the skill to trade the "family capital" as something connected with the public good guarantees these students a positive distinction, an A grade.
17. Katherine Verdery, *What was socialism and what comes next?* Princeton: Princeton University Press, 1996, 37–58.
18. "Activity" is the word I use here to translate the Bulgarian *meropriiatie*, which the interviewee used. "Meropriatia" (literally—taking measures) were events, the participation in which was always obligatory, organized by the Communist Youth League (Komsomol). These activities were supposed to give a meaningful direction to the youth's free time, to strengthen collective living and the loyalty of young Bulgarians to the party's creeds. The ultimate purpose of these was again not to leave a moment of the young citizens' time unsupervised, to keep them preoccupied so that they could not get into bad ways.

19. This means that she was a member of the class subdivision of the Komsomol committee, which was responsible for the proper conduct and excellent academic results of all the classmates.

20. This was said in English in the interview because in this school the Sciences were taught in English and English was expected to be used in the classroom.

21. The interview was recorded on September 22, 2005; the interviewee is a woman, graduation year 1969 (years spent at the school 1964–69).

22. The interview was recorded on October 11, 2005; the interviewee is a woman, graduation year 1981 (years spent at the school 1976–81).

23. In fact, if I have to be precise, the second interviewee did not talk about the experience as something that had happened to her. This was only implied in her story as something she knew about, but it was so difficult to believe and explain that she preferred to present it in a very impersonal way. Another possible interpretation is that she wanted to hide the fact that there were students who were the teacher's pets—and she was one of them. I will return to this later on in the text.

24. The archive of the school is available in SGODA (Sofiyski Gradski y Okra-zhen Darzhaven Arhiv—Sofia City and County State Archive), archive stock 1892, lists 1–5.

25. SGODA, stock 1892, list 2, archival unit 35, sheet 7, minutes from a teach-ers' meeting—June 12, 1960.

26. SGODA, stock 1892, list 2, archival unit 37, sheet 107, minutes from a teachers' meeting—September 30, 1963.

27. SGODA, stock 1892, list 2, archival unit 40, sheet 68, minutes from a teachers' meeting—July 4, 1975.

28. A detailed study of the organization and the overall effects of the festival on the lifestyle and the experiences of the young Bulgarians of that time, see Karin Taylor, *Let's Twist Again: Youth and Leisure in Socialist Bulgaria*, Berlin: LIT, 2006; Ibid. "At the Socialist Frontier: The 1968 Sofia Festival of Youth and Students," *Historia*, vol. 7, 2004, 191–206.

29. SGODA, stock 1892, list 2, archival unit 14, sheet 60—a letter from the city council to all Sofia schools from May 11, 1968.

30. SGODA, stock 1892, list 2, archival unit 70, sheet 16—a report of the headmistress on the academic 1973–74.

31. SGODA, stock 1892, list 2, archival unit 72, sheet 12—a report on the academic 1975–76.

32. SGODA, stock 1892, list 2, archival unit 38, sheet 48—a report of the headmistress on the fulfillment of the Common State Pedagogical Requirements.

33. SGODA, stock 1892, list 1, archival unit 59, sheets 34–38—The party organization of the school complains that the head teacher exercises her power to make some teachers change the grades of students with "distinguished" parents; SGODA, stock 1892, list 2, archival unit 37, sheet 321—minutes of a teachers' meeting from December 29, 1966. A teacher complains that the father of one of his students has threatened him with a punishment from the Central Committee of the party, if he supports the student's expulsion from the school.

34. See endnote 8.

5

Contested Normality: Negotiating Masculinity in Narratives of Service in the Yugoslav People's Army

Tanja Petrović

The *normal biography* of the majority of men who grew up during the socialist period in the former Yugoslavia included service in the Yugoslav People's Army (*Jugoslovenska narodna armija*, henceforth the JNA). Military service was mandatory for all men after they turned eighteen and/or graduated from high school.[1] The shared JNA experience and memories and narratives related to it still connect men in various parts of the former state and of different ethnic, educational, and social backgrounds—the same men who fought against each other in the wars following the breakdown of Yugoslavia.

According to Daniela Koleva, the characteristics of *normal biography* include the following: they are widespread, predictable to a great extent, and concern all or almost all. Additionally, the normal biography is considered *normal* because it is predefined by institutionally set norms.[2] Narratives constituting normal biographies may therefore be regarded as a cultural discourse, understood as "widely shared 'background' assumptions or 'truths' about how the world works."[3] A cultural discourse on masculinity, as Andersson emphasizes, "would refer to how people assume that the majority of men in society act, talk, and feel (Kiesling 2005): in other words, how *normal men* are, and should be."[4]

Army service in the former Yugoslavia became one of the key elements of the normal biographies of socialist men because of its mandatory and universal character. On the other hand, because of

83

the very same characteristics, it defined *normality* in normative terms (vis-à-vis pathological or deviant) as far as male worlds of Yugoslav socialism were concerned: only those men who served in the army were considered *normal*, that is, capable of taking over the responsibilities of an adult man: getting married, having children, taking care of a family, and so forth.

This kind of relation between normal as common and normal as nondeviant was made possible by a feature of socialism that was already noticed by numerous pieces of research on various socialist societies in Europe: the socialist states went far beyond the political domain and influenced and significantly controlled spheres of private and individual life. Thereby, "the communist establishment kept to some extent the directness of traditional social relations" and not only tolerated, but also maintained a "quasi-patriarchality" in which familial patriarchal authorities were replaced by the authority of the state.[5] In most socialist states, this thorough control was most visible in such domains as property relations,[6] freedom of movement (inside and outside the country), and birth control.[7] Although Yugoslavs were in many aspects in a different position,[8] quasi-patriarchal relations between the state authority and its citizens were also a characteristic of Yugoslav socialism. One of the best illustrations of such relationship is found in a New Year's letter written at the very end of 1963 by a peasant from Braničevo (Serbia).[9] The letter begins with "Dear Lord Comrade Tito" (*Dragi gospodaru druže Tito*) and thanks Tito for his "dedicated work" and for everything he has done for his people. Describing contemporary life in his village, the peasant writes thus:

> We have now seen that we need furniture in our rooms that we need a kitchen. Now we eat enormous amounts of sugar, rice, and all sorts of sweets, which we knew nothing about. And you made possible all of that. Now there is a noise in our village, coming from radios, TVs, tractors, motorcycles.

He proceeds with a description of progress and improvement in the country and in all branches of industry, stressing that "this progress does not belong to us, but to you, Comrade Tito. If you had not cleared our path for us we would have drowned in our own work and everything would be pointless just like it was in the previous Yugoslavia."[10]

In a system in which there was no mediator between the state and individuals, the Yugoslav socialist state used rather subtle mechanisms to blur the boundaries between public and private, official and personal. It not only colonized spheres of private and individual life, but also skillfully used existing values, narratives, socially established identities, and patterns from traditional life to build up socialist ideology.[11]

This was also the case in the process of building up and maintaining the role of the Yugoslav soldier, as one of the ideologically strongest figures symbolizing Yugoslav socialism. In this essentially hybrid role, the image of the Yugoslav socialist man was entangled with images construed by tradition, family practices, and values as well as by the reproduction of gender roles. Army send-offs were celebrated in a manner similar to weddings, and on local radio stations, one could greet the future soldier with an appropriate song—a practice that existed also for birthdays, the beginning of primary school, a wedding, the birth of a child, retirement, and other milestones in a person's life. The role of the JNA soldier, established by this integration of the personal and the collective, the family and the state, has proven to be much more resistant than the state of Yugoslavia and Yugoslav socialism: the former Yugoslav soldiers' narratives about their army experience show that they still closely identify with this role, despite the rival roles, identities, and narratives that compete in the post-Yugoslav societies, which are characterized by strong nationalist ideologies, ethnic homogenization, and neglect of the socialist and Yugoslav legacy.

Although the identity of a JNA soldier was shaped by the institution of the Yugoslav army and was thus an ideological product of Yugoslav state socialism, it also essentially belonged to the family domain. JNA service was one of the rites of passage of a male family member. Photographs depicting a young man in the JNA uniform are found in family albums in virtually every former Yugoslav home, placed among photographs depicting other rites of passage of the boy/man.[12]

In this chapter, which is largely based on the narratives of former Yugoslavs about their JNA experience collected by interviewing or found on Internet forums, as well as in pieces of Yugoslav and post-Yugoslav popular culture, I deal with normality and the ways it is negotiated from a twofold perspective. First, the chapter aims to explore how former Yugoslav men negotiate their identity as JNA soldiers in the realm between institutionally set norms and subversive strategies that challenge or ridicule these norms and how these subversive strategies relate to the fact that the JNA soldier's identity is simultaneously deeply rooted in the domain of the traditional and the familial. The second perspective treats narratives of JNA service as a memory practice, taking into account the present-day positioning of JNA memories; it seeks to highlight the ways criteria of normality, and *normal masculinity* in particular, shaped during the socialist period, are justified and negotiated in the postsocialist and post-Yugoslav period, when everything socialist and Yugoslav is dismissed, ridiculed, or at best ignored.

Before turning to these two questions, it is necessary to say a word on the nature and cultural function of the narratives of JNA experience that still circulate in the former Yugoslav space and that are known as "army stories." They are found in virtual space[13] as well as heard around, especially in casual, men-only conversations, in which sooner or later the question "Where did you serve in the army?" arises. In relation to their contents and structure of narration, many of these stories seem to fit the same familiar mold regardless of their narrators' ethnic, social, and educational backgrounds. The best audience for these stories is other men who share the same experience, while others usually find them unbearably boring.[14] The Croatian writer Miljenko Jergović describes this storytelling habit in the following way:

> *Sooner or later, every Croatian male feels the need to tell of his experience in the Yugoslav National Army. We mostly do that in the most inappropriate social situations. Then the ladies scold us and roll their eyes and those nice boys, who were released or have served their time recently by cleaning windows in dorms or bringing kindergarten teachers snacks from the shop, think that our stories are completely outdated. Fuck, perhaps they are right, those who object because of their conscience, but we cannot give up a year of our lives just like that, just because it is not trendy anymore.*[15]

"Army story" is a narrative genre that can arguably be designated a "male story": not only that in the former Yugoslav context these stories are told only by men[16]—more importantly, they serve a narrative function of performing masculinity,[17] which essentially indicates a gendered narrative practice. According to Brickell, "those performing masculinity are (. . .) constructs and constructors of symbolic orders; simultaneously productive and produced, loci of action and participants of interaction, they may perpetuate and/or resist hegemonic social arrangements."[18] Masculinity is therefore "performed within a restricting order of symbolic meaning, constantly negotiating, producing and reproducing what it entails to 'do masculinity' in relation to the surrounding culture and social structures."[19] This may also explain the pervasiveness of the "JNA stories" in post-Yugoslav reality: despite their outdatedness and the impossibility of fitting them into current dominant narratives, the stories are still around because for their authors they are means to prove, emphasize, negotiate—all in all to *perform*—their masculinity.

Against the System? How Subversive Subversions Were

The former JNA soldiers usually build their "army stories" along the following three story lines[20] that connect individuals' narratives with cultural discourses:[21] the narrative of male friendship, the school-of-life narrative, and narratives of subversive strategies undertaken by soldiers during the army service to make it easier or simply to confront the authorities.

Friendship among men is an ideological constant related to the Yugoslav People's Army. It is otherwise typical for all-male groups and institutions, but in the context of the Yugoslav People's Army, it took on additional value and became both a symbol and a realization of friendship among Yugoslav nations and nationalities, ideologically expressed by the well-known motto of *brotherhood and unity*. Army friendship as one of the central contents of army service found an important place also in popular culture: in former Yugoslav films, songs, and so on. For example, *Vojnici* (*The Soldiers*),[22] a film directed by Stjepan Zaninović, is a eulogy to friendship and solidarity among JNA soldiers. One of the protagonists in the film was the famous Serb musician Đorđe Balašević. In one of this singer's popular songs, there is a line that subsumes this narrative of army male friendship: "u vojsci sam stekao druga do groba" (I found a lifelong friend while serving the army).

In memories of JNA service, friendship occupies an important place:

> My best friend was Zoran, he was with me during training. Then we went to different places and lost contact. He was a great guy. Zoran Milivojević. I often think about trying to find him. (M. J., Ivančna Gorica, Slovenia)
>
> After we finished the six months of tough training for officers in Karlovac, they separated us and we were all crying because we became good friends who slept, ate, and had fun and suffered together. (http://www.forum.hr/showthread.php?t=127325&page=8, posted January 18, 2006, accessed May 17, 2006)

A film director from Novi Sad, Serbia, stressed friendships made during JNA service as the most important positive aspect of this *otherwise boring experience*:

> *What is most important, in the army I made some friends whom I would not have a chance to meet in other circumstances. And we have remained friends until today. One of them is from Surdulica, he calls me whenever he comes to Vojvodina. I have friends in Zagreb and I still visit them—some of them changed a lot meanwhile, some even became Tuđman's supporters, but we are still friends from those times.* (Ž. Ž., Novi Sad, Serbia)

In 2010, the Serbian weekly *Vreme* published a series of articles related to the JNA and memories of it, motivated by the fact that since January 1, 2011, the mandatory service is abolished in Serbia and a professional army has been introduced.[23] Persons participating in public life in Serbia who were interviewed for these articles also stressed the importance of friendship in their JNA experience. The Serb actor Petar Kralj stated: "I had some wonderful friends there and made many great friendships," while politician Nebojša Čović said thus:

> *When I was leaving to perform army service, there was a lot of tears because I was married already and had a 14-month-old baby daughter. When I was leaving the army, there were many tears again, because good friends were parting.*[24]

Another narrative that was produced and supported both by socialist institutions and by people experiencing Yugoslav socialism was the narrative of army service as a school of life that makes men mature and responsible, capable of facing the challenges of adulthood. Former soldiers perceived JNA service as an initiation necessary for boys to become men: the harder the experience of military service, the more one could demonstrate his masculinity. This image of the JNA was also a part of the official narrative and was reproduced in socialist popular culture as well: the film *Vojnikova ljubav* (*Soldier's Love*)[25] is about a young Belgrade playboy, the spoiled child of a rich family, who changes for the better as a result of his service in the JNA.[26] This narrative is present in the former soldiers' memories as well. In the opinion of Petar Kralj,

> *The army teaches a young man to adapt to very different circumstances. In some sense, the army service was very, very useful: one*

learns to share there. We had only one bowl for eight of us, and in the beginning those who would take the food first would take all of it and there was nothing left for those who came later (...) But two days later everything was nicely stabilized, and those who were greedy realized that the others were hungry, too. I am talking about the educational role of the army, which was very important for me. One learns there an order that is useful also later in life, and that cannot do harm, but only be of use.

In reaction to one of these articles in *Vreme*, a reader stressed in his letter that *for all generations, the army was a kind of school—a school where one learns about order, respect, friendship.*

In the narratives of former JNA soldiers, the story line of the JNA as a school of life is also indicated by stressing one's ability to live under difficult circumstances and fulfill tasks that require a high level of both physical and psychological fitness:

The whole torture of getting up at 5, exercising outside only in T-shirts at temperatures below zero, washing with freezing water and education—all this resulted in my case in such physical condition that I felt as if I could jump over the world. I was always hungry and I would fall asleep before I touched the pillow. I was full of energy... The army made a young man strong. It is not a sanatorium, after all. It is useful for a young man to experience army service. Without that, they remain weak their whole life (http://www.forum. hr/showthread.php?t=127325&page=1, posted January 17, 2006, accessed May 17, 2006).

"Subversive" strategies during army service were often stressed in former JNA soldiers' stories. Usually they ascribe to the dominant ideology of the army service as a "school of life" where masculinity is "measured" by the ability to go through severe army training and to survive a year under tough circumstances. Yet avoiding obligations and finding one's own way to outwit the system can also be taken as a proof of capability and smartness as male features. The narratives of the JNA experience often contain stories about alternative practices and ways to avoid the rules:

Since we were in the middle of nowhere, we were getting money instead of food each month. We would drive to the town and buy supplies that we liked. The cook used to cook for only 10 of us. The place we lived in was like a holiday house. It did not resemble a barracks at all except that it had a fence. There were carpets in the rooms, civilian furniture in the living room, "civilian" kitchen like those we have at home. I would wake up and go wherever I wanted to, and we were making real coffee there, not that trash that was usually drunk in the barracks. I lived like a king (http://www.forum. hr/showthread.php?t=127325&page=5, posted January 17, 2006, accessed May 17, 2006)

Since I was in the rear . . . I got as much food as I wanted from the cook . . . I had my own shower and TV set. Others had to pay me to take a shower . . . (http://www.forum.hr/showthread. php?t=127325&page=5, posted January 17, 2006, accessed May 17, 2006)

An ethnomusicologist from Zagreb describes how he used his army service to accomplish personal professional goals while serving in Prizren, Kosovo: during his army year, he completed a research project on Roma music in Prizren and its surroundings. He even used army equipment to record Roma songs.

These stories about easy army days or about using the time spent in the army to do other things have the same function as those in which the individual's ability to live under tough circumstances is stressed: both express the competitive nature of male narratives.

A similar type of narratives tells about the resistant behavior of the soldiers during their JNA service; in these narratives, the refusal to obey orders and the ability to bear the consequences of such behavior are depicted as another manifestation of masculinity:

I had to report at least once or twice a week. They were threatening me with jail and saying that I would not find any job when I finish army service. But all that was in vain, because I understood that if I am punished, my officers and other superiors will be punished as well, since a soldier's failure is also the officer's failure. That is why they tried to hide every misbehavior (from ignoring orders to escapes to the town), unless you have done something really serious. (http://www.forum.hr/showthread.php?t=127325&page=7, posted January 19, accessed May 17, 2006)

Former JNA soldiers regard performing army service as a proof of masculinity, and male solidarity and competitiveness (in competing over who had either more difficult or easier service) are dominant contents in the narrative construction of maleness[27] through "army stories." Although individual practices and narratives of avoiding hard work or disobeying orders contradict the state-supported image of the "ideal JNA soldier," they are not in real conflict. As performance of masculinity, they both support the dominant ideology of the socialist Yugoslav army that is built upon the image of a man as a warrior who protects his family by protecting the nation and the land. While in socialist Yugoslavia these two kinds of masculinity worked in harmony, with the dissolution of Yugoslavia, the balance was disrupted and the image of man as a protector and master of family was threatened. Due to economic impoverishment, many former Yugoslav men were unable to take care of their families and had difficulties adjusting to the new circumstances.[28] This "economic emasculation," as some anthropologists label the crisis of masculinity in the former Yugoslavia in the late 1980s and early 1990s, "probably reinforced feelings of inadequacy, and often resentment, among men."[29] Going hand in hand with the ethnicization[30] of the former Yugoslav societies and the re-traditionalization of gender roles, it opened up space for "another traditional venue for regaining masculinity (. . .)—going to war."[31] *True men* returned to their traditional roles as defenders, guardians, and heroes of the nation,[32] while a woman was expected to "fulfill her destiny of self-denial and motherhood, (. . .) to be hardworking and modest, (. . .) passive and silent, aware of her duty to the fatherland."[33] In this light, Aleksandra Milićević's finding that in Serbia "the proportion of married men was significantly higher among war volunteers than among draft dodgers" comes as no surprise.[34] Neither is it a surprise that the same men who served the Yugoslav people's army together with their buddies from all over former Yugoslavia later fought each other in ethnic conflicts following the federation's dissolution.

Justifying the Past, Negotiating Masculinity: Former Yugoslav Soldiers in National Times

Many men who served in the JNA can be recognized by a visible souvenir from their army days—a tattooed heart on their arms with the inscription "JNA" and the start and end dates of their service. Dragan, a Macedonian who presently lives in Slovenia and works there as a software engineer, served in the JNA in the late 1980s in the Croatian town of Pula; he also has such a tattoo on his right arm. In the summer, he frequently travels from Ljubljana to the nearby Croatian coast, to the same area where he performed his military service. Each time he goes to the beach, he covers the JNA tattoo with a Band-Aid, afraid that some Croats might express a negative reaction to the symbol of the once-common army that in the 1990s was widely identified as an instrument of Serbian aggression in Croatia.

Tattoos are visual markers that indicate membership in a group of people who performed service in the JNA; less explicit signs of membership in this group reveal themselves in cultural practices such as narrating memories from the army. What is common to both the visible signs of belonging to the group of JNA soldiers, such as tattoos, and the narrated memories of army days is a discomfort felt by those who possess them. They feel that their JNA experiences are outdated, problematic, and inadequate in the new, post-Yugoslav circumstances. The JNA was an institution organized and ideologically shaped both as a central embodiment and as a main agent of the unity of all people living in socialist Yugoslavia. It was considered one of the most important pillars of Yugoslav unity and often referred to as *the forge of Yugoslavism* (*kovačnica jugoslovenstva*) and the *school of brotherhood and unity*.[35] In the post-Yugoslav states and societies, where the pluralistic ideology of Yugoslavism[36] was replaced by national(ist) ones, official discourses, which set up criteria of acceptability and normativity and which are supposed to simultaneously reflect and create the attitudes of the majority of society members, were highly unfavorable toward any positive attitude toward the legacy of the Yugoslav state and society, as well as any manifestation of an inherited supranational identity. In academic discourses dealing with these societies, it is often stressed that this replacement was followed by processes such as the suppression or erasure of positive memories of the common Yugoslav past, "collective amnesia"[37] or "confiscation of memory."[38] Any positive stance toward the Yugoslav past is seen as a lack of patriotism and is stigmatized as Yugo-nostalgia.

Closely associated with the ideology of "brotherhood and unity" of the former multinational state, the JNA is seen as one of the most salient symbols of Yugoslav socialism; in addition, it was symbolically opposed to the newly established national armies that, as Miroslav Hadžić stresses, had an essential role in the process of formation of national post-Yugoslav states.[39] Under the pressure of the prevailing views and ideologies in the Yugoslav successor states, a positive self-identification as a JNA soldier is perceived as problematic, even by the former soldiers themselves. On the other hand, this identification is persistent, despite being in conflict with the other identities, especially national identity, which an individual may bear in the former Yugoslav lands. The contested nature of the memories of JNA service is partly a consequence of the end of socialism, which in the former Yugoslav lands coincided with the end of the common state and was followed by the outbreak of ethnic violence. If socialism had never disappeared and the former Yugoslavia still existed, these memories of the JNA would have been just another kind of story about an exceptionally male experience from the past—quite universal and rather boring for everyone except other men who shared the same experience. In the post-Yugoslav context, however, they are negatively marked and usually labeled with the pejorative term of Yugo-nostalgia.

New means of communication enabled by the Internet have enabled a broad group of former JNA soldiers to exchange JNA memories across the current national borders. In the Internet forums that contain JNA-related topics, belonging to the group of former JNA soldiers reveals itself as a dominant aspect of the identity of people participating in the forum, while their national identity does not play an essential role. This makes it possible for Serbs, Croats, and others from the former Yugoslav nations to share their army experiences, even though some of them fought against each other in the wars of the 1990s.

Members of these forums post information about where and when they performed their JNA service; they try to make contact with their army buddies or at least with those who served in the army at the same place or time; they tell anecdotes from their army days, ridicule characteristic army jargon, and compete with each other in measuring the extent of their "manhood" by comparing the toughness of their service and thus reproducing the widespread narrative of JNA service as a "school of life" that "turned boys into men." While they remember both good and bad things from the army, their ethnicity and even their role in ethnic conflicts do not play a significant role in the way this memory is shaped through re-narrating their army stories in the Internet forums.

These forum messages are characterized by independence from the present-day perspective—they could also have been articulated while Yugoslavia still existed. There are only a few references to the 1990s' wars and the role these men had during that period. The contested role of the JNA in these wars, widely identified as an instrument of Serbian hegemony, is mentioned only a few times. These stories are thus primarily a means of social construction of masculinity and are void of political contextualization, in reference to both the present and the past.

Although the army stories of the former Yugoslav soldiers are void of political contextualization and stress the personal aspects of remembering one's experience in the army in socialist Yugoslavia, the former JNA soldiers nevertheless feel the need to justify their memories, thus showing awareness of the inappropriateness of these memories in the new circumstances. For example, after sharing his JNA memories with the others, one of the www.forum.hr forum members writes as follows:

> *Whatever service in the JNA looked like, it took up one of the best years of our lives, and we must not let our memories from that time be thrown away.* (http://www.forum.hr/showthread.php?t=127325&page=1, posted January 21, 2006, accessed May 17, 2006)

Expectations that the memories of socialism should be "thrown away" and the reluctance of individuals to do so are a consequence of the discrepancy between prevailing "official" attitudes toward the socialist past and the experience of *really lived communism*.[40] While the former are characterized by prescriptivism and assess socialism as a totalitarian system and an illusion and Yugoslavia as a "wrong" country and a false project, the perceptions of people who lived in socialism and participated in the "Yugoslav project" provide different accounts and construct a different hierarchy of values. Quite often, one's personal memories of socialism do not correspond with the dominant narratives that have an "official" character and tend to be normative and totalizing. The same is true of remembering the JNA experience: while in totalizing, impersonal discourses coming "from above" the JNA are seen as a mirror of the totalitarianism of the Yugoslav socialist system, and the people who "lived the army" attach different meanings to their own experiences in the JNA. And as the quoted Internet post shows, they feel that they have the right to keep their memories and not let them be "thrown away," thus giving meaning to their personal past and justifying the role they had in that past. The Belgrade journalist Teofil Pančić put it in the following way: whether we call it nostalgia or not, we have the right to keep our memories of socialism, since they are proof that "everything from our past that we remember so well was not a dream or an imagination, a proof that we were and remained somewhere and someone."[41]

The vitality and persistence of the "army stories" in the narrative spaces of former Yugoslavs should also be observed through a generational prism and understood as negotiation and justification of a certain kind of masculinity, in opposition to other, newly emerged and competing masculinities. As Toerien and Durrheim point out, "masculinity is no longer regarded as a particular way of being, but as a field of conflict that men have to traverse in a quest for coherence."[42] The postsocialist era in the former Yugoslav lands brought not only nationally defined and professionalized armies, but also new patterns of masculinity, based on a different relation between masculinity and army service. This is often reflected in discussions on the Internet forums, where forum members belonging to different generations provide different and frequently opposed opinions on whether JNA service was a useful experience or a wasted year. Most of the former JNA soldiers argue that their army service was a valuable experience, thus arguing for the legitimacy of their own past and the then-valid version of masculinity. One of these Internet discussions is found at the Serbian portal b92.net:

> (. . .) all that is great—that you ate Euroblok and spam, but— abandoning mandatory army service means that the state gave you back a year of your life. You can use this year to see Europe, to fall in love, to find a job, to complete your studies, to learn to play an instrument, to learn a foreign language . . . without having to clean restrooms or suffer torture from uneducated officers . . . during this year, you may watch TV whenever you want, you may eat whatever you want, you may go out freely and dress as you like . . . (http://blog. b92.net/text/14242/Uspomene-iz-JNA-i-Rojters/, posted February 9, 2010, accessed March 11, 2010)

This post provoked a series of replies from former JNA soldiers:

> Mandatory service can be and should be abolished, but it seems that you would like to "abolish" people's memories as well. (http://blog.b92.net/text/14242/Uspomene-iz-JNA-i-Rojters/, posted February 9, 2010, accessed March 11, 2010)
> There are no good and bad experiences, there are only experiences. Of all things (both useful and useless) that I have learned serving in the JNA (in the year you were born) I would like to stress the following: in these 12 months, I met so many different people and destinies, so many different ways of thinking, that I find that fascinating. It was a "best buy" for me (. . .) If you ask me now if I am sorry to have served in the army, my answer is: not for a moment. If you ask me if I would do it again—the answer is the same. (http://blog.b92.net/text/14242/Uspomene-iz-JNA-i-Rojters/, posted February 9, 2010, accessed March 11, 2010)

A similar discussion, in a somewhat sharper tone, is found on the Croatian forum:

> *What an idiotic topic and those who remember 365 days of forced imprisonment are idiots too. Only a mentally sick person or those who did not move from their village can find something good in it. I served in the JNA 5 times for one day, in a recruit center.* (http://www.forum.hr/showthread.php?t=127325&page=7, posted January 17, 2006, accessed May 17, 2006)
>
> *I cannot say whether you praise or pity yourself. That you qualify as sick persons those who remember (gladly or not) what you called the forced imprisonment, says much more about you than about the army* (http://www.forum.hr/showthread.php?t=127325&page=7, posted January 17, 2006, accessed May 17, 2006)
>
> *A person who knows everything about the army without serving in it must be a genius* (http://www.forum.hr/showthread.php?t=127325&page=7, posted January 17, 2006, accessed May 17, 2006)
>
> *It seems to me that someone who managed to get as far in the soldier career as to the recruit commission has no right to any judgment about the army service* (http://www.forum.hr/showthread.php?t=127325&page=7, posted January 17, 2006, accessed May 17, 2006).

While JNA soldiers proved their masculinity by testing their capabilities of endurance and by being able to survive a tough year in the army far away from home, "modern" young men choose instead to serve in kindergartens, hospitals, and schools; their service is performed near their homes and lasts much shorter. In some former Yugoslav republics (Slovenia, Montenegro, Serbia), mandatory service has been completely abandoned and replaced by professional armies. According to my interviewees, these new circumstances are doubly problematic and "wrong": not only do they mean that boys cannot be transformed into men by army service (and that they consequently remain immature, "soft," "mama's boys")—they also prevent young men from developing a sense of patriotism and a correct and honorable attitude toward his country and people.[43] A former JNA officer from Slovenia, where the professional army was introduced in 2004, points out:

> *Some ten days before the ten-day war, there was a flood in Laško. And the JNA soldiers and officers went into the water to save people's property and to build dams. And where is the army now when it comes to an earthquake or a flood? They do not help anymore, because they are*

paid soldiers. JNA soldiers were not only there for carrying weapons, they were also helping people and building the country. Slovenians should not forget that.

Another JNA officer described the difference between the JNA and the professional army in the following way:

I have a very bad opinion about the professional army. It is named professional army, but in fact it is a legion. There is no patriotism any more. This army is not dedicated to the well-being of its own country, but to some global interests.

Comparisons between the JNA and the "new armies," in which the latter are usually seen as "too soft," "not hard enough to make real men from immature boys," and "a kindergarten in comparison with the real army," can be observed in various discursive domains. In everyday communication in Slovenia, one can frequently hear the question, "Have you served in the real army (meaning JNA) or in the Slovenian army?" A similar attitude is noticeable in the other former Yugoslav republics, even in Croatia, where the Croatian national army took on a heroic aura of defender and liberator of the nation (from the Serbs, who were equated with the JNA) during the war in the 1990s. According to one of my Slovenian interviewees, it was not a good decision to abolish mandatory army service in Slovenia for, as he stresses, "people in the countryside still use to say: 'If one is not good enough for the army, one cannot be good enough for a wife either.'"

The narrative of the JNA as "the only real army"—as opposed to today's existing national armies in the former Yugoslav lands—can be interpreted in many ways. It is certainly a part of the nostalgia for the past, universal and found in all domains of life; in such a discourse of nostalgia, which Michael Herzfeld labels structural nostalgia,[44] the selectively remembered past is seen as better and laden with real qualities and values that do not exist in the present. In the post-Yugoslav context, as in other instances of remembering life in the socialist period, this nostalgic narrative of the JNA experience takes on additional quality and weight: it becomes contested and engages in a dialogue with dominant discourses that emphasize the importance of national armies for the "national projects" in each of the former republics, aiming to constitute them ideologically as the main factors of protection of the nation and its stability. The opposition between the JNA and the "new armies" can also be interpreted in the more general context of the modern world's "changing masculinity": initiation into manhood through the successful accomplishment of "tasks of endurance, infliction of pain and suffering"[45] is found in "primitive societies," but was also a characteristic of many mandatory military services in the world.[46] In the post-Yugoslav societies, the shortening and eventual abolition of mandatory military service, the performance of service near one's home, and the possibility of civil service all resulted in the disappearance of the last collective initiation rite, which the army was perceived to have been.

That none of these explanations excludes or can be reduced to any other underlines the complexity of the JNA soldiers' identity and its positioning in the present-day social and axiological coordinates, in which different criteria of normality (in the sense of both what is acceptable and what concerns all) prevail. This on the other hand conditions the necessarily multilayered practices of negotiating male identity: in this particular case, narratives and cultural practices that are used to negotiate the masculinity of former Yugoslavs, as well as the normality of this kind of masculinity, cannot possibly avoid entering into discourses of (re)approaching socialism, nationalism, patriotism, and reconsidering criteria of normality and acceptability in much broader terms than a simple renegotiation of gender roles.

Notes

1. Aleksandra Sasha Milićević, "Joining the War: Masculinity, Nationalism and War Participation in the Balkans War of Secession, 1991–1995," *Nationalities Papers*, vol. 34 (3), 2006, 267–87.

2. Daniela Koleva, *Biografija i normalnost* [Biography and Normality], Sofia: LiK, 2002, 40.

3. Scott F. Kiesling, "Homosocial Desire in Men's Talk: Balancing and Re-creating Cultural Discourses of Masculinity," *Language in Society*, vol. 34, 2005, 695–726. Cf. Kjerstin Andersson, "Constructing Young Masculinity: A Case Study of Heroic Discourse on Violence," *Discourse & Society*, vol. 19 (2), 2008, 140.

4. Andersson, "Constructing Young Masculinity," 140.

5. Koleva, *Biografija i normalnost*, 51–52.

6. Cf. Katherine Verdery, *What Was Socialism, and What Comes Next?* Princeton: Princeton University Press, 1996.

7. Cf. Gail Kligman, "The Politics of Reproduction in Ceausescu's Romania: A Case Study in Political Culture," *East European Politics and Societies*, vol. 4 (3), 1992, 393–438; Susan Gal and Gail Kligman, *The Politics of Gender after Socialism*. Princeton: Princeton University Press, 2000; Verdery, *What was Socialism*; Anelia Kassabova-Dintcheva, "Neue Alte Normen. Die versuchte Normierung der Sexualität in sozialistischen Bulgarien," *Ethnologia*

Balkanica, vol. 8, 2004, 155–75; Ulf Brunnbauer and Karin Taylor, "Creating a 'Socialist Way of Life': Family and Reproduction Policies in Bulgaria, 1944–1989," *Continuity and Change*, vol. 19 (2), 2004, 283–312.

8. For many of them, freedom of movement was much greater during socialism, when they used to have the legendary "red passports," than it is nowadays, when visa requirements and bad economic circumstances make traveling difficult (cf. Tanja Petrović, "The Territory of the Former Yugoslavia in the Mental Maps of Former Yugoslavs: Nostalgia for Space," *Sprawy Narodowościowe*, Seria Nova, Zeszyt 31, 2007, 263–73).

9. The letter is part of the collection stored in the Josip Broz Tito Memorial Center. It was published in *VlasTito iskustvo: Past Present*, Belgrade: Samizdat B92, 2004, 158–59.

10. Boris Buden sees this patriarchal father image of Tito as an essential characteristic of the ideology of Titoism: "The Yugoslavs were created as a mass of people whose collective identity was pressed within a political discourse which began and ended with ritually staged scenes of pledging oaths of allegiance to the leader. On the other hand, Tito, as an indisputable authority, guaranteed security and communal spirit, as does the patriarchal father of a complex family. As an internalized father-figure authority, he played the role of a symbolic representative of general moral norms, socially recognized values, and phylogenetically acquired cultural achievements, thus laying the foundation for the development of collective consciousness" (Boris Buden, *Kaptolski kolodvor*, Belgrade: CSUb, 2002, 20–22).

11. Katherine Verdery notes that the socialist state had the position of "parent-state," or "the paternalistic state," transmitting the patriarchal gender roles from the nuclear family into public discourse (Verdery, *What was Socialism*, 64).

12. Marianne Hirsch argues that "photographs, as the only material traces of an irrecoverable past, derive their power and their important cultural role from their embeddedness in the fundamental rites of family life" (Marianne Hirsch, *Family Frames: Photography, Narrative and Postmemory*. Cambridge, MA and London, UK: Harvard University Press, 2002, 5).

13. There are Internet forums in all the former Yugoslav republics where the former soldiers tell their "army stories"; army experiences and various aspects of the JNA service were also described in the Lexicon of YU mythology, a project initiated by Dubravka Ugrešić and Vladimir Arsenijević (cf. *Leksikon YU mitologije*: Belgrade-Zagreb: Rende, Postscriptum, http://www.postyu.info, accessed on October 10, 2009).

14. It also became apparent during my fieldwork when I conducted interviews with former JNA soldiers about their army service: although all my interviewees were very glad to share their memories of the JNA with me, it was rather difficult to maintain dialogues; they were unsure about how much I understood and went into details explaining army realia, ranks, jargon expressions, and so on. On the contrary, in cases when I was simultaneously interviewing two men or a group of them, they would soon "forget" about my presence and start a lively exchange of their memories, with the usual elements of performing masculinity (competing, teasing each other, telling jokes, etc.).

15. Miljenko Jergović, O romanu (On the novel) [*Ništa nas ne smije iznenaditi* by Ante Tomić, Zagreb 2003]. http://www.karaulafilm.com/novel.php, accessed on October 12, 2009.

16. There was a short-lived attempt to introduce army service for women between 1983 and 1985. It was voluntary and lasted 2 months and 22 days for female soldiers and 6 months for officers. The practice of including women in the JNA, justified with a need "to improve the status of women in the Yugoslav society," was eventually abandoned in 1985, as it faced numerous difficulties and women's interest in service declined significantly. Thus the idea of transforming voluntary service for women into mandatory was never realized (Gombač, 2011).

17. Judith Butler (1990) sees gender as performativity and a culturally and discursively produced social category. Within the Butlerian tradition, gender is regarded as "an emergent feature of social situations" (Andresson, 2008: 140; Candace West and Don H. Zimmerman, "Doing Gender," Gender and Society, vol. 1, no 2, 1987, 125-151).

18. Chris Brickell, "Masculinities, Performativity and Subversion; A Sociological Reappraisal," *Men and Masculinities*, vol. 8, 2005, 37.

19. Andersson, "Constructing Young Masculinity," 140.

20. Drawing on Bronwyn Davies, *Frogs and Snails and Feminist Tales. Preschool Children and Gender*. Sidney: Allen and Unwin, 1989, Søndergaard defines story lines as "collective and culturally dependent narratives that make up the pillars upon which individuals build their own personal stories" (Dorte Marie Søndergaard, "Poststructuralist Approaches to Empirical Analysis," *International Journal of Qualitative Studies in Education*, vol. 15, 2002, 187–204, quoted after Andersson, "Constructing Young Masculinity," 145).

21. Andersson, "Constructing Young Masculinity," 145.

22. *Vojnici* [Soldiers] 1984: Stjepan Zaninović dir. 105 min. Yugoslavia.

23. Cf. Aleksandar Ćirić, "Zbogom, gušteri," *Vreme* 996, 4 February 2010; Zoran Majdin, "Vojničke priče: nikad više ili nikad gore," *Vreme* 996, 4 February 2010; Ibid., "Zbogom, gušteri," *Vreme* 1040, 9 December 2010.

24. Majdin, "Vojničke priče."

25. *Vojnikova ljubav* [Soldier's Love] 1976: Svetislav Pavlović dir. 103 min. Yugoslavia.

26. This narrative is not specific to the socialist Yugoslav context only. It was exploited also in post-Yugoslav societies, but with different ideological references: instead of the Yugoslav ideology of defense based on World War II (people's liberation war), the ideological foundations of national post-Yugoslav armies were in the legacies of the establishment of post-Yugoslav states. In his speech on the occasion of the Day of the Army of Bosnia and Herzegovina, a member of the Sulejman Tihić government addressed the soldiers who were taking the oath with the following words: "Dear soldiers! I wish you good health and success in your army training. I have no doubt that you will be able to meet the challenges of new times, like your fathers, brothers, and sisters did. Performing army service is not only a debt to the homeland, but also a school of life! I urge you to preserve and keep the legacy and moral values of the defensive

war of liberation!" (Sulejman Tihić, Prvi put u novijoj historiji imali smo bosansku vojsku koja se borila samo za svoju državu [For the first time in our history we had an army that fought for its own country], 2003. http:// www.tihic.ba/Tekst/Govori/Dan%20armije%202003.html, accessed on 24 May 2007).

27. Competitiveness and solidarity are important features of male talk in general (cf. Coates, 2003).

28. Milićević, "Joining the War," 271.

29. Ibid.

30. Milićević (ibid., 268) stresses that the ethnicization of society is often accompanied by masculinization, which shapes "aggressive, controlling, competitive, power-oriented, rationalistic, instrumental behaviors in men" (Huggins and Haritos-Fatouros, "Bureaucratizing Masculinities Among Brazilian Torturers and Murderers," in: *Masculinities and Violence*, ed. L. H. Bowker, Thousand Oaks, CA: Sage, 1998, 30).

31. Marko Živković, "Introduction: Ex-Yugoslav Masculinities under Female Gaze, or Why Men Skin Cats, Beat up Gays and Go to War," *Nationalities Papers*, vol. 34 (3), 2006, 259. Claudia Koonz points out that there was "intense anxiety about the erosion of traditional gender arrangements in Germany after World War I, and this contributed significantly to the support of Nazism. Similarly, periods of social, economic, and political upheaval, such as the collapse of communism, can push men into what Peggy Watson called 'masculine anomie.'" (Claudia Koonz, *Mothers in the Fatherland*. London: Methuen, 1988 quoted after Jill A. Irvine and Carol S. Lilly, "Boys Must Be Boys: Gender and the Serbian Radical Party, 1991–2000," *Nationalities Papers*, vol. 35 (1), 2007, 96).

32. Irvine and Lilly, "Boys Must Be Boys," 133; Milićević, "Joining the War," 268.

33. Milićević, "Joining the War," 273.

34. Ibid., 275.

35. Mile Bjelajac, *Jugoslovensko iskustvo sa multietničkom armijom 1918–1991* [Yugoslav experience with multiethnic army 1918–1991], Belgrade: Udruženje za društvenu istoriju, 1999, 13.

36. On the idea of Yugoslavism, its birth, evolution, and fall, see Dejan Đokić (ed.), *Yugoslavism. Histories of a Failed Idea 1918–1992*. London: Hurst & Company, 2003; Hannes Grandits, "Dynamics of Socialist Nation-Building: The Short-Lived Programme of Promoting a Yugoslav National Identity and Some Comparative Perspectives," *Dve domovini/Two Homelands*, vol. 27, 2008, 15–28.

37. Stef Jansen, *Antinacionalizam* [Antinationalism] Belgrade: XX vek, 2005, 220.

38. Dubravka Ugrešić, *Kultura laži: Antipolitički eseji* [The Culture of Lies] Belgrade—Zagreb: Samizdat B92—Konzor, 2002, 275. Although a perception that remembering socialism is prohibited and morally questioned is common for postsocialist societies in Europe (cf. Maria Todorova, "Daring to Remember Bulgaria, pre-1989," *Guardian*, November 9, 2009), the violent and traumatic breakdown of the country in the 1990s makes it particularly strong in the former Yugoslav societies.

39. Miroslav Hadžić, *Sudbina partijske vojske* [The destiny of the party army], Belgrade: Samizdat B92, 2001, 173.
40. Maria Todorova uses this term in order to "distinguish it from (. . .) communism as an intellectual/ideological endeavor" (Maria Todorova, "Remembering Communism," *Centre for Advanced Study in Sofia Newsletter* 2/2002 (autumn), 15).
41. Teofil Pančić, "Leksikon YU mitologije—knjiga smeha i pamćenja," *Vreme*, 699, May 27, 2004.
42. Merran Toerien and Kevin Durrheim, "Power Through Knowledge: Ignorance and the 'Real Man,'" *Feminism & Psychology*, vol. 11, 2005, 36 quoted after Andersson, "Constructing Young Masculinity," 139.
43. There is a close link between ideologies of masculinity and patriotism, as stressed by Nielsen: "Patriotism is an ideology, like masculinity, that posits specific behaviors and beliefs as best for a nation and an individual." Kim. E. Nielsen, "What's a Patriotic Man to Do: Patriotic Masculinities of the Post-WW-1 Red Scare," *Men and Masculinities*, vol. 6 (3), 2004, 240–41. And just as patriotism is contested, so is masculinity.
44. Michael Herzfeld, *Kulturna intimnost* [Cultural Intimacy], Belgrade: XX vek, 2004.
45. Lynne Segal, *Slow Motion. Changing Masculinities, Changing Men*. New Brunswick: Rutgers University Press, 1990, 32.
46. Segal discusses the case of the British National Service in the same vein. Ibid., 132–33.

6

Experiencing Socialism: Female Singers in Southeastern Serbia

Ana Hofman

This chapter examines the strategies in performances of socialist femininity by exploring personal narratives of women involved in amateur cultural activities in their villages from the beginning of the 1970s to the end of the 1980s. My focus is on the older generation of women (born prior to and during World War II)[1] in the area of Niško Polje in southeastern Serbia, who were the protagonists of important changes in Serbian rural society, its discourses, and practices.[2] My interlocutors[3] were all very good singers who took an active part in the villages' cultural activities, mostly at stage cultural events organized by cultural institutions established to suit the demands of the new socialist cultural policy, such as Culture Houses (*Domovi kulture*), Collective Houses (*Zadružni domovi*), Cultural-Educational Associations (*Kulturno-prosvetne zajednice*, KPZs), or Cultural-Artistic Societies (*Kulturno umetnička društva*, KUDs). These events contributed to the development of "culture and entertainment" (*kulturno-zabavni život*) and amateur activities (*amaterizam*) in rural areas as a part of the larger project of modernization and emancipation of Yugoslav cultural policy.

Applying the oral history method, my intention was to keep a record of the women's personal histories, points of view, and interpretations of the past.[4] The autobiographical testimonies made it possible to present women as individuals differentiated by age, attitudes, and background. However, although the emphasis was on the "polyvocality" of their accounts, the fieldwork revealed that my interlocutors shared common experiences as members of village amateur groups, which shaped their

103

discourses in a similar way. Drawing on the phenomenological feminist approach and on "the narrative musical ethnography,"[5] this chapter shows the ways in which personal experience and individual discourses can be used as sources of insight in researching the interplay between ideology and practice in socialism. I have employed the approaches of some post-structuralist feminist theorists who have criticized the essentialist concept of experience as an "authentic truth" as introduced by the standpoint theory.[6] They have suggested the category of experience not as a true and authentic subjective testimony, but as a discursively created active, volatile, and creative force.[7] Therefore, my aim is not to argue for an essentialist approach to women's identity and experiences, as suggested by the concept of *women's oral history*, which claims a particular "women's history" based on women's specific voices and experiences.[8] Employing the phenomenological approach based on a self-reflexive and dialogic research methodology, my goal is to offer polyvocal and multifaceted research strategies of many complex and contradictory experiences of socialism. I will examine the role of experience in the processes of re-creation of the female singers' subjectivities and negotiation of power relations and gender hierarchies as a result of the interplay between ideology and everyday life strategies. This will make it possible to understand the complex relation between political discourses, on the one hand, and the lived experiences of my interlocutors, on the other. Therefore, the focus will be on the links between the personal and the political, since the changes in self-perception and the restructuring of social relations can be perceived as an integral part of political change.[9]

"State Feminism"

Gender politics of equality was introduced as an important part of the socialist modernization project: the creators of the new ideology felt that economic changes would eventually improve women's social position. The "new woman" established by socialist identity politics was made equal to man, not only in battle and the socialist revolution, but also in the building of the new society. At the Anti-Fascist Congress of the National Liberation of Serbia (*Antifašistička skupština narodnog oslobođenja Srbije, ASNOS*) held between February 22 and 24, 1944, social equality was proclaimed and women obtained the formal right to vote at the constitutional meeting in 1945.[10] The 1946 Yugoslav Constitution guaranteed for the first time in history a political, economic, and social equality between men and women. Women were given the right to vote, to be educated, and to be employed without discrimination.[11] By 1946, civil marriage had become obligatory in the entire territory of Yugoslavia. Customs regarded as discriminatory toward women, such as dowry or "selling of the bride," were forbidden.[12] Women were permitted to choose between keeping their father's name and adding their marital partner's family name after marriage. State law safeguarded the reproductive rights of women, equal prospects for employment of men and women, and various aspects of social protection (such as maternity leave or eldercare).[13]

Legal emancipation of women was realized through employment, which provided for economic independence and represented a crucial factor of women's emancipation. In the public discourse, employed women were recognized as the main driving force of the modernization of Yugoslav society, which enabled women's self-recognition on two levels: as a mother/daughter/wife and as a productive individual working outside the home.[14] The discourse of "woman–mother" was transformed into "mother–worker,"[15] the price of which was the well-known double burden—taking on responsibilities both at work and at home.

Through their activities, the newly founded women's and feminist organizations particularly tried to reach women in rural areas: "The first and basic interest is that women, through modernization of agriculture and participation in the communal movement, improve their cultural level and get involved in the socialist transformation of the village."[16] The association called the Union of Women's Societies of Serbia (*Savez ženskih društava Srbije*)[17] established its branches in villages with the purpose to support rural women emancipation.[18] Education, as the most important element of the new Yugoslav peasant family idea,[19] set about rooting out illiteracy among the elderly (particularly women) in villages.[20] One of the crucial acts the activists singled out was the ban on the wearing of veils as a part of the new identity and body politics.[21]

These changes offered new chances to rural women, but the Communist Party program and the state strategy for gender equality in Yugoslavia found different obstacles in putting the ideas into practice. The fast economic transformation in Yugoslavia after World War II and the women's emancipation did not proceed apace—while the economic reforms were being carried out rapidly, the customs and patriarchal relations were changing very slowly.

Increasing fragmentation of the extended family after World War II resulted in the division of land and the establishment of the nuclear family. This affected not only the disintegration of traditional forms of agricultural production but also changes in the lives of peasant population. Electricity and mechanization introduced in farming made work much easier and improved the position of women in many respects. On the other hand, as a consequence of the fast process of industrialization, their husbands who were employed in factories moved away to town; hence much of the agricultural work fell on women's shoulders—in addition to household and childcare duties, they had to do the farm chores formerly done by men.[22] Thus women became the main agricultural labor force, but their "job" was seen as inseparable from the joint work within the kinship group or kin obligation in general; it was considered simply a part of rural women's life.[23] Unlike their husbands, rural women rarely got employment at local factories, since employment outside the home was considered inappropriate for them. The women I am focusing on remained housewives.[24] A few of them who started working after World War II had to quit their jobs because maternity leave, childcare, and eldercare were inexistent in rural environments:

> *I worked in the company "The 22nd December" for four years and six months. We sewed in the sewing-factory and I also worked as a student. I quit the job a long time ago; I did not have anyone to take care of my children.* (Mladenka Ristić, Vukmanovo village)

The data from the beginning of the 1960s also show that although women were formally members of the Socialist Alliance of Working People of Yugoslavia (*Socialistički savez radnog naroda Jugoslavije, SSRNJ*) and other organizations, they did not participate in elections, celebrations, and working actions.[25] Instead, their husbands, considered to be the heads of the family, participated at alliance meetings and other actions, in accordance with the general opinion that women were not capable of taking part in political and social life.[26]

The essentialist "we" of socialist feminism considered women as a homogeneous social group, propagating their equality regardless of all regional, ethnic, religious, and other differences.[27] Rural areas, far from the centers of power, were particularly ignored: "Opportunities reached only a very small number of women: the urban middle class predominantly in the northern regions."[28] Official reports concerning women's position in rural society illustrate a tension between the official policy and the real state on the ground, where women were still in almost a slavish subordinate position.[29] As the official records confirm, even though young rural women were strongly against the "old" patriarchal norms, they were rarely supported by the wider community or local institutions:[30] "Although not openly promoted, this patriarchal mentality was in fact the easiest way of exploiting traditional views, incorporating them into ideological texts, and consequently redistributing power, without exposing such views to unfavorable communist criticism."[31]

To summarize, in the new political system women—as less mobile social subjects—started to get fresh opportunities (education, employment). On the other hand, the presence of women in the public sphere was by and large symbolic, unable to challenge the existent gender hierarchies.

Overstepping the Boundaries

Supporting women's contribution to educational–cultural, cultural–artistic, and sports activities was one of the new gender policy goals. Authorities appealed for effective actions to encourage women's active participation in village cultural life, claiming a low number of female participants in any kind of a state-supported social activity. As the main goal, policy makers emphasized the establishment of cultural and entertainment forms suitable for women, since their cultural activities were still strongly connected to the "old" and "primitive" types of entertainment such as religious customs, weddings, or informal gatherings (*prela, slave*).[32] Amateur activities were presented as the most important feature of the inclusion of rural women in the "cultural development" of villages, which was also a way of their emancipation and enlightenment (*prosvećivanje*). The local schools, KPZs, and KUDs were the main vehicles of education and emancipation particularly of older rural women.[33]

On the other hand, the very possibility for women to be engaged as protagonists in state-supported cultural manifestations was not accepted with approval by their families and the wider community. At the beginning of the amateur activities in their villages, the women participants had to ask their husbands' permission for every performance.[34] Dragan Todorović, an amateur collector of folk music, stresses that many of them did not allow their wives to be active in vocal amateur groups. Those who agreed to let their wives perform, usually asked for a group to be accompanied by male supervisors, in some cases also insisted on their own presence. For that reason, female amateur groups usually had a male guide who was accountable to their husbands for their safety and proper behavior. The story I heard from Milorad, the husband of Ilinka Despotović from the village of Trupale, illustrates such attitudes toward amateur activities: Ilinka was invited to perform at an event in Macedonia together with her vocal group, and the local cultural workers asked them to prepare a suitable program. Yet influenced by the villagers' commentaries about the immorality of women who sang in public, her husband did not allow her to perform. Telling this story, Milorad admitted that he had made a big mistake and that today he regretted having paid too much attention to other people's opinion. He told me that he had ruined the opportunity for his wife to develop her career further and perhaps go abroad to perform.

Female singers' activities were closely supervised by family members whose reactions toward their performances varied. It was particularly important not to disgrace one's family by performing in public ("They were afraid I would shame myself," Sevlija Stanković, Trupale village), and many women had problems not only with their husbands but also with their sons and sons-in-law:

> He [my son] did not allow me to sing, he was ashamed, he said: What will you do there, you just open your mouths like fools. He threatened me: Just show up on the stage, you'll see what will happen! (Sevlija Stanković, Trupale village)

Apart from being active in public in the way that was unusual for women in the rural community, the singers started to perform alongside their husbands and other male relatives and to expand their repertoires, appropriating vocal genres that were usually reserved for men. This practice further destabilized the boundaries between gender-segregated performances characteristic for the musical practices in Niško Polje villages.[35]

Therefore, the female singers destabilized the strong boundaries between the "normal" male and female spheres of activities.[36] As a consequence, they were considered by their families and wider society as "immoral women"—peculiar persons, whose behavior disturbed the given norms and rules. The villagers tended to view their performances as frivolous and shameful:

> They tell us: where are you going, they will make fun of you. Oh, we suffered, me and her. They were gossiping and saying all kinds of things. Our neighbors did not understand that. (Ilinka Despotović and Sevlija Stanković, Trupale village)

Cultural events as displays of the official discourse provided an opportunity for these women to transmit their activities from the periphery to the center of social happenings. The stage, as an optimal place for the production and representation of meaning, social legitimization, and power renegotiation, brought a new representation of female subjectivities in rural cultural environment. Did the women import that "new role" into their personal lives? Did the reality that they staged become legitimate in their communities? Was the imaginary line drawn between performance and everyday life overcome?

New Concepts of Identity, Subjectivity, and Self-Representation

As their stories reveal, the involvement in amateur musical activities was an extremely important factor of rural women's personal identification. Through performing on stage, they got an opportunity to challenge their position on the margins of society, thus opening up possibilities for reinterpretation, reconsideration, and "resignification" of their subject positions. Their specific experiences influenced a new self-awareness and self-image of female singers, which caused a shift in their understanding of the social environment. Their accounts became mediated by the dominant institutional discourses of gender equality, which they experienced as empowering.

The female singers' stories confirm that their amateur activities and stage performances brought them satisfaction. They spoke very proudly about the situations where representatives of the authorities came to their houses to insist on their participation in organized cultural activities. Gradually, as organizers confirmed, women who were initially too shy to sing started joining in by themselves:

> I went to the village fountain and women asked me: "Dragane, can I sing, I see that it is very beautiful." And I said: "Yes, but would your husband allow it?" And she answered: "I will ask him to let me, but if he doesn't, you come and ask him." There were women whose husbands agreed after they talked to them and everything was ok. (Dragan Todorović, Vukmanovo village)

Women mostly spoke about their most memorable performances describing the reaction of the audiences and juries. At the beginning of our conversation, Velika Jovanović from Gornji Komren told me that she had won the first prize in three villages ("We in *Gornja Studena* sang best and our songs were the best," Rada Zlatanović, Petrija Vučković).

The female singers I talked to were particularly proud of their travels. Bearing in mind the restrictions on women's mobility characteristic of the rural society,[37] travels with amateur groups marked a big step in gaining their independence. The important parts of their stories were travels and contacts with people who were enchanted by their singing:

> *I have pictures from the Village Gatherings when I went to Bubanj and three days in Aleksandrovac. There was a banquet, the wine . . . you just pour it and drink. I have pictures, I will show you later. I have traveled, I have seen things, so, if I die now, I would not be sorry.*
> (Grozdana Đokić, Leskovik village)

The media also played an important role in the construction of the new self-identification of the female singers. Their performances were shown on the local and national television, broadcast on radio, and presented in newspapers. All of them showed me newspaper clippings, particularly the ones with their pictures. TV shows were a particularly significant experience as a source of personal gratification. Public acknowledgment of their talents on the highest level brought them very close to professionals:

> *In Belgrade we barely danced one dance (kolo). You had to turn over to the audience and cameras, so we hardly persisted. They pursued us very much; we danced according to the clock, because they had already prepared the program. First went the News and then the rest. But we performed first.* (Ilinka Despotović, Trupale village)

Through stage performances, the women expressed their personal attitude, challenged the patterns of "propriety" and "impropriety" in the patriarchal environment of Niško Polje, and gained power in an officially recognized way. That enabled the re-signification of the female singers' social environments and contributed to their visibility and legitimacy as social subjects.

The socialist identity politics influenced the shift in the representational discourse of gender, at the same time producing new discourses on women's subjectivities. Public manifestations represented an arena in which the notion of the "old" roles of woman was challenged by the new socialist femininity. With regard to the concept of social temporality, where every identity is performed,[38] new female roles were performed as a part of the new gender politics—socialist woman is equal to man and is the new driving force of socialist society. From that viewpoint, new gender relations promoted by official politics influenced the new dynamics of social relations and the new ways of self-recognition of the women in Niško Polje.

The Interplay between Ideology and Practice

However, despite the ideology of emancipation and creation of the "new femininity" in the official discourse, the representation of women at cultural events maintained the construction of gender relations that were based on a traditional matrix. First, there were no drastic changes in the field of musical activities: although they started performing male vocal genres, the women stayed in the field of vocal practice, only transmitting performance from the "private" to the "public space."[39] For them, the predominantly male domains such as playing instruments still remained a non-legitimate sphere of activity.[40] Moreover, in contrast to the official narratives of women's active participation in village cultural life, the leaders of amateur groups as well as the main organizers of Village Gatherings were men. Women did not have a say in deciding which songs they would perform; the final choice of the repertoire was usually made by the local organizers. As a rule, a few days before their performance at a Village Gathering, women would go to the House of Culture, the local KPZ, or another local administrative office to present the repertoire and get the opinion of the organizers:

> We went down to the Center and got started. They told us to get on the stage, but without microphones; they just listened to us. And we started to sing one song, and after that another song, and then the third. After that they said: you will sing this song. (Sevlija Stanković, Trupale village)

Thus, the women were still dismissed and marginalized as "mere" performers, rather than amateur group leaders or organizers of the events. This illustrates the general presumption that older women in rural environments remained in the traditional domain of music-making. Although they were portrayed in a new role in the public sphere, their activity essentially did not transgress the existing norms. In such a way, the socially constructed matrix was transmitted on stage, and the representation of women still retained the same framework.[41] As some authors point out, despite the ideology of gender equality, rural women were still displayed as custodians of folk culture, protectors of the family and the household, and keepers of traditional values and virtues.[42] This supports the dominant scholarly narratives regarding the position of women in socialist societies claiming that despite the formal rights they got, women remained subordinated.[43]

On the other hand, by performing the socialist female subjectivity in the public sphere, my interlocutors personally experienced emancipation and transgressed patriarchal norms. For the first time in their lives, they got a sense of active participation in social life by taking responsibility for their autonomous actions. They challenged women's position within the community, achieving some level of individual autonomy and restructuring their values and priorities. The extraordinary experience they shared made it possible for these women to transgress the existent norms of the rural society and enabled them to occupy a specific social position as the embodiments and promoters of the rural culture. As mentioned above, by expressing their individualities through cultural activities, they developed new ways of understanding the world and new perceptions of themselves. This implies that the female singers started to be *active* in the process of meaning-making and understanding cultural and social change. This is not to say that the old female cultural roles disappeared. Rather, new roles were allowed to coexist with the old ones, opening possibilities for the future (or further) political reconsideration.

This chapter illuminates the interplay between ideology, discourse, and practice on the level of personal experience. Even though the socialist ideology of gender equality was politically proclaimed and conceptualized as holistic and collectivist, on the level of individual experience and everyday life the women portrayed in this chapter received the benefits and obviously experienced socialism as a period of emancipation. Their stories qualify the assertion that the "emancipation" of women was realized only at the surface of gender relations, without penetrating into the private sphere and interfamily relations, and that therefore "gender equality was not understood, or lived, in cultural terms."[44] Through their personal experiences of socialism, the women used the dominant policy to achieve a better personal social position and subvert gender hierarchies within their social environments in spite of the "double burden." In this respect, "the totality created the possibility for a transformation by the particular."[45] The main idea of this chapter is not to "prove" or "disprove" the discrepancy between official socialist narrative and local practices, but rather to destabilize a fixed and static conception of "socialism"[46] and to offer a multifaceted picture of the everyday life in socialism and to question the tendency of "categorizing" and producing one-dimensional and univocal narratives of this period. The female singers' personal experiences of social transformation transgress the binaries usually present in thinking about socialism such as public/private, ideology/practice. Their stories speak about the complex and contradictory relations among personal, interpersonal, and political levels and emphasize the interlacement of political and lived realities. The female singers' accounts show the interplay between ideology, representational, and social practices at the level of everyday life strategies and challenge the strong division between ideology and practice in socialist societies presented in scholarly narratives.

Archival Resources

Archive of Yugoslavia (AJ) League of Communists of Yugoslavia, funds:

142—Federal Conference of Socialist Alliance of Working People of Yugoslavia

List of Villages and Interlocutors with their birth years

Brenica	Ruža Gocić, 1929, Kamenica
	Vera Đorđević, 1937
	Milica Cvetanović, 1941
Brzi Brod	Životka Stanković, 1926
	Zorica Stankovic, 1938
Čukljenik	Ilinka Mladenović, 1934
	Rada Stankovic, 1938
Donja Vrežina	Rusanda Arsić, 1914
	Vukosava Gocić, 1923
	Kostadin Gocić, 1923
	Javorka Radovanović, 1934, Jasenovik
Donja Studena	Živadinka Tasić, 1926
	Vidosava Stojanović, 1927
	Olga Marković, 1934
	Savka Milenović, 1938
	Olga Stanković, 1939
	Dragiša Stojanović, 1953
	Miodrag Tasic, 1946
Donji Komren	Radivoje Petrović, 1913
	Jelica Jovanović, 1936, Čamurlija

Gornja Studena	Petrija Vučković, 1937
	Radica Zlatanović, 1946
Gornja Vrežina	Desanka Petrović, 1924, Donja Vrežina
	Mladenka Živković, 1927
Gornji Komren	Velinka Jovanović, 1943
Gornji Matejevac	Zagorka Igić, 1926
	Ljiljana Cvetković, 1938
Hum	Dobrisavka Jankovic, 1935
Jelašnica	Milunka Đorđević, 1930, Rautovo
	Svetlana Makarić, 1950
	Miodrag Tasić, 1946
Kamenica	Verica Mitić, 1920
	Emilija Gocić, 1932
Leskovik	Grozdana Đokić, 1945
Malča	Miroslava Jovanović, 1933
	Jelena Mitrović, 1948, Knez Selo
Niška Banja	Bata Belević, 1943, Bijelo Polje (Montenegro)
Novo Selo	Stojan Stošić, 1921
	Ljubica Andjelkovic, 1939
	Nikodije Andjelkovic, 1941
Prosek	Verica Miljković, 1933, Ostrvica
	Ljiljana Radonjić, 1944, Manastir
	Sava Radonjić, 1939, Kamenica
	Stanković D. Velibor, 1939
	Jevica Bogdanović, 1924
	Božidar Bogdanović, 1923
Rujnik	Slavka Petkovic, 1922
	Ruža Zdravković, 1924, Hum
	Jagodinka Mitrović, 1930, Kravlje
Trupale	Vukašin Mitić, 1952
	Ilinka Despotović, 1939, Jabukovik (Crna Trava)
	Sevlija Stanković, 1936, Darkovce (Crna Trava)
Vukmanovo	Dragan Todorović, 1956
	Grozdana Zlatković, 1934
	Mladenka Ristić, 1945

Notes

1. For the names of women and the list of villages, see the Appendix.
2. Niško Polje belongs to a wider region called the Valley of the Južna Morava River (*Pomoravlje Južne Morave*). It is a passive and poor area relatively ethnically homogeneous, with a dominant Serbian population and the Roma as the largest minority group.
3. Taking into account the interactive nature of the biographical method, I avoid the terms such as interview, interviewers, or informants. I rather use the terms conversations and interlocutors.
4. Authors such as Paul Thompson, Liz Stanley, and Donald A. Ritchie argue that the main purpose of this method is not to get information of "objective" value, but to "make a 'subjective' record of how a man or a woman looks back on his or her life as a whole, or part of it" (Paul Thompson, *The Voice of the Past—Oral History*. New York: Oxford University Press, 1978, 199). See also: Liz Stanley, *The Auto-Biographical I*. Manchester and New York: Manchester University Press, 1992; Donald A. Ritchie, *Doing Oral History*. New York: Twayne Publisher, 1995.
5. In ethnomusicological research, several scholars have focused on the musical experiences of individuals including Timothy Rice, Jeff Titon, and Jonathan Stock. The notion of "the study of people experiencing music" stems from the philosophical tradition of phenomenology and hermeneutics, which attempt to confine knowledge within the limits of the world of lived experience (Jeff T. Titon, "Knowing Fieldwork," in: *Shadows in the Field: New Perspectives for Fieldwork in Ethnomusicology*, eds. Gregory F. Barz and Timothy J. Cooley, New York and Oxford: Oxford University Press, 1997, 90). See also: Timothy Rice, *May It Fill Your Soul: Experiencing Bulgarian Music*. Chicago: Chicago University Press, 1994; Jonathan P. J. Stock, "Musical Narrative, Ideology, and the Life of Abing," *Ethnomusicology*, vol. 40 (1), 1996, 49–74; Jonathan P. J. Stock, "Toward an Ethnomusicology of the Individual, or Biographical Writing Ethnomusicology," *The World of Music*, vol. 43 (1), 2001, 5–19. More about this methodology see in: Ana Hofman, *Staging Socialist Femininity: Gender Politics and Folklore Performance in Serbia*. Leiden: Brill Academic Publishers, 2010.
6. The standpoint theorists (Dorothy Smith, Sandra Harding, Carol Gilligan, and Particia Hill Collins) claim that because of their common subordinate position, women have universal experience. They asserted that "women's experience" could be used as a research material for writing the history of repressed identities. Post-structuralists, African-American feminists, Third World feminists, and Queer theorists criticized the idea of common female experience, which unifies women regardless of ethnic group, class, or generation. In her text *Experience*, Joan Scott held an opinion that although the main quality of the standpoint theory is that it challenged the idea of an "essential truth" and one-sided perceptions of the world, its main insufficiency is the premise of essentialism (the concept of the unified female subject). Scott problematizes the "objective evidence of experience" and argues that the subject is constructed through discourse and only from that position is he/she able to produce his/her experience (Joan W. Scott,

"Experience," in: *Feminists Theorize the Political*, eds. Judith Butler and Joan W. Scott, New York: Routledge, 1992, 22–40).

7. Victor W. Turner and Edward M. Bruner, *The Anthropology of Experience*. Urbana and Chicago: University of Illinois Press, 1986, 17.

8. Sherna Berger Gluck, "What's So Special about Women? Women's Oral History," in: *Women's Oral History: The Frontiers Reader*, eds. Susan H. Armitage, Patricia Hart and Karen Weathermon, Linkoln and London: University of Nebraska Press, 2002, 3–20.

9. Nancy C. M. Hartsock, *The Feminist Standpoint Revisited and Other Essays*. Boulder, CO: Westview Press, 1998, 19.

10. Neda Božinović, *Žensko pitanje u Srbiji u XIX i XX veku*, Beograd: "Devedesetčetvrta," Žene u crnom, 1996, 151.

11. Susan L. Woodward, "The Right of Women: Ideology, Policy, and Social Change in Yugoslavia," in: *Women, State, and Party in Eastern Europe*, ed. Sharon L. Wolchik and Alfred G. Meyer, Durham: Duke University Press, 1985, 240.

12. Božinović, *Žensko pitanje*, 151.

13. Ibid.

14. Despite the ideology of equal employment possibilities and equally paid work, women remained in certain professions and were completely absent from others. They were employed in social services, textile, health care, and elementary schools, and underrepresented among journalists, professors, administrators, and judges (Garth Massey, Karen Hahn, and Duško Sekulić, "Women, Men and the 'Second Shift' in Socialist Yugoslavia," *Gender and Society*, vol. 9 (3), 1995, 363).

15. Ulf Brunnbauer and Karin Taylor, "Creating a 'Socialist Way of Life': Family and Reproduction Policies in Bulgaria (1944–89)," *Continuity and Change*, vol. 19 (2), 2004, 230.

16. Božinović, *Žensko pitanje*, 171.

17. The League of Communists of Yugoslavia (LCY) founded around two thousand societies at federal, republic, provincial, district, and communal level in all Republics of Yugoslavia (Sabrina P. Ramet, "In Tito's time," in: *Gender Politics in the Western Balkans*, ed. Sabrina P. Ramet, University Parc, Pennsylvania: Pennsylvania University Press, 1999, 94).

18. AJ-142, The status of women in villages, materials from 1959 to 1962, F-616.

19. Woodward, "The Right of Women," 244.

20. In 1961, the proportion of illiterate women in Yugoslavia was reduced to 28.8 percent over the age of 10, and 75 percent of those over the age of 35 (Suzana Đurić and Gordana Dragičević, *Women in Yugoslav Society and Economy*. Beograd: Međunarodna politika, 1965, 10).

21. Božinović, *Žensko pitanje*, 171.

22. So-called "feminization of the agriculture" (Vlado Puljiz, *Jugoslavensko selo: problemi i perspektive*, Osijek: Centar za idejno-teorijski rad, 1989, 20).

23. As Maria Todorova asserts, rural women's double burden was deeply embedded in rural life and culture, due to the long tradition of their active participation in the labor process (Maria Todorova, "The Bulgarian Case: Women's Issues or Feminist Issues," in *Gender Politics and Post*

Communism, ed. Nanette Funk and Magda Mueller, New York: Routledge, 1993, 33).

24. The situation changed with the change of generations and their daughters mostly started working outside the home. However, the daughters also had problems because of ambitions in their professional lives: Ljiljana Radonjić from the village of Prosek told me that her daughter could not get married in the village since she had been working in a company situated in the city of Niš. The main problem was to find a husband who would accept her night shift working hours.

25. AJ-142, The status of women in villages, materials from 1959 to 1962, F-616.

26. In spite of formal commitment to gender equality, women stayed unrepresented in leadership institutions. For example, in 1957, women presented just 17.2 percent of all members of LCY (Ramet, "In Tito's time," 100).

27. Gail Kligman, *The Politics of Duplicity: Controlling reproduction in Ceausescu's Romania*. Berkeley: University of California, 1998, 26.

28. Woodward, "The Right of Women," 240.

29. Results presented in Vera St. Erlich's book *Jugoslovenska porodica u trasformaciji—studija u tri stotine sela* [Family in Transition: A Study of 300 Yugoslav Villages] Zagreb: Filozofski fakultet, Izdanja Isntituta za kniževnost, 1971 illustrate how rural women remained in a subordinate position within their families, particularly in relation to their husbands and mothers-in-law. They did not complain about their problems, moreover, they did not express any demands for changing that inferior position (ibid., 227).

30. AJ-142, The status of women in villages, materials from 1959 to 1962, F-616. For example, in 1965, the husbands and fathers obstructed the enrollment of rural girls in high schools since they did not want to accept a female social role other than that of the housewife (Đurić and Dragičević, *Women in Yugoslav Society*, 14).

31. Svetlana Slapšak, "Identities under Threat on the Eastern Borders," in: *Thinking Differently—A Reader in European Women Studies*, eds. Gabriele Griffin and Rosi Braidotti, London and New York: Zed Books, 2002, 148.

32. AJ-142, The status of women in villages, materials from 1959 to 1962, F-616.

33. Ibid.

34. Organizers emphasized that during the first few years of holding the Village Gatherings, it was very difficult to introduce this new activity to villagers. The emergence of new patterns of cultural life was not generally met with approval, and villagers were not open to new tendencies and the socialist concept of "modernity."

35. Women's appropriation of repertoire that previously belonged to men and vice versa is noticeable in various societies in the second half of the twentieth century such as Kosovo (Svanibor Pettan, "Male, Female, and Beyond in the Culture and Music of Roma in Kosovo," in: *Music and Gender: Perspectives from the Mediterranean*, ed. Tullia Magrini, Chicago and London: The University of Chicago Press, 2003, 287–305), Corsica (Caroline Bithell, "A Man's Game? Engendered Song and the Changing Dynamics of

Musical Activity in Corsica," in: *Music and Gender*, 33–66), and Greece (Gail Holst-Warhaft, "The Female Dervish and Other Shady Ladies of the Rebetika," in: *Music and Gender*, 169–94).

36. Carol Silverman's research of state-ensemble female singers in Bulgaria shows the same practice: women who sang professionally were considered to lack morality and were not respected. For that reason, many families did not allow their daughters to join the state ensembles in the 1950s (Carol Silverman, " 'Move Over Madonna:' Gender, Representation, and the 'Mistery' of Bulgarian Voices," in: *Over the Wall/After the Fall: Post-Communist Cultures Through an East-West Gaze*, eds. Sibelan Forrester, Magdalena J. Zaboowska, and Elena Gapova, Bloomington and Indianapolis: Indiana University Press, 2004, 220).

37. In the villages of southeastern Serbia, through marriage the husband became "the master of his wife" and she was not allowed to go away from home without his permission or that of the oldest man in the house.

38. Judith Butler, *Gender Trouble: Feminism and the Subversion of Identity*. New York and London: Routledge, 1999, 33.

39. Drawing on Susan Gal's definition of the public/private distinction as a communicative phenomenon that is a product of a semiotic process (Susan Gal, "A Semiotics of the Public/Private Distinction," in: *Transitions, Environments, Translations: Feminisms in International Politics*, eds. Joan W. Scott, Cora Kaplan, and Debra Keates, New York: Routledge, 1997, 261), these terms will be employed in the same manner that my interlocutors used them in their narratives. The notions of public and private are employed to demarcate important boundaries and especially to underline the "official–unofficial" and "visibility–invisibility" interrelation.

40. Data from the mid-1980s on female instrumentalists exist, but with reference to school children who learned to play at music classes or went to the music school. They usually performed as part of school orchestras in the part of the program reserved for "children's folklore."

41. For instance, despite the above-mentioned actions against traditional clothes, the female singers were dressed in traditional dress (*narodna nošnja*) for their performances.

42. Laurie Occhipinti, "Two Steps Back? Anti-Feminism in Eastern Europe," *Anthropoloy Today*, vol. 12 (6), 1996, 15.

43. Scholars assert that the ideology of equality was just a thin layer over almost untouched patriarchy. See Daša Duhaček, "Women's Time in the Former Yugoslavia," in: *Gender Politics and Post Communism*, eds. Nanette Funk and Magda Mueller, New York: Routledge, 1993, 135; Nanette Funk, "Introduction: Women and Post-Communism," in: *Gender Politics and Post Communism*, 6; Hana Havelkova, "A Few Prefeminist Thoughts," in: *Gender Politics and Post Communism*, 70; Andjelka Milić, "Women and Nationalism in the Former Yugoslavia," in: *Gender Politics and Post Communism*, 111; Occhipinti, "Two Steps Back," 14; Mirjana Morokvasic, "The Logics of Exclusion: Nationalism, Sexism and the Yugoslav War," in: *Gender, Ethnicity and Political Ideologies*, eds. Nickie Charles and Helen Hintjens, London and New York: Routledge, 1997, 72; Kligman, *The Politics*

of Duplicity, 26; Ramet, "In Tito's Time," 105; Frances Pine, "Retreat to the Household? Gendered Domains in Postsocialist Poland," in: *Postsocialism: Ideals, Ideologies and Practices in Eurasia*, ed. Chris M. Hann, London and New York: Routledge, 2002, 103; Slapšak, "Identities Under Threat," 149; Brunnbauer and Taylor, "Creating a 'Socialist Way of Life,'" 230.

44.   Kligman, *The Politics of Duplicity*, 28.
45.   Funk, "Introduction: Women and Post-Communism," 1.
46.   Ibid., 3.

7

Eating Well in Times of Scarcity: Reactions, Perceptions, and Negotiation of Shortages in 1980s' Romania

Simina Bădică

The 1980s in Romania are largely remembered as a period of scarcity and shortages of all kinds: from food to books, from electricity to TV broadcasts.[1] And it is not only that they are remembered this way but autochthonous scholarly analyses also lean into the direction of remembering, capturing the anecdotic, the laughable, or horrible[2] instead of putting forward coherent theoretical frameworks that might lead to a comprehensive view on Romanian communism.[3]

Everyday life during communism is not yet a proper historical topic in Romanian academia. The historian is only one among the many voices to talk about the communist past, which remained a matter of personal and public memory, of intellectual debate engaged among people whose expertise comes only from having lived through it.[4] This makes the subject highly sensitive and sometimes suffocated by taken-for-granted concepts and theories. Most of them originate in the dissent discourse and operate with binary oppositions such as oppression versus resistance, official versus unofficial, public versus private, and ultimately truth versus lie.[5] These concepts were not only restricted to the intellectual sphere, but applied to the most mundane aspects of everyday life as well: from telling a joke to the illegal purchase of a pig for Christmas, more and more actions are considered, in nowadays accounts of the period, subversive.[6] One of the reasons for this inflexibility of arguments when historicizing the communist past is the political standing behind these accounts. Most of them are anticommunist pamphlets written in a time when the acknowledgment of the "crimes of communism" was still far from sight.[7]

This chapter enquires into the everyday life of the Romanians in the 1980s using the queue (the omnipresent food line) as its starting point of enquiry into the perceptions of and reactions to shortages. I count among the reactions to shortages the long debated "solidarity" among citizens of socialist states; I argue that the queue can be described as a form of community activity whose organization was left almost entirely in the hands of the community itself. Officially nonexistent, the queue provided an opportunity for Romanian citizens to exercise their organizational and communitarian skills. This is of course a reading that emphasizes "the bright side" of queuing; a more complex description of the phenomenon is provided in the body of the chapter.

The second part of the chapter is concerned with perceptions of shortages. An account of the answers to the question "Why are we queuing?" is presented at both official and unofficial level. Analyzing the unofficial answers (extracted from oral history sources), I argue that they were mainly a reworking of the state propaganda, successfully internalized by the citizens.

The main arguments of this chapter, that is, the existing agency of Romanian citizens even in harshest times and a level of belief in state propaganda higher than previously remarked upon, support a broader conviction that the binary oppositions derived from dissent discourse are no longer useful theoretical tools in accounting for the realities of everyday life in socialist states.

The Research: Methodology and Sources

My research consisted of interviewing members of a community formed by the inhabitants of a block of flats in Bucharest. The district (Tineretului) is a central one and its inhabitants are proudly thinking of it as a neighborhood of mainly intellectuals (i.e., people with higher education).[8] The interviews focused on experiences of queuing, according to a set of questions (see Appendix) that nevertheless had the status of guidelines and were not restrictive for the interviews. One of my purposes was also to see what personal connections arise from memories of queuing and how each interviewee embeds these narratives in his/her own life story.[9]

Some brief comments about the memory issues involved should be made at this point. First, my sources, the interviews, speak of the 1980s from the distance of more than fifteen years.[10] These are not firsthand testimonies, contemporary stories about life in the 1980s. They are *memories* of the 1980s and the distance that separates the moment of the telling from the moment of the happening is not only temporal but also, and maybe more important, cultural. It is the distance that separates two worlds. The world of the 1980s with all its written and unwritten rules, with its sophisticated ways of coping with the system collapsed in 1989. Thus, what my interviewees are recalling is practically another world, but one that is deeply embedded in their youth and still influences their present lives. It is a world that they try to integrate into contemporary realities, to explain and understand not only for themselves but also for a whole generation that does not understand it anymore since it was never theirs.

Working with oral history sources is both challenging and disturbing for a historian always on guard on source criticism and authenticity. The fragility of this kind of sources led to very sophisticated theoretical developments on the nature and uses of oral history.

Paul Thompson names two basic forms of interpretation, "the narrative analysis" and the "reconstructive cross-analysis." The narrative analysis focuses on the interview as a text, on its language, themes, repetitions, and silences. Its aim is not to establish the relevance of the oral text for the broader social context but to reconstruct a personal world or experience. In the reconstructive cross-analysis, which is most common among oral historians, "the oral evidence is treated as a quarry from which to construct an argument about patterns of behavior or events in the past."[11] Even those historians who do not define themselves as oral historians but use oral evidence as part of their research use this second approach. Sometimes, especially illuminating and challenging life stories emerge during fieldwork and special attention is granted within the wider analysis to these life stories using the methodology of the narrative analysis. It is in this in-depth approach that the special value of oral history can best be seen. It is here that the "different credibility" of oral sources, as Alessandro Portelli calls it, emerges:

> *Oral sources are credible but with a "different" credibility. The importance of oral testimony may lie not in its adherence to fact, but*

rather in its departure from it, as imagination, symbolism, and desire emerge. Therefore, there are no 'false' oral sources.[12]

Oral history is extremely useful if one tries to follow Daniel Barbu's invitation in analyzing real socialism:

> *The history of Romanian communism must be seen less as a whole global and totalizing history of the Party, the industrialization, the collectivization, the repression, of doctrinaire and ideological elaborations but rather as a chain explosion with immediate effect of concrete, multiple, incoherent, intersected and conflicting histories of real people, of specific interests, of individual careers. Summing it all, a history of the way Romanians have 'coped' [s-au descurcat], better or worse, but each for himself and for those near him.*[13]

The Queue: An Everyday Site in 1980s' Romania

While talking about the 1980s, most of my interviewees would spontaneously bring into the conversation the subject of queuing, an activity and a site that they considered essential for the period. I will first reconstruct from their memories the scenario according to which the queue functioned, including the "plot" and the characters that most queues were relying on. I will then analyze the special solidarity, the networks created around queuing, in support of it and in spite of it.

The sociologist Leon Mann considers that the underlining principle of queuing is "distributive justice" that he defines as the belief that

> *There is a direct correspondence between inputs (time spent waiting) and outcomes (preferential service). Generally, if a person is willing to invest large amounts of time and suffering in an activity, people who believe there should be an appropriate fit between effort and reward will respect his right to priority.*[14]

He also describes the queue as an "embryonic social system" that reflects the broader social organization. If one is to use both his remarks in analyzing the Romanian queue of the 1980s, the resulting image becomes contradictory. For, if the queue reflects the society at large, then any notion of "distributive justice" cannot be applied since it contradicts the broader reality. My hypothesis is that the queue does reflect society's organization, thus including all the privileges some groups of people had and all the bypasses other people employed and also a deep feeling of "queuing justice" and solidarity among fellow queuers.

I will provide in the next pages a description of the Romanian queue of the eighties, its functioning, its characters, and its unwritten rules. One informant considers the Romanian queue to be a special type of queue: "I often stood in queues, but the Romanian one was corrupted by other rules than an ordinary line."[15] He does not explain what "an ordinary line" is, but it is probably connected to the notion of "distributive justice" that Mann proposes. That is, an ordinary line means respecting the right to priority, in the order of arrival, of the people who spent equal amounts of time waiting next to each other.

Peculiarities of the Romanian Queue

There are several aspects of the Romanian queue that make it distinct from the standard image defined above. First, most of the queues in the 1980s formed before the desired product actually arrived. Through a complicated system of spreading information within the community and also much presuppositions, people formed long queues before closed shops. The queues for milk, which was more or less brought daily, started at 4:00 or 5:00 a.m., even though the shop opened only at 7:00 or 8:00 a.m. If a special product was supposed to come next day, the first members of the queue would be there from the previous evening, spending their night on the spot. The existence of a socialist queue can be thus split into two distinct phases: the first phase in which the queue grows only by addition of new members and there is actually no movement toward purchasing the commodity and the second phase when the products are actually put on sale. The first mode is more waiting based than the second part since there is no physical movement toward the beginning of the queue and there is also no certainty whether or not and at what time the products would arrive. As testimonies show, this is the more relaxed part of the queuing process. Order is loose and people find time to discuss and socialize. When products actually arrive and the selling begins, the atmosphere suddenly becomes tenser. The passage from one situation to another is remembered as a short moment of chaos when anything can happen. People start squeezing into each other, pushing toward the interior of the shop.

> *And then there was this well-known thrill in the crowd: somebody announced that the meat car might have parked in the back. And it seemed like everybody became more focused and occupied their place*

more firmly. . . . Then the children were taken out of the line; we had to wait somewhere aside because when the doors of the butcher's or shop opened, everybody started pushing in an awful manner, they would step on each other's feet, and the children risked being squashed unaware.[16]

This is the moment when queuing becomes an active process, involving physical strength and determination. It is no more about waiting, but about fighting, as this man remembers:

Whenever I planned to buy meat, I woke up round one or two a.m., and I was there at half past two or three a.m.; . . . so we waited there in the hall, and, at the right time, those inside pushed the gates open and ran. But, the crazy thing was that they did not have the time to actually open the gates, they just drew the bolt. The moment people heard the clacking of the bolt, the throng started through the gate. If you were among the first, and had the bad luck to have an old lady that stumbled and fell in front of you, it was a disaster. And let me tell you how things went, doing these things many times I developed a strategy. Whenever I queued, I noticed who was next to me, and I always behaved almost like a stag or a deer. I gathered some speed and I pushed on one side, yet I immediately withdrew and thrust myself on the other side, and in this way I made three, four zigzagged steps to get among the first.[17]

Nancy Ries characterizes stories like this as "tales of heroic shopping."[18] However, they are not characteristic for queuing stories in the Romanian 1980s. The narration of the queuing process, in the Romanian case, mostly relies on the waiting component as a painful and humiliating experience. In these narratives, *queuing* and *waiting* are usually used as synonyms, testifying to the major importance of time, seen as wasted time, in the queuing process. This is one of the interesting points that Leon Mann makes in his analysis: the queuing system reflects the surrounding society in as much as it dwells on "the importance of time as a value in Western society."[19]

The imposition of waiting, as Barry Schwartz explains it,[20] is a manifestation of power, thus leading to feelings of humiliation.

The queues for meat were the most humiliating, one could have wasted a night and a day, and when one got to the door or to the counter, it was finished. So many times I came back home with an empty bag after hours and hours of waiting![21]

This testimony includes key words like *waiting* and *wasted time* and also another important aspect of these queues: one could not be sure that after having invested a large amount of time, the desired commodity would be in his/her possession. This is because these queues also included some virtual members, people that were not physically present but whose existence was always to be taken into consideration.

The most numerous group of virtual members were those who would have their place "kept" by other members of the queue. This practice could double the number of people who were actually present in the queue. As one interviewee states:

> When I was about to get to the counter, almost every time, two or three persons stepped before me, saying that they had been there before and they had asked the old people, who queued almost every day, to reserve a place for them, and thus, there was not enough for me anymore.[22]

Another group of virtual members were the ones with whom the seller had a special relationship. The shop employees would always keep a small part of the stock for their personal arrangements, products later to be exchanged for other products or services. Even if these people did not actually join the queue, they represented nevertheless a decrease in the stock that the members of the "real" queue were about to acquire.

And there were also some citizens with a privileged status who would go directly to the counter and buy the products without having to queue. (S)He could be the local policeman who proudly recalls how he would get in the shop apparently to reestablish order and then get out with his bag full or other "authorities" that no one dared to submit to the "distributive justice" of the queue.

Solidarity Within the Queue and Against It

Solidarity is a concept that can be used and understood in at least two different definitions, which I can differentiate as the philosophical and the sociological one. The "human solidarity," a philosophical and ethical concept, mainly Kantian, is based on the recognition of humanity in fellow human beings and the duty one should feel toward that human quality. This understanding of solidarity has been challenged on account of universalistic claims even from within the discipline of moral philosophy.[23] However, this concept, even in its current restricted understanding, is quite useless as a historical variable. The level of "human solidarity" of a past society eludes any analysis, precisely because it is very personal and should be judged rather on intentions than on outcomes.

Social solidarity, on the other hand, a concept used by sociologists ever since Durkheim, might prove to be helpful. "The classical form of solidarity refers to the cooperation of concerned people with the goal of improvement of their own fate."[24] The basic difference between the sociological understanding of the term and the philosophical/ethical one is that the former does not downplay the personal interest solidarity is based upon. The claims that the communist regime destroyed the feeling of solidarity among Romanian citizens mainly refer to the moral/ philosophical understanding of the term. However, the existence of this kind of solidarity, at any time and in any place in human history, even more Romanian history is much debated today and would be indeed impossible to sustain with plausible arguments.

Returning to the subject of queuing and reacting to shortage, I argue that solidarity is one of the reactions shortages triggered. I will argue for this solidarity of the queue, manifest in its organization, left entirely in the hands of the queuers who assumed responsibility for achieving the common goal: buying the desired products. There is also a solidarity expressed in the informal networks meant to decrease the amount of queuing in one's life. So far in my research, I have not encountered a single informant who would admit to relying only on merchandize bought from state shops. Everybody had other sources of food products. Some were so well "organized" that they did not even have to queue: "To put it bluntly, between 1980 and 1989, I never stood in a queue to buy meat from shops."[25] The purpose was not only to have a full refrigerator; the higher accomplishment was not being forced to queue for that.

One of the paradoxes of this shortage period is that, even though the shops were empty, people were convinced that there was sufficient food in the country. The basis of this belief was that nobody was actually dying of hunger[26] and having a refrigerator or a storage room full of food products was a common occurrence in that period. Thus, the problem seemed to be more a shortcoming in the distribution of these products than a real lack of basic foods.[27] It is in this context that small networks of people in a position of obtaining different commodities or providing different services were created. Some of these networks actually replaced activities that should have been conducted by the state, especially the distribution system. This is why these networks and the secondary economy developed were necessary for the survival of the system.

As Polish sociologists observed, "the basic difference between the informal economy in the West and in the socialist countries is the fact that in the West, informal economic activities are marginal, while in a socialist planned economy, they are a fundamental part of the activity of state-owned enterprises."[28] As these activities were mainly illegal, the kind of solidarity that they entailed refers back to the etymological meaning of the term: the *obligatio in solidum* meant that the community as a whole was held accountable for the deeds, especially the debts of any one of its members.[29]

Ordinary Stories in Extraordinary Times

A couple remembers how they would pay somebody in the countryside to raise a pig for them.[30] In 1989, it was in a village in Sibiu county, in the center of the country, where they "raised" their pig and the Revolution "caught" them on their way to bring the pig to Bucharest. They successfully got hold of the pig but they could not also reach Constanta, at the seaside, where they were supposed to collect some wine. Earlier in the 1980s, the same couple knew somebody who had an illegal slaughtering place in his own house. Every Thursday he would slaughter a cow. Mr. BP would come and take his fifty-kilo share. There was no negotiation; it was fifty kilos or nothing. So, Mr. BP also had to organize a network of his own to distribute the extra meat. In other periods, his neighbor, Mr. SP, who was a member of one of the national sports teams and had access to the special food store for sportsmen, would provide foods for him. All of these arrangements did not spare the family of having to queue from time to time, but the amount of wasted time and humiliation was seriously diminished.

Mrs. DV is married to a TV repairman. "He had lots of clients; he had bread-salesmen and food store-salesmen so we had some relations . . ."[31] But these relations helped only with flour (each year she had to gather one hundred kilos of flour to send to her parents in the countryside who had difficulties finding bread in the winter), corn flour or sugar. For meat they still had to queue. Queuing for meat was also organized in a small community formed by her work colleagues, as she was an accountant in a health institute.

One of my colleagues who came from the neighborhood, when she came in the morning, stopped at the meat-store, kept a place there, came to the institute, signed the register, we gathered two or three women, went there to register to the queue too and then we took shifts. One of us stayed one hour, she came back, then . . . At three o'clock when the program was finished, we all went there. And by five, five and a half the meat truck came.

Q: So these queues started in the morning . . .
From morning to evening. And of course, there were lots of people who did the same thing. If I went there and I had 20 or 30 persons ahead of me, by five o'clock it was double, they kept coming from work and so on. And I would also telephone him [her husband] and say I am at the meat-store. And then he appeared at six, seven and we stayed there, they started giving . . . And he would take too and this meant that for that month we were assured. So once a month we made this effort but this meant that we arrived home at half past nine, ten in the evening.[32]

Surveillance and Organizing of the Queue: A Community Activity

As explained earlier, these queues did not always respect the "distributive justice" system. There were people who attempted to join the queue from the middle or access the salesman with whom they had a special arrangement. And as these queues did not officially exist, there was no organized surveillance of the queue, except the one people organized themselves.

The queues were very rarely orderly; they surged periodically so an ad-hoc police was in charge of maintaining the order. One or more men would place themselves near the counter or office and prevented the ones who wanted to rapidly get in front of everybody else.[33]

This *ad-hoc police* would not only control the queue, but also the salesman from keeping too much of the stock for himself.

At a store, they had brought beer; immediate queue and extraordinary scandal. They did not bring large quantities and this generated a lot of problems . . . . A few representatives of the queue insisted in witnessing the whole thing until the beer sold out.[34]

These people, the "representatives of the queue" stayed longer after they managed to buy their share of the products only to ensure that all the stock was sold to the population. It was not easy to be a queue representative; it took a lot of time, knowledge of the functioning of the queue, and the ability to exercise one's authority.

> There were some queue-supervisors, people that had learned how queuing goes (cum se face coada) and they were keeping the discipline. So, if the queue supervisor happened to be at the beginning of the queue and he sacrificed himself, it was a very ordered queue. So this guy came in the evening, around eleven, put his little chair there, brought a book, something, a neighbor to talk to. He slept during the day and stayed the night there. And everybody who passed by talked to him; he would let them go from time to time. There was a list, of course.[35]

To be able to take part in such elaborate activities, one needed a lot of time. Not everybody could afford, in as much as time is concerned, to spend twelve hours or more in front of a shop. As this system was time, and not money, consuming, people who had more time at their disposal became more important in the household economy. And these were the elders, the already retired grandparents, and the children. Besides providing for their own family, some elders found in queuing an alternative activity that could earn them some extra money. Instead of staying at home, they stayed in queues transforming the passage of time into a money-earning activity. If time is a value, then it can also be sold.

> There were especially the retired people, they stayed in the line, like I tell you, a whole day, took two kilos of meat to give them to somebody who couldn't stay and take some money so . . . instead of 37 [lei] that he gave for it, he would sell it with 50. He won some extra money like this. It wasn't only the gypsies who speculated.[36] There were also some other categories of people who had the time to stay.[37]

Even before the rations were introduced, a system of unofficial rations functioned in order to ensure that the stock brought at a certain moment in the shop would be divided among as many people as possible. Usually, the quantity, two kilos of meat, one chicken, one kilo of oranges per person, was established by common agreement between the salesman and the "representatives of the queue." This "ration" was a function of the quantity of products that were brought to the shop; however since the quantities supplied were usually the same, these unofficial rations had the tendency to become fixed as the later introduced official rations. When recalling the ration system of the 1980s, people have trouble distinguishing between the two types of rations, testifying thus to the strong establishment of these unofficial rations.

> *Q: Do you remember if there were rations in the 1980s?*
> *Yes, of course, there were. They introduced them. Rations for meat.*
> *Well, even the other products, flour, corn flour, these, you couldn't buy*
> *more than two kilos, this was the ration, two kilos of flour. And you*
> *kept going from one food store to another, when they brought, because*
> *it wasn't there always, it wasn't on the shelves. Oil was "rationalized"*
> *too, two kilos of oil. And when it was brought you queued for it. You*
> *went to this food store and took two kilos, then to the other and took*
> *two kilos.*[38]

When the official rations were introduced, one was assigned to one food store in the neighborhood and was not allowed to buy the products on ration from any other store. What Mrs. DV is referring to is the system of unofficial rations when one could actually go to several stores and buy small quantities of flour, oil, or sugar in order to increase one's stock. Or one could stay in the same line, if it was not that large, several times. Or one could bring one's children along since the rations were established per person. There are testimonies of parents queuing with their very young children, two or three years old, in order to buy a larger quantity. Sometimes, children were also "borrowed" from one person to another within the queue.

Kathy Burrell has examined the problem of queuing in 1980s' Poland, also relying on oral history material. She documents a situation that I have not encountered in the Romanian case. It is the story of a Polish woman who recalls that she did not have to queue since "it is a tradition that old persons and the mothers with the small children or babies are put first. So if there was something and I would take [my daughter] in my arms, then I could skip the queue, and people were putting me at the front."[39]

The Romanian socialist queue was saturated with old people and children but no documented situations when they would be allowed to skip the queue. Children were sometimes assigned the role of informing their parents about new deliveries in the neighborhood stores.

> *Many times, instead of playing in the parks by our blocks of flats, we*
> *had to play near the stores because the car with products could arrive*
> *any time. When this thing happened, we would run to our houses and*

let our parents know, mainly mothers. As most of us lived in blocks of flats, it was easier to shout from down there that the car had arrived and thus we announced all the neighbors. In maximum five minutes, everybody was there, their bags in their hands, ready to run towards the store, where we got there before them and "kept a place for them in the line." The problem is that it did not matter whether there were children, old men; everybody was dashing, as if blind, for fear they might be left without that product.[40]

Was Solidarity Just Another Victim of the Communist Regime?

These children, as it becomes evident from the example above and the practice of "borrowing" them among queuers, were also used in the functioning of a community working together in facilitating access to food. This community could be formed by the inhabitants of a block of flats, colleagues of the same workplace, or members of the same family, in an extended meaning of family. Everyone was part of one or more of these networks. The exchange and reciprocal help went from spreading information about upcoming deliveries to keeping a place in the queues and to facilitating access to informal, usually also illegal, sources of commodities.

The debate about the meaning and extent to which solidarity functioned in these societies is still ongoing. One of the most influential theories states that within these societies, different types of solidarity were among the first victims of the regime. David Kideckel claims it strongly as the basis of his study *The Solitude of Collectivism. Romanian Villagers to the Revolution and Beyond*: "The title of this book reflects on one of the basic contradictions of life in many socialist communities: the socialist system, though ostensibly designed to create new persons motivated by the needs of groups and society as a whole, in fact created people who were of necessity self-centered, distrustful and apathetic to the very core of their beings."[41] This perspective does not only belong to Kideckel. It is widespread among scholars of socialist and postsocialist societies, among which the phenomenon is also held responsible for the apathy and lack of civil society in post-1989 Eastern Europe. It is an opinion that needs, in my view, a reevaluation.

Daniel Barbu, a political scientist, attempted to do this in an article published in Lucian Boia's collection of essays entitled *The Myths of Romanian Communism*. The article breaks the apparent unity of the contributors by boldly suggesting from the beginning that an analysis of the communist period is as much subjected to myth making as the communist regime itself: "I wonder if the analysis that, for decades, is focused on the system of symbolic representations and ideological imaginary of the totalitarian regimes of the Soviet type has not itself generated a new series of myths."[42] Looking at the problem of the supposed solidarity promoted by the regime and the lack of solidarity observed by the analysts, Barbu proposes a third way, a "dependent individualism born under totalitarianism,"[43] which would account for the situations both within the socialist states and after their collapse. Regarding the common image of an imposed regime over a helpless society, he notes that the degree of acceptance by Romanian society greatly surpassed the degree of its resistance. Also the lack of power of the society cannot be argued for if one understands power as Foucault does, not only as political power. Barbu claims that "to cope with the regime," "to manage" (*a te descurca*), a frequent word when people refer back to those years, "is only another way to name participating at power, access to the normal functioning of it."[44] What Barbu is arguing against is an image of Romanian communism as "an anonymous and impersonal ghost that drove unexpectedly on a population forced to improvise its resistance."[45]

As I have explained in this chapter, establishing a community of common interests was an essential, necessary feature of everyday life in communist Romania. Other researchers have noted the special solidarity that queuing entailed. "Albeit much hated and ridiculed, the queue outside the shop produced forms of sociality that might be coded to demonstrate the existence of values and close-knit solidarity in spite of the alienating effects of socialism."[46] This type of solidarity is usually dismissed as only being based on the short- or long-term project of obtaining food or other commodities. However, using the sociological understanding of solidarity that relies precisely on "the cooperation of concerned people with the goal of improvement of their own fate," this counterargument becomes invalid. As Tita Chiper remembers the 1980s, "In the time of rationing, they would move 'the community of the block' (spiritul scării) to the queue, reciprocally informing on the products that were to arrive, keeping the place in the queue for each other, discovering a solidarity that functioned perfectly against the 'intruders.' "[47] It is, thus, a solidarity directed against the outsiders (and what type of solidarity is not?) in the everyday contest of coping more easily with the system.

These types of small-scale solidarities within the socialist system, even when constructed for personal gain, should not be disregarded. The ephemeral solidarity of the queuers reflects the contradictions of the society at large. People interacted with each other with a degree of caution and self-surveillance that they employed in other circumstances as well. Thus, there are testimonies of queues as that type of ancient peasant evening gathering (şezătoare) where people would tell stories, discuss politics, in a word—socialize.

> For the rest, I liked very much to queue, especially with my grandfather, who would stand in the line telling stories to other old men, boasting about all sorts of youth adventures . . . . There was a real contest of wonderfully embellished stories.[48]

Or other memories:

> At the queue there was big cheerfulness. Yes, whistling, curses, jokes. Everybody was talking.
>
> Q: So you were not afraid of the people you didn't know.
> No, no. Then, as now, there were people who were against you. But there was no restriction. Who has the courage to talk, talks anywhere. And then, in a collectivity like this where you see that one talking, the other one talking . . . Especially since the discontent was general. How was I not to talk?[49]

On the other hand, there were people who thought that it was better not to get involved in these kinds of discussions.

> The people around, especially since most of them were retired, talked only about troubles and scarcity and . . . generally, it was much better not to listen. It happened to me once, while I was standing in a queue for butter, to witness how a man in front of me started to swear: "The hell with Ceauşescu and everything, and . . ." I do not know what else. Suddenly two men came to him and took him away.[50]

Without disregarding the contradictory testimonies on this issue, the queue was both a space that reflected the rules and restrictions of the broader society, and, in the same time, a space where a greater degree of individual freedom might be experienced. It was a space of continuous negotiation among fellow queuers and between the queuers and the state representatives.

Why Are We Queuing? Internalizing the Official Discourse

One of the most influential theories of life in socialist countries was put forward by Václav Havel: *living within truth* versus *living within a lie* was for him the daily dilemma of the socialist citizen. Havel, a playwriter, the leader of the Czech dissent movement and the first president of the Czech Republic wrote the story of the greengrocer in his highly influential essay *The Power of the Powerless*.

His character, the greengrocer is fictional but he presents him as the most ordinary man in the Czech Socialist Republic, part of the Czechoslovak Federation. The reader does not find out much about the greengrocer. Only that, on official holydays, he "places in his window, among onions and carrots, the slogan: "Workers of the World, Unite!"[51] Why does he do it?, Havel asks. It is not that he believes in the slogan, not that he actually ever thought about what it means that all the workers of the world should unite. Rather, the sign he puts in the window actually reads: "I, the greengrocer XY, live here and I know what I must do. I behave in the manner expected of me. I can be depended upon and I am beyond reproach. I am obedient and therefore I have the right to be left in peace."[52]

Dwelling on this example, Havel explains how these post-totalitarian systems, as he calls them, derive their strength from widely accepted lies: "Individuals need not believe all these mystifications, but they must behave as though they did, or they must at least tolerate them in silence, or get along well with those who work with them. For this reason however, they must *live within a lie*. They need not accept the lie. It is enough for them to have accepted their life with it and in it. For by this very fact, individuals confirm the system, fulfill the system, make the system, *are* the system."[53]

Along with his theory of living "within a lie" and his plea for living "within the truth," Havel develops in the same essay the concept of post-totalitarianism. The Czech society of the 1970s that he describes is no longer a dictatorship in its classical form. This means that it is no longer based on military power, but on something subtler: ideology. As Havel understands it: "the primary excusatory function of ideology, therefore, is to provide people, both as victims and pillars of the post-totalitarian system, with the illusion that the system is in harmony with the human order and the order of the universe."[54]

As I understand it, this function of ideology, and therefore of propaganda[55] goes way beyond truth and fakery. The slogan in the window is not there because it is true or fake; it is there because this is how it should be, because "the system is in harmony with the human order and the order of the universe." There is no question here of whether that human order, or even less, the order of the universe is right or wrong. It simply is and it should be obeyed by virtue of its mere existence. However, this is my reading of Havel's story, since he insists that truth and fakery are still valid concepts even within these systems; that people actually knew what was right and wrong, true or fake and unfortunately chose the latter.

I argue in the following pages that the border between lies and truth, official and private discourse is not as sharp as Havel, and many of his followers would claim. By looking at the answers people gave me when asked why they had to queue, I argue that most of their answers are forms of internalized official discourse. And one of the reasons for this phenomenon is the fact that, sometimes, official discourse was true, or at least seemed plausible or comfortable to believe in.

One of the most frequent answers is related to the goal of paying the country's foreign debts announced by Ceaușescu in the early 1980s. The final goal was to achieve the total independence of Romania, not only political, but also economical.[56] The absurdity of such an economic policy, in the context of the emerging global market, needs no further explanations. However, in a country practically cut off from communication with Europe and the world, the development of world economy was not so widely understood. The issue of the independence of the country was closely related to an upsurge in nationalism that the government successfully promoted.[57] This is why the project of paying all the debts of the country was generally positively assessed; it was seen as a goal worth sacrificing personal comfort for.

> *There was no food because it was in small quantities, because they were giving a lot for export and it was this period when we were paying the debts that the Romanian state had. And these were paid from what? From the earnings of the populations, they had no other source.*
>
> Q: Why do you think they insisted so much on paying the foreign debts?
> *Why they wanted to pay them? I don't know. I suppose Ceaușescu had a purpose. If he would have lived to do it, what do I know...? It got into his head that he has to pay them. And he finally did. And? It was no use since the ones who came after them made them all over again.*[58]

137

There were hardly any official explanations for the shortages. Journals and the two-hour TV broadcast presented the ongoing increase in living standards, productivity, and enthusiasm for the *multilateral developed society* in Romania. Nicolae Ceaușescu's last international interview, published in *Newsweek* in August 1989, presents a totally distorted image:

> *N.C.: I believe we are among the first countries when it comes to consumption per capita. And we are exporters of food and clothing. But this is not done at the expense of consumption. It is based on productivity. We don't have problems regarding the consumption of food.*
>
> *Q: When do you think some of the empty shelves will be full?*
> *N.C.: We don't have empty shelves. On the contrary, we have lots of stock in our shops. It's possible that we started having negligence in the shops and we don't want to put extra stock in the shops. You can go in any shop and you can buy anything including products that you find in the United States, because we export some of those to the United States.*[59]

This is more or less what the Romanians were hearing every day, with the notable exception that no one really dared to ask when would some of the empty shelves be full.

There were, however, two events that were meant to put the shortages in a more favorable light. One incentive was the *Program for scientific alimentation of the population (Programul de alimentație științifică a populației)*. The idea of "scientific alimentation," basically meaning reducing the number of calories per capita, appeared in the early eighties, thoroughly explained in an issue of *Scânteia* on July 14, 1982. The idea became a program, approved by the Grand National Assembly, only in 1984 and it was published in *Scânteia* on June 30 that year.

It was not clear how the new program had to be implemented. How can the state control the number of calories that a citizen is eating? The answer was simple: by providing less. The purpose was to change the obvious conclusion, "We are eating less and worse" into "We are eating healthier." Even though the program did not meet the approval of the population, it was nevertheless "implemented." First by providing less food in the shops, rationing some products, and then by building those huge cantinas in Bucharest, nicknamed the Hunger Circuses,[60] which were supposed to feed entire neighborhoods thus making home-cooking and food-shopping useless. Building the Hunger Circuses began only in the late 1980s, so they never actually functioned.[61] The idea of controlling, in such a direct manner, the meals of the population is only an exacerbation of the "dictatorship over needs." In a socialist economy, the state holds a monopoly on the distribution of food products; however, to seek to establish a daily menu, the same menu, for the entire capital of Romania was a new idea, even for a socialist country. As one of my interviewees put it:

> You go there [to the Hunger Circus], you take your three little boxes, you go home, you heat them and you eat them. The bad thing is that behind this project there was a terrible idea. Since everything can be found like this, there is no more need for markets, for raw products. So by this system, he would manage to control even what you ate. So he[62] would tell you what you eat Monday, Tuesday, Wednesday. This idea with the fish, one day only with fish, would have become reality. Plain reality.[63]

The Program for scientific alimentation of the population is thus closely linked with the Hunger Circuses growing overnight in different parts of Bucharest. Neither of them were the cause of the shortages; they were merely a response, a justification for the obvious lack of basic products. The same interviewee thinks that the program was realized, but only on a theoretical level, in calculating the amount of food that was necessary to maintain the subsistence level of the population:

> This program was only achieved at a global level. That is, some calculations were made. How many Romanians are we? 22 millions. How big is the cereal production? How many calories must a Romanian consume? 3,000. Well, 22 million to multiply by 3,000 it means I don't know how many giga-calories. Let's see, we keep in the country that much grains, that much rice, that much meat, that many eggs and that's it! Everything else goes for export.[64]

Hoarding and Speculating: Cause or Effect of the Crisis?

Another propaganda-disseminated idea regarding the shortages was that they were the result of some people actually hoarding food in order to resell it at a higher price. A law against hoarding was issued in October 1981. Hoarding was defined as having in one's possession more than one month's supply of oil, sugar, flour, corn flour, rice, coffee, and other food products. The announcement on the radio, broadcast on October 9, also warned the Romanians that they should return excess food to the stores for refund at official prices by October 12.[65]

Contrary to the widespread lack of trust in the official discourse, it seems that this justification convinced some. Not as far as to say that this was the cause of the shortages, but that it was an important factor that influenced the crisis.

> *Meat was brought, you had to queue. And this is where the problem of speculating intervenes. There were some people who were staying there and they were taking. This is why there was not enough for me to buy a piece of meat when I finished my working hours. Because they were systematically taking it[66] and selling it on the black market. But I would still buy it. Even on the black market, I would still buy it.[67]*
>
> *But I think that it is not only Ceaușescu that led to this thing. I say that we as individuals, as a nation . . . after a while, when you see that there is no more, you hide it, isn't it? When you see that you can't find in the market as much as you need, you hide it.[68]*

It is difficult to establish where the border between hoarding and speculating is. The official discourse made anyone possessing more than one month's supply of food a potential speculator. Even though everybody was trying to keep their refrigerators as full as possible, it was not for speculation purposes. However, the ambiguity between a hoarder and a speculator persists in fragments of interviews like this one:

> *So that is when food disappeared, the cheese and so on. And then speculating began, because the Romanian never died of hunger. He always used to say: there's no meat, there's no that, there's no I don't know what. Vasile, can you keep in your refrigerator for two days three kilos of meat? Well, I don't have place. So why don't you have place? It was, it was also this panic.[69]*

People used to have refrigerators and storage rooms filled with food products, despite or, better said, exactly because of the shortages. Most of my interviewees confess to this at some point during our talks:

> *Now, saying this in brackets, I always said that we eat too well in our house . . . We eat too well, my wife having a real genius of administrating, saving and transforming, to put it this way.[70]*

Having supplies for a long enough period of time, exceeding a few weeks, gave them a feeling of safety that allowed them to accomplish other activities.

> *After 1980, our only preoccupation was the lack of food. The food. If we knew that we had butter in the refrigerator or that we had meat, we were very happy. . . . If the storage room was full, then we were calm. We would meet, talk, we would read a lot.*[71]

This is the reason why one can encounter frequently, apparently astonishing statements like this one:

> *The problem was with the alimentation. Because you had to queue to buy something. And yet, you see, there is this paradox. There wasn't [food], but I had the refrigerator full. Full because of foreseeing. When I would find, I would buy and put it in the refrigerator.*[72]

There are two points to be made to clarify the situation. First, the reason why stressing hoarding seems to have been a success idea of state propaganda in those years is that it was true. People were hoarding food, and not only food. Janos Kornai describes the functioning of the *shortage economy*[73] (the term belongs to him) as a mixture of bargaining and hoarding. He explains how this functions for enterprises, not only for individuals. Hoarding is, however, only a result of the shortages not their cause and this is where the official discourse was very effective. It managed to substitute an effect for a cause. Consciously or not, the authorities relied in this issue on some very ancient popular beliefs related to periods of dearth. They were identified by R. C. Cobb in his research on eighteenth-century France. Among them, "the belief in the existence of vast and preferably underground supplies at home"[74] is exactly what the Romanian propaganda in the 1980s suggested and partially succeeded to promote as a cause of the food shortages confronting the country.[75]

It must be underlined, in the end, that providing explanations for the shortages was not a habit of the Romanian authorities in those years. They were actually more inclined to deny that an alimentation problem existed, as Ceauşescu does in the *Newsweek* interview, than to acknowledge and explain the situation. The queues were usually formed behind the stores, especially when the stores were on the big boulevards of the city. The image of people standing in long lines waiting for food was not congruent with the allegedly prosperous Romanian economy.

For this reason, when asked what the official explanations for the shortages were, my interviewees usually answer that there were not any. Or, at most, they remember some of the most absurd ones that stuck in their memory precisely because of their absurdity:

> *The first thing that started to disappear was sugar. They blamed it, this was the motivation, on the peasants who were making brandy (țuica) in the countryside and sugar disappearing because it is used there. This is non-sense. They started with an excuse, like this. And then there were no more problems for them to start removing slowly, slowly everything.*[76]

Whatever explanations my interviewees may have given—the foreign debts, the hoarding, the speculators—I could not help but notice that this was one of the most startling questions they were asked. They usually took a pause, repeated my question slowly, *Why were there no more food products?* And then provided one of the explanations enumerated above, explanations that mostly came, as I have shown, from the official discourse of those years. My hypothesis in this matter is that they were not really thinking, in the 1980s, of possible explanations for the shortages. They were accepting them like everything else: the cutting of electricity, the cold in the apartments or the mandatory participation in political meetings and celebrations. This attitude is closely related to the usage of pronouns (explained in endnote 62); it is either "them" or "him" who brings these misfortunes upon them, misfortunes that they experience like natural calamities. There is nothing to be done about an earthquake or a flood. Asking why the food started disappearing was a bit like asking why an earthquake had occurred.

This type of attitude was observed by Slavenka Drakulić in one of her essays on communism in Eastern Europe, and she connects it to the experience of World War II and everything that came afterward.

> *One of the things one is constantly reminded in these parts is not to be thoughtless with food. I remember my mother telling me that I had to eat everything in front of me, because to throw away food would be a sin. Perhaps she had God on her mind, perhaps not. She experienced World War II and ever since, like most of the people in Eastern Europe, she behaves as if it never ended. Maybe this is why*

they are never really surprised that even forty years afterwards there is a lack of sugar, oil, coffee, or flour.[77]

I hope to have shown in this chapter that some of the main topics in analyzing the Romanian communist regime are still controversial: resistance and collaboration, living within a lie and constructing one's own truth, constructing solidarities or individualistic pursuits. I argued that even one of the most hated activities of the 1980s, queuing, is retold by former queuers in conflicting memories: some emphasize the solidarity, others the alienation that queuing developed. Most of my interviewees actually testify to both. Instead of sticking to black and white, they prefer to remember the gray. The same applies to their explanations of the shortage situation. The answers to the question *Why did you have to queue?* span from purely official explanations, like the paying of the national debt or hoarding, to unbelievable rumors. This shows, in my opinion, that the former black and white, good and bad image of the communist regime, originated in the dissent discourse, is no longer academically sustainable and has reached a dead end.

Appendix. My Interview Guidelines

How old were you in 1980?

Where were you working in the 1980s?

Were you married? Who were the members of your family? (It is important to determine how many people the family had to sustain)

When you think about the 1980s, is there any particular image/event/story that comes to mind?

How did you acquire the necessary food?

What did you queue for?

What did you queue for except food?

Was queuing for food different from queuing for other products?

Who used to queue more often in your family? Were children also joining the queues?

When did you queue? In the morning, during daytime, or nighttime?

Some people were asking others to keep their place in the queue? How did that function?

Were there rules of the queue? Was there anybody establishing an unofficial order?

How much time did a queue last? Were you always standing or did you bring something you would sit on?

How did you explain the fact that you had to queue?

What do you remember about the "Hunger Circus"? How were they to function?

Do you also have some good memories about the queue?

Do you remember when you first had to queue?

Do you still have to queue now?

Do you sometimes talk about the communist period (the 1980s) in your families? What topics do you talk about? In which moments?

How would you characterize your life in the 1980s?

How would you characterize the period as a whole? (This question repeats the question in the beginning. The image that the interviewee provides as a frame at the beginning may be reshaped as memories unfold during the interview)

Notes

1. This chapter is the result of research started in 2001 with Irina Nicolau at the Romanian Peasant Museum, continued as an MA student at the Central European University in Budapest (2003–2004) and then as *Europa* fellow at the New Europe College, Bucharest (2006–2007). The first version of this chapter has been published as "Beyond Hunger. Perceptions of and Reactions to Shortages in 1980s Romania" in *New Europe College* Europa *Program Yearbook 2006–2007*. Bucharest: New Europe College, 2007, 143–73.

2. Romanian publications on the increasingly fashionable topic of everyday life during Socialism fit this description: Paul Cernat, Ion Manolescu, Angelo Mitchievici, Ioan Stanomir, *Explorări în comunismul românesc*, vols. 1, 2 [*Explorations in Romanian Communism*], Iaşi: Polirom, 2004, 2005; Irina Nicolau, Ioana Popescu et al., *Anii '80 si bucureştenii* [*The 1980s in Bucharest*], Bucureşti: Paidea, 2003; Tom Sandquist, Ana Maria Zahariade, *Dacia 1300. My Generation*. Bucureşti: Simetria, 2003; Adrian Neculau, *Viaţa cotidiană în comunism* [*Everyday Life During Communism*], Iaşi: Polirom, 2004; Gabriel H. Decuble, ed., *Cartea roz a comunismului* [*The Pink Book of Communism*], vol. 1, Iasi: Versus, 2004; Carmen Chivu, Mihai Albu, *Noi si Securitatea. Viaţa privată şi publică în perioada comunistă aşa cum reiese din tehnica operativă* [*Us and the Securitate. Private and Public Life in the Communist Period as in the Securitate Files*], Pitesti: Paralela, 45, 2006.

3. There is terminological overlap between *communist* and *socialist* regimes that forces me to use both terms referring to the same reality. Romanian academia and everyday speech prefer to call the 1948–89 regime communist. Western and also Hungarian or Bulgarian academia call it socialism, actually existing socialism, real socialism, and so on (see also Daniela Koleva's remarks on this in the introduction to this volume). I personally prefer *socialism* as it is a historically more accurate term. Even in the Romanian case, the regime never claimed to have reached the stage of communism

and the country was called Romanian Socialist Republic. However, the ruling party called itself communist.

4.   For a more detailed account on the context and common places of the debates on communism in post-communism, see my article "The Black Hole Paradigm. Exhibiting Communism in Post-Communist Romania" in: *History of Communism in Europe*, new series, vol. 1/2010 "Politics of Memory in Post-Communist Europe," edited by the Institute for the Investigation of Communist Crimes and the Memory of the Romanian Exile, Bucharest: Zeta Books, 83–101.

5.   See Václav Havel's influential essay *The Power of the Powerless: Citizens against the State in Central-Eastern Europe*. London: Hutchinson, 1985. For a critique of using these binary oppositions in assessing the communist regimes see Alexei Yurchak, *Everything was Forever, Until it was no More: The Last Soviet Generation*. Princeton, NJ: Princeton University Press, 2005.

6.   So much so that even joining the Communist Party is sometimes decoded as a "subversive" action.

7.   I developed this argument in an article written together with Gabriela Cristea, "Raising the Cross. Exorcising Romania's Communist Past in Museums, Memorials and Monuments" in: *Past for the Eyes. East European Representations of Communism in Cinema and Museums after 1989*, eds. Oksana Sarkisova and Peter Apor, CEU Press: Budapest, 2007.

8.   I interviewed eleven people, five women and six men, most of them in their fifties and sixties. They all inhabit the same block of flats so they all depended on the same shop (Alimentara) for basic food. During the 1980s they were also queuing together.

9.   I have published this analysis of the same oral history material in "What Are They Talking About When They Talk About Queuing in 1980s Romania" in: *Erinnerungen nach der Wende. Oral History und (post) sozialistische Gesellschaften. Remembering After the Fall of Communism. Oral History and (Post-)Socialist Societies*, eds. Julia Obertreis, Anke Stephan, Klartext: Essen, 2009, 359–70.

10. My sources include excerpts from the published archive on everyday life in the 1980s gathered by the Romanian Peasant Museum (the project that triggered this research) and published in *Martor. The Museum of the Romanian Peasant Anthropology Review*, VII [*The Eighties in Bucharest*], 2002 and in Serban Anghelescu, Cosmin Manolache, Anca Manolescu, Vlad Manoliu, Irina Nicolau, Ioana Popescu, Petre Popovat, Simina Radu-Bucurenci, Ana Vinea, *Anii '80 și bucureștenii* [*The 1980s in Bucharest*]. Bucharest: Paideia, 2003.

11. Paul Thompson, *The Voice of the Past. Oral History*. Oxford: Oxford University Press, 2000, 271.

12. Alessandro Portelli, "What Makes Oral History Different" in: *The Oral History Reader*, eds. Robert Perks and Alistair Thompson, London and New York: Routledge, 1998, 68.

13. Daniel Barbu, "Destinul colectiv, servitutea involuntară, nefericirea totalitară: trei mituri ale comunismului românesc" [Collective destiny,

forced servitude, totalitarian unhappiness: three myths of Romanian communism] in: Lucian Boia, ed., *Miturile comunismului românesc* [*The Myths of Romanian Communism*], Bucharest: Nemira, 1998, 183.

14. Leon Mann, "Queue Culture: The Waiting Line as a Social System," *The American Journal of Sociology*, vol. 75 (3), 1969, 346. Leon Mann bases this article on analyzing Australian lines for football tickets.

15. Testimony of Dragoş Olea, *Martor. The Museum of the Romanian Peasant Anthropology Review*, vol. 7, 2002 [The Eighties in Bucharest], 70.

16. Testimony of Gabriela Şulea, student, *Martor*, p. 134.

17. Testimony of Stancu Daniel, designer, *Martor*, p. 103.

18. Nancy Ries, *Russian Talk: Culture and Conversation during Perestroika*. Ithaca: Cornell University Press, 1997, 51.

19. Mann, "Queue Culture," p. 350.

20. "To be kept waiting—especially to be kept waiting an unusually long while—is to be the subject of an assertion that one's own time (and therefore, one's social worth) is less valuable than the time and worth of the one who imposes the wait." Barry Schwartz, "Waiting, Exchange, and Power: The Distribution of Time in Social Systems," *The American Journal of Sociology*, vol. 79 (4), 1974, 841.

21. Testimony of Victor Bărbulescu, electrician, *Martor*, p. 101.

22. Ibid.

23. Richard Rorty, one of the most acclaimed and controversial contemporary philosophers challenges this universalistic view on human solidarity: "My position entails that feelings of solidarity are necessarily a matter of which similarities and dissimilarities strike us as salient, and that such salience is a function of a historically contingent final vocabulary." Richard Rorty, *Contingency, Irony and Solidarity*. Cambridge: Cambridge University Press, 1989, 192.

24. Hans W. Bierhoff and Beate Küpper, "Social Psychology of Solidarity" in: *Solidarity*, ed. Kurt Bayertz, Dordrecht/Boston/London: Kluwer Academic Publishers, 1999, 133.

25. Testimony of Dragoş Olea, *Martor*, 70.

26. There is however medical evidence of numerous disease and growth problems in the 1980s and 1990s related to the poor quality of food in the 1980s.

27. This feature of socialist regimes is explained in Ferenc Fehér, Agnes Heller, and György Márkus, *Dictatorship over Needs*. Oxford: Basil Blackwell, 1983, an attempt to analyze East European societies with the tools provided by Marxist theory. The economies of socialist countries do not function toward the maximization of profit, which would imply an effective distribution system. On the contrary, they function toward enforcing the "dictatorship over needs," that is, the state seeks to control most of the means of production and thus actually needs a defective distribution system. These theories are successfully tested on the Romanian socialist queue in Pavel Campeanu, *Coada pentru hrana. Un mod de viata* [*The Queue for Food. A Way of Life*], Bucuresti: Litera, 1994.

28. Elżbieta Firlit, Jerzy Chłopecki, "When Theft is Not Theft" in: *The Unplanned Society. Poland During and After Communism*, ed. Janine R. Wedel, New York: Columbia University Press, 1992, 96.

29. "The term "solidarity" has its roots in the Roman law of obligations. Here the unlimited liability of each individual member within a family or other community to pay common debts was characterized as obligatio in solidum." Kurt Bayertz, "Four Uses of <<Solidarity>>" in: *Solidarity*, 3.

30. AP, BP, interview by Simina Bădică, tape recorder, Bucharest, Romania on April 18, 2004.

31. DV, interview by Simina Bădică, tape recorder, Bucharest, Romania on April 19, 2004.

32. Ibid.

33. Testimony of Şerban Anghelescu, ethnologist, *Martor*, 131.

34. Testimony of Dragoş Olea, *Martor*, 133.

35. RC, interview by Simina Bădică, tape recorder, Bucharest, Romania on February 25, 2002.

36. I will further discuss on the belief in these speculating activities and the way they were attributed to "outsiders." (Roma people are still considered non-Romanians and outsiders to Romanian society).

37. DV, interview by Simina Bădică, tape recorder, Bucharest, Romania on April 19, 2004.

38. Ibid.

39. Kathy Burrell, "The Political and Social Life of Food in Socialist Poland," *The Anthropology of Eastern Europe Review*, vol. 21 (1), Spring 2003, 4.

40. Testimony of Ana-Maria Bucium, *Martor*, 134.

41. David A. Kideckel, *The Solitude of Collectivism. Romanian Villagers to the Revolution and Beyond*. Ithaca: Cornell University Press, 1993, xiii.

42. Barbu, "Destinul colectiv" [Collective destiny], 175.

43. Ibid., p. 183.

44. Ibid., p. 185.

45. Ibid., p. 192.

46. David Crowley and Susan E. Reid, "Socialist Spaces. Sites of Everyday Life in the Eastern Bloc" in: *Socialist Spaces. Sites of Everyday Life in the Eastern Bloc*, eds. David Crowley and Susan E. Reid, Oxford, New York: Berg, 2002, 15.

47. Tita Chiper, "Provincia pe verticală" [The Counties on the Vertical], *Dilema*, 312, 1999.

48. Testimony of Gabriela Şulea, student, *Martor*, p. 134.

49. DV, interview by Simina Bădică, tape recorder, Bucharest, Romania on April 19, 2004.

50. Testimony of RR, Romanian language teacher, *Martor*, 137.

51. Havel, *The Power of the Powerless*, 27.

52. Ibid., p.28.

53. Ibid., p.31.

54. Ibid., p. 29.

55. My understanding of propaganda attempts to elude ethical judgments. I agree that "any act of promotion can be propaganda only if and when it

becomes part of a deliberate campaign to induce action through influencing attitudes" (Terence Qualter, *Opinion Control in the Democracies*. 1985). However, "whether or not that which is being presented is true or false, it is the way in which it is used (and not its 'truthfulness') that determines whether or not it is in fact propaganda" (Reeves Nicholas, *The Power of Film Propaganda: Myth or Reality?* London: Cassell, 1999, 238).

56. On March 31, 1989, Nicolae Ceausescu announced to the Central Committee of the Romanian Communist Party the integral payment of foreign debts.

57. For Ceausescu's national communism, see Dragoş Petrescu, *The Collapse of Romanian Communism an Explanatory Model*, PhD thesis, Budapest: CEU, Budapest College, 2003.

58. EB, interview by Simina Bădică, tape recorder, Bucharest, Romania on September 10, 2002.

59. Nicolae Ceauşescu, interview in *Newsweek*, August 21, 1989, HU OSA 300-60-1, 3200 Standard of living, General 1980–1989, Open Society Archives, Budapest, Hungary.

60. They were built around a huge, circus-like, cupola.

61. The unfinished building sites can still be seen in Bucharest, although some of them were finished and transformed into shopping malls, which is actually not very far from their initial purpose.

62. When speaking about the 1980s, the interviewees either use "he" or "they" for state decisions or measures that had disastrous effects. "He" is obviously referring to Ceauşescu, but to establish who are "they" is more difficult. It does not designate members of the Communist Party, for they use it also. Most probably, it refers to the leadership of the party, the nomenclature. Today, "they" are also mentioned in conversations about the current unfortunate situation, economical or social, in Romania. Some people maintain that "they" are the same.

63. CR, interview by Simina Bădică, tape recorder, Bucharest, Romania on February 25, 2002.

64. Ibid.

65. HU OSA 300-60-1, 3200 Standard of living, Hoarding 1981, Open Society Archives, Budapest, Hungary.

66. In the 1980s, the verbs *to buy* and *to sell* were replaced by *to take* (a lua) and *to give* (a da). The shops were giving and the customers were taking. The proper question was never "Did you buy meat?" but "Did you take meat?" or, even better, "Did you catch meat?" when there was long queuing involved.

67. MM, interview by Simina Bădică, tape recorder, Bucharest, Romania on April 18, 2004.

68. SP, interview by Simina Bădică, tape recorder, Bucharest, Romania on May 4, 2004.

69. EM, interview by Simina Bădică, tape recorder, Bucharest, Romania on December 3, 2002.

70. ZT, interview by Simina Bădică, tape recorder, Bucharest, Romania on January 7, 2004.

71. AP, interview by Simina Bădică, tape recorder, Bucharest, Romania on April 18, 2004.

72. MM, interview by Simina Bădică, tape recorder, Bucharest, Romania on April 18, 2004.
73. János Kornai, *Economics of Shortage*. Amsterdam: North-Holland Publishing, 1980.
74. R. C. Cobb, *The Police and the People. French Popular Protest 1789–1820*. Oxford: Clarendon Press, 1970, 278.
75. The issue of rumors related to shortages is fascinating and insufficiently researched. One very telling example comes from an anonymous letter sent to Radio Free Europe: "I find the children yellow and sleepy, because the kindergarten food is scarce and bad. However, the children ask for it, so the party takes care and gives each child a small pill to take away the appetite." Letter from "a group of workers and peasants from Romania," August 29, 1982, Records Relating to Romanian Opposition and Protest Movement, HU OSA 300-60-3, Open Society Archives, Budapest, Hungary.
76. AP, interview by Simina Bădică, tape recorder, Bucharest, Romania on April 18, 2004.
77. Slavenka Drakulić, *How We Survived Communism and Even Laughed*. London: Vintage, 1992, 14–15.

8

Resistance in Consumption: In Search of a Negotiating Agent

Valentina Gueorguieva

What can the purchase of a TV set "Opera" in 1963 or the first bottle of Coca-Cola in 1966 tell us about socialism? Does the consumption of such emblematic mass culture products signify an act of resistance or an act of compliance with the socialist regime? To address this question, I offer a case study of individual consumption that tests the applicability of Western theories to practices of consumption under socialism and after.

The History of an Archive

In the spring of 2007, the Institute for Studies of the Recent Past in Sofia (ISRP) published a call for participation in its first contest for collecting memories from the socialist period. The call, titled "This is my past" was placed in the announcements section of a couple of newspapers and addressed individuals who were willing to submit their personal archives of the socialist period, including memoirs, diaries, correspondence, as well as any other personal documents testifying to the lived experience of Bulgarian socialism. The ISRP received a note by Mr. Kumanov, a retired secondary school teacher from a small town in southern Bulgaria; he was willing to make publicly available his individual record of daily expenses, which he kept for a period of more than forty years. Dimitar Dimov from the ISRP first met Mr. Kumanov and collected the major part of the archive. I joined him at the last stage of collecting and organizing documents, and was thus able to work with the originals from December 2007 through January 2009 at the Institute for Studies of the Recent Past, where the archive is now preserved.

The archive of Mr. Kumanov consists of thirty-two volumes comprising his records of daily expenses (the consumption diary); two volumes of his unpublished autobiography entitled "When the Watermills Freeze";[1] the history of the Kumanovi family written by his granddaughter; and a number of short writings by Kumanov himself published or intended for publication in local newspapers (copies of the manuscripts are deposited at the ISRP).

The consumption diary is kept in notebooks of eighty or one hundred pages, each one corresponding roughly either to a calendar year or to a school year (September–July). The first record dates from October 1, 1963. Records are kept most often daily, but following the rhythm of shopping tours (i.e., for certain dates there are no records). Entries usually correspond to expenses for food (bread, milk, fruits, and vegetables), daily press (newspapers and magazines), trips (to and from his and his wife's native village, to and from Sofia), medicines, clothing, book purchases, theater and cinema visits, and other items related to leisure activities. A separate page in each notebook is devoted to the annual newspaper and magazine subscriptions. Another page lists the radio stations with their respective frequencies. Different notes and memos can randomly be found everywhere in the notebooks. The exact amount of family incomes is noted at the beginning of each month, consisting of Kumanov's and his wife's monthly salaries.

It is interesting to see how the agent himself sees the practice of keeping a consumption diary. What was his motivation for persisting in the daily practice of meticulously taking note of every sixpence he and his wife made during the day?

More information about the daily ritual of keeping record of expenses can be found in the unpublished autobiography. He mentions there that his father had the habit of keeping notes of his expenses and that one of his father's notebooks is still preserved (indicating the purchase of the first radio set in 1943). Kumanov mentions that on October 1, 1963, at the age of thirty-six, he began taking notes of his daily expenses, but nothing is said of the motivation and purpose of this activity.

To understand Kumanov's motivations, I interviewed other people in his age group and specifically asked them whether they had the habit of keeping records of family expenses. They all confirmed that they did at certain periods of their lives or that they still do but have not preserved the notebooks. Some informants told me that they were taught to keep such records and to calculate their monthly balance when they were in secondary school, in the 1930s or 1940s. For most of them, keeping track of daily expenses was a way to organize and reasonably distribute the family budget. But they assumed it was worth doing it for the same month or the same year of budget. So usually they did not preserve these accounts, but threw them away as soon as the monthly or yearly notebook was finished. My grandmother was deeply surprised when I asked her about her old notebooks that I remember her keeping. For her, as for my other informants, these notebooks were valuable only for a particular budget period and, hence, there was no reason to preserve them after the period ended.

Evidence to the effect that keeping a record of daily expenses was a common practice of family budget management can be found also in practical guides on housekeeping. In a handbook containing descriptions of good practices for housewives, published in 1978, I found instructions about how to keep such balance and practical guidance for better distribution of expenses.[2]

So most probably in keeping his consumption diary Kumanov simply continued the family tradition or did what all reasonable people used to do when calculating their family budget. It was a usual practice, but he was particularly persistent in keeping notes and in preserving them.

Kumanov, however, began his diary at a difficult point in his life. His autobiography indicates that the period 1962–64 was a difficult time for him. Since 1951 he had occupied a position in the official state trade union and had gradually made a career in the regional branch of the organization. Kumanov reported that in 1960 he had conflicts with one of his superiors. These escalated in 1961 during a visit to the Soviet Union and in 1962 the author was forced to leave the trade union. For a couple of months he was unemployed (at that time he was thirty-five, married with two children) and decided to accept the only job offer he received—a traveling speech and language therapist. So the well-established ex-unionist suddenly found himself without prospects for career development. His income quite likely was lower as well. In 1964 he settled in the newly opened school for children with special needs and later was appointed as, first, its financial director and, afterward, its principal (from 1970 to 1987, the year of his retirement). This brief sketch of his professional development indicates that 1963 was difficult financially and professionally, marking the switch to a new job, which forced him to be constantly on the road. It is not surprising then that he would carefully calculate even the smallest expenses of his family.

But can the rupture in his career account for his practice of keeping a diary for forty-three years? More evidence can be found from other items in Kumanov's archive. In a short piece of writing, titled "Declare our incomes, but also our expenditure," and intended for publication in a local newspaper, Kumanov describes the practice of keeping a record of expenses. The text dates from July 2006. In it he presents this activity as a sort of necessary supplement to the annual income tax declaration. He states that not only revenue, but also expenditures have to be declared, because only a parallel calculation of incomes and expenditures can provide a fair idea of the difficult economic situation of "the two million Bulgarians my age who live on the scant pensions" that the state provides. He continues by insisting that the same parallel declaration of incomes and expenditures is to be demanded from those in power; once the incomes and expenditures of the rulers and the ruled are

Table 1 Translation of the Appendix to the Text "Declare Our Incomes, But Also Our Expenditure"

	February	March	April	May
I. Pension incomes				
GK	183.14	207.32	191.20	191.20
EK [*his wife*]	122.73	138.93	128.13	128.13
Total	305.87	346.25	319.33	319.33
II. Major expenses January–April 2006				
Medical check-ups and medicines	158.83	102.22	121.72	153.18
Electricity	72.47	77.35	76.38	33.02
Telephone bill	20.80	17.24	22.26	17.16
Newspapers	16.90	18.10	17.60	18.75
Small household services	15.36	36.00	–	–
Birthdays of relatives: flowers, photos, others	–	10	17	–
Photocopying	–	–	–	11.22
Water-supply bill	–	–	–	7.02
Credit bill	10	30	10	10
Total	294.00	290.91	264.96	250.35
III. Remaining expenses for food, clothing, shoes, household items, cultural needs, etc.				
	11.87	55.34	54.37	68.98

Reference to the income and major expenses in leva of Kumanov's family for February, March, April, and May 2006, as recorded in his notebooks.

compared, it will be possible for Bulgaria's retired population to receive just pensions. He provides an example from his consumption diary for the period January–April, 2006; the example makes it painfully clear that his expenses outstrip his pension thereby providing testimony to the financial difficulties of his family (see more in Table 1).

This short note on incomes and expenses does not represent a mere personal habit of dealing with the family budget. Rather it is intended to serve as evidence, addressed to the Bulgarian public, that the life of a retired person in postsocialist Bulgaria is financially untenable. Kumanov's note on his family's consumption practices aims to challenge the system of social security in Bulgaria.

There is no doubt then that Kumanov assigned special meaning to the action of keeping a diary of expenses. Especially after 1989, not only when his economic situation became worse but also when he could voice his discontent, the diary of expenses turned into a tool of social criticism.

Reading the Consumption Diary

The best way to give an idea about the kind of information that can be found in the diary is to present a sample of daily expenses. Figure 2 is a snapshot of the entries from September 23, 1982 (vol. 17

Figure 2 The Daily Expenses from September 23, 1982

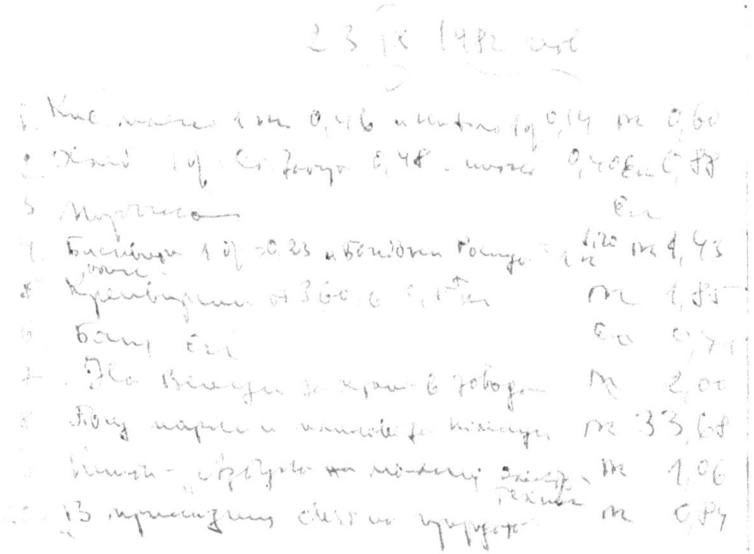

Volume 17 of the archive.

Table 2 Transcript and Translation of the Daily Expenses for September 23, 1982

[Transcript] 23.IX. 1982 четв.		[Translation] September 23, 1982 Thursday	
1. Кис.мляко 1 к. 0,46 и кифла 1 бр.0,14	ГК 0,60	1. Yoghurt 1 container 0,46 and a sweet bun 1 pc. 0,14	GK 0,60
2. Хляб 1бр. Ст.Загора 0,48 и питка 0,40	ЕК 0,88	2. Bread 1pc. [type] Stara Zagora 0,48 and flat loaf 0,40	EK 0,88
3. Поръчка	ЕК	3. Order	EK
4. Бисквити 1 бр. 0,23 и бонбони „Росица" 1 к. 1,20	ГК 1,43	4. Biscuits 1pc. 0,23 and candies "Rositza" 1 box 1,20	GK 1,43
5. Кренвирши от 3,60лв. 0,5хх кг.	ГК 1,85	5. Frankfurt sausage 3,60 lv. per kilo 0,5xxkg	GK 1,85
6. Баня ЕК	ЕК 0,75	6. Bath EK	EK 0,75
7. На Васко за храна в завода	ГК 2,00	7. [money given] to Vasko for food at the factory	GK 2,00
8. Пощенски марки и пликове за колекци	ГК 33,68	8. Post stamps and envelopes for collection	GK 33,68
9. Книга „Азбука на малкия електротехник"	ГК 1,06	9. Book *ABC of the young electro technician*	GK 1,06
10. „В приказния свят на природата"	ГК 0,84	10. "In the Wonderland of Nature"	GK 0,84

of the archive), accompanied here by a transcript in Bulgarian and its translation into English (see Table 2).

Some explanations are needed in order to make sense of the information contained in this excerpt. Items are described in the left column and the exact sum of money spent is provided in the right column (in Bulgarian leva), preceded by the initials of the member of the family who purchased the particular item (GK, Kumanov himself, or EK, his wife). The daily expenses of food are listed in lines 1–5. Prices are given for each item separately and in sum for all items purchased. The line "Order" (here line 3) appears almost everyday and will be discussed separately later. The exact weight or quantity of sausages on line 5 cannot be read but can easily be calculated since the price per kilo is carefully noted (it should be 0.510 kg). The initials EK appear also in line 6—"Bath EK." Similar entries can be found on different dates in the same year, and with different names ("Bath" EK and GK; or Vasko[3]—their son born in 1960; or Sylviya—their elder daughter born in 1951; or also Peter and Irina—the son and daughter of Sylviya and her husband whose name is not mentioned). I read the entry "bath" as price paid for the ticket at the public baths, meaning that the family probably did not have a bathroom in their house at that time. Line 7, money given to Vasko, reveals additional information about the life of the family. In 1982, Vasko was already twenty-two years old and obviously worked in a factory, but his parents give him money to buy food at his workplace, probably to pay for his lunch at the canteen of the factory. Vasko's salary is never mentioned in the entries related to the income of the family whereas Kumanov's and his wife's monthly salaries are carefully noted. Nor is his name present in the right column of the diary as the person who shopped for the household. Most probably the son did not contribute to the family budget. The same is valid for the elder daughter; her income is not mentioned and she is not cited among those who did the shopping. But unlike the son, she married early and probably had to set up a separate family budget with her husband.

Lines 8 to 10 (line 10 is probably a book title) are related to cultural consumption. The major expense of the day is the purchase of post stamps and envelopes for Kumanov's collection; his hobby during that period was philately. The sum of 33,68 lv. listed here corresponds to 19 percent of his monthly salary of 179,46 lv. (listed in the same volume of the archive, under the entry dated from August 5, 1982).[4]

This example shows how the data in the notebooks are scarce and elusive, but at the same time can reveal much more information than they literally provide. From this document, we learn little about the work and leisure activities of Kumanov's wife. He mentions in his autobiography that she was employed in the sector of education, but nothing is said about her training and career. The exact amount of her salary is noted every month (it is slightly higher than Kumanov's salary for the cited period), and she does an equal portion of the purchases as listed in the right column of the diary. But unlike her husband, she did not buy special articles for her hobbies. Apart from one or two titles of women's magazines listed in the annual subscriptions of the family, we learn nothing about the interests and activities of the women in the family, the wife EK and the daughter Sylviya.

The example above suggests two distinctive characteristics of this family's pattern of consumption. Firstly, there is a certain discrepancy between the budget for food and the budget for hobbies and leisure activities (or the consumption of cultural goods). It seems that the consumption of cultural goods prevails over the consumption of food. And secondly, food is present in the record of expenses not so much in the form of shopping lists of supplies that will be cooked later (such as vegetables, groceries, meat) but in the form of ready-made snacks (sweet buns, biscuits and candies), of sausages, lunch in the factory canteen, and so on. I will attempt to explain these two peculiarities below.

Let me first introduce my analytical tools. In order to explain the consumption practices outlined above, I will use the model of the French theorist Michel de Certeau, who analyzes everyday actions of ordinary people as forms of creative consumption to explain the microphysics of resistance in the everyday war of strategies and tactics.

The Everyday War of Strategies and Tactics: The Model of Michel de Certeau

Michel de Certeau's model emerged from his reports on the creativity of cultural practices published between 1968 and 1972. The vocabulary of strategies and tactics appeared in an article first published in 1974, which later formed the conclusion of the book *Culture au pluriel* (1974). However, de Certeau's theory of ordinary people's tactics against the constraints of the system is fully developed only in *The Practice of Everyday Life* (1980).[5] The book was prepared as the report of a larger group research project on leisure and recreational activities among the French; the project commissioned by the state directorate for scientific research was awarded to Michel de Certeau and his team.

Michel de Certeau's model of everyday practices is a replica of Michel Foucault's concept of the discipline of the body, developed in *Discipline and Punish* (1975).[6] In it Foucault pays particular attention to microscopic "mechanisms," "operations," "techniques," and "procedures," which form what he calls "the microphysics of power." Michel de Certeau employed the same logic of microscopic operations, but used it instead as an analytical tool to understand the subversive practices of the weak. De Certeau terms these practices microphysics from below, or a microphysics of resistance to power. He takes over Foucault's idea of a "microphysics of power" to turn to the dark side of cultural production. The metaphor of darkness is used to specify the creative practices that remain in the shadow of reason, of the central, expansionist, spectacular and loudly proclaimed cultural production, which obfuscates another production of a completely different type qualified as consumption or usage. In this passage to the dark side, de Certeau introduces the idea of an anti-discipline. Whereas Foucault studies discourses of power, de Certeau's object are the arts of the weak, that is, the same microscopic mechanisms, techniques, operations, and so on, but from below.

As already mentioned, de Certeau defined his object of study as the cultural practices of consumption. But "consumption" has for him a broader meaning. In a way, de Certeau's theory of everyday practices deconstructs the binary production–consumption.

First, he challenges the conception of popular culture as mere assimilation of media messages. "In any case, the consumer cannot be identified or qualified by the newspapers or commercial products he assimilates: between the person (who uses them) and these products (indexes of the "order" which is imposed on him), there is a gap of varying proportions opened by the use that he makes of them."[7] As de Certeau points out, assimilating does not necessarily mean "becoming similar to" what one absorbs. It can also mean "making it similar" to what one already is, or appropriating it. The idea of passive consumption is a restrictive version of the act of consuming media messages. "Inclined to believe that its own cultural models are necessary for the people in order to educate their minds and elevate their hearts, the elite upset about the 'low level' of journalism or television always assumes that the public is moulded by the products imposed on it. To assume that, is to misunderstand the act of 'consumption.' "[8] Furthermore, the only freedom left to the consumers, or the masses, "is that of grazing on the ration of simulacra the system distributes to each individual."[9] And it is precisely this vision of the consumers that de Certeau finds unacceptable.

This vision of passive consumption results from a theoretical fallacy—it is our scientific apparatus that creates the illusion of the masses molded by the culture industry. De Certeau concludes his chapter XII on reading as poaching by insisting that we as researchers should not assume that people are only passive consumers.[10] The emergence of this theoretical (and political) fallacy of taking people for passive consumers is traced in the historical practices of education and their impact on contemporary practices of reading, and of consuming popular culture.

> The efficiency of production implies the inertia of consumption. It produces the ideology of consumption-as-a-receptacle. The result of class ideology and technical blindness, this legend is necessary for the system that distinguishes and privileges authors, educators, revolutionaries, in a word, "producers," in contrast with those who do not produce. By challenging "consumption" as it is conceived and (of course) confirmed by these "authorial" enterprises, we may be able to discover creative activity where it has been denied that any exists, and to relativize the exorbitant claim that a certain kind of production (real enough, but not the only kind) can set out to produce history by "informing" the whole of a country.[11]

De Certeau rejects the conception of the passive consumer and replaces it with the conception of creative consumption. What is "creative consumption" then?

Consumption is actually usage in the sense that it refers to what the cultural consumer "makes" or "does" with the message or product s/he receives. This is equally valid for cultural commodities as well as for symbols, rules, strategies, that is to say, the discourse of the dominant occupying the point of view of enunciation. It is in the ways ordinary people "use" products and discourses that they fill in the gap between dominant production and individual consumption. And it is in this gap that their creativity operates. The "use" or "making" is also production, but the hidden production of "the silent majority."[12] The dominant production has left it without place of enunciation in the cultural field. Production and consumption reiterate the opposition between dominant discourse and popular culture, the elites and the common people, the powerful and the weak.

Everyday "uses" (or also "ways and customs," practices of "making do," "actions" in the military sense)[13] should not be understood as routinized activities or repeated manners, that is, typical solutions to typical problems. Everyday "uses" have their own formality and inventiveness. There are no routine ways of consumption; in every case consumption takes different forms. It is unexpected and unpredictable. This is what Michel de Certeau calls "the enigma of the consumer-sphinx." Inventiveness is the secret weapon of the users; it opposes dominant strategies and discourses:

> In reality, a rationalized, expansionist, centralized, spectacular and clamorous production is confronted by an entirely different kind of production, called "consumption" and characterized by its ruses, its fragmentation (the result of the circumstances), its poaching, its clandestine nature, its tireless but quiet activity, in short by its quasi-invisibility, since it shows itself not in its own products (where would it place them?) but in an art of using those imposed on it.[14]

Strategies and tactics are another binary used to express the same opposition between the powerful and the dominated: those who have a place of their own, a point of enunciation (from where they speak), producing a discourse, dominating the field, on the one hand, and on the other—those who are deprived of place, but have the opportunity to seize the right moment to interpret, reappropriate, modify, distort the discourse, and create something else, a more practical and easy-to-use version of cultural products. These tactics are called "Ways of operating," or "making do" or "*art de faire*" or victories of the "weak" over the "powerful."

In sum, for Michel de Certeau, consumption is an act of inventiveness, a skill, or "a tactical and joyful dexterity" that ordinary people develop in their efforts to "make do" or circumvent the rules of a constraining setting. Consumption creates "opacities and ambiguities—places of darkness and trickery" and is thus invisible to the eyes of the system. Sometimes it takes repetitive forms, but its weapon is to take advantage of time and circumstances, and therefore it has "innumerable ways of playing and foiling the other's game."[15]

I can now return to my case study: the consumption pattern of Mr. Kumanov's family. I will analyze this pattern according to the model of creative consumption, that is, the inventive ways of using available resources, which form particular tactics of "making do."

The Consumption Tactics of the Kumanovs

As we have already seen in the example from September 23, 1982, the diary points out two distinctive expenditure practices of the family. First, a significant part of the family budget is spent on cultural goods, such as books and items related to hobbies. Second, there is a peculiar absence of shopping lists from the diary, of lists indicating the purchase of meat, groceries, vegetables, and other products necessary for cooking.

I propose the following interpretation of the consumption practices of the Kumanovs: (1) Regarding groceries, they found a creative way of "making do" with less. (2) By analyzing the purchases of cultural goods, I reconstruct the interests and passions of the family during the socialist period in order to disclose the forms of creative consumption (or inventive uses, or tactics of resistance).

"Making Do" With Less, or Expenses for Food

The most voluminous part of the records in the diary is related to nutrition, but also clothing, items for personal hygiene, and medicines. The daily purchase of bread and milk is noted; cheese, cold cuts, fruits and vegetables, and candies are to be found once or twice a week in small quantities. The amounts mentioned can scarcely cover the needs of the four or five members of the household (after 1978, Mr. and Mrs. Kumanov shared their house with the family of their daughter Sylviya, her husband, and their child). Groceries are not mentioned. Such typical items for Bulgarian cooking like dry beans, lentils, potatoes, rice are absent from the lists of purchases. Meat and fish appear only randomly, in quantities that can only serve as a complement to the main diet.

For example, in January 1982, the family bought chicken only twice for the whole month (vol. 17 of the archive, diary entries from January 10 and 31: one chicken each time, in total 2.6 kg for the whole month); minced meat—only once (January 15, 0.5 kg), different types of cold cuts once or twice per week for a total quantity of 2.4 kg for the whole month. In February 1982, the family bought the total amount of 3.4 kg of sausages (*krenvirshi, nadenitsa*) and minced meat; chicken is not mentioned, 0.7 kg of fish fillet. The situation is not very different during the autumn season. In September 1982, the variety and quantity of meat products is very similar: 1 kg of minced meat, 1 kg of Frankfurt sausage (*krenvirshi*), 2 kg of sausage (*nadenitsa*), two chickens.

The year 1982 was chosen for this example because it was not a year of scarcity. The average data from the official statistics show that the consumption of main food and beverages for 1982 is significantly higher, compared with the same values in 2007. For example, in 1982 the household consumption of meat (average per capita) was 68.3 kg,[16] whereas for 2007 it was 42.2 kg (the sum of 27.4 kg of meat and 14.8 kg of meat products, the latter is not calculated separately in the yearbook from 1982).[17]

The calculations above show that all meat products for the January 1982 amounted to 5.5 kg. If we assume that the family consumed similar quantities each month (which is not actually the case, for in February we see 3.4 kg and in September the total is 6.6 kg), we can roughly calculate the annual consumption of meat and meat products for 1982 at 66 kg. But this quantity is for the whole family and not per capita, as in the official statistics, which give us similar numbers—68.3 kg. And in 1982 the family consisted of at least four adults and one child aged four. My calculations here are very rough, though, nevertheless indicate that the quantities are small for a household of five people.

To sum up, the quantities of food purchased according to the diary were definitely not enough to make up a reasonable regimen for the family. If we take into account the income of the family, this is not due to financial difficulties.[18] Moreover, it was improbable that they were in shortage of food, since for the same day or period they spent more money on newspapers and other items related to leisure activities, than for food. This opacity in the records of expenses can disclose a different tactic of making do.

In contrast to the absence of groceries, food, and vegetables, there is one entry that is present every day, which literary translates as "order" (*porychka*). Most of the time this is the major expense of the day. It relates to the money spent for lunch in the canteen of the place of work. Sometimes the author of the diary provides a list of what he actually ordered at the canteen, and these lists usually include three or more main courses, or double portions of one or two main courses accompanied by soup and dessert (see Figure 3). This suggests that he regularly brought home food from the canteen. Cooked meals brought home from Mr. and Mrs. Kumanov's working places' canteens most

Figure 3 *Kotelki* or a set of containers, designed to fit one on top of the other, with lid and handle on top

Similar sets of vessels were used to transport cooked meals. These *kotelki* are currently in use. Photo by the author.

probably represented the main part of the nutritive regimen of the family, complemented by milk and bread, small quantities of sausages, cheese, fruits, and vegetables bought in addition.

The food from the canteen was a different and easier way of making do. It saved time on cooking. But also the prices of meals at the canteen were low because canteens at workplaces were subsidized by the state, or by trade unions, or factory management. The goal was to make cooked food affordable. The canteen at Mr. Kumanov's school was part of the state educational system and was thus subsidized by the state. We can assume that this was also the case for his wife. So the practice of buying more food from the canteen to take home was one small way of taking advantage of the system in coping with daily needs. It was not formally forbidden, though each canteen could have special regulations. It was not a fraud, rather taking advantage of a gap in the system, a petty trickery that spared time and effort, and offered more time for leisure activities.

What happened after 1987, when Kumanov retired and no longer had access to the canteen? And what happened after 1989, when the canteens of factories and institutions were gradually closed down, along with the factories and institutions themselves? Other tactics of making do had to be invented, if the family wished to keep to their old ways.

At first, Kumanov continued using the canteen at the school for children with special needs from where he retired as principal, probably relying on his personal relations with his older colleagues and friends. Starting from the early 1990s, most likely this was no longer an option. Occasionally, Kumanov mentions in the diary where they took the "orders" from, as well as the raising of prices. By 2002, they tried a number of solutions: the canteen of the trade union of health practitioners, then the canteen of the hospital (both subsidized by the Ministry of Health); in 1998 and afterward, the canteen of the city garrison (supported financially by the Ministry of Defense), then the canteens of a couple of high schools (receiving funds from the Ministry of Education); then again the city garrison in 2002, and then he mentions that the canteens of these schools became private (and therefore do not receive financial support by the state). He gradually abandoned the practice of buying canteen food since the prices became unaffordable.

Access to these canteens was not open; rather, their subsidized prices were a form of support for the employees in the respective institutions provided through state subsidies earmarked for "social activities." Kumanov might have gained access to the canteens with the help of his older connections (if someone who previously worked in the canteen of his school moved to work in another canteen). But eventually they would also reach the age of retirement (Kumanov's connections have to date before 1987, when he himself retired). He might simply try at random at different places, by hit or miss. But no doubt, it implies some inventiveness: taking advantage of time and available resources to get around the rules of a constraining social arrangement (the restrictions of access to canteens).

If we take the practice of buying meals from subsidized canteens to be an example of an everyday tactic of making do with the system requirements, it appears that this tactic of poaching or ruse was applied systematically during socialist times and persisted even after 1989.

Creative Uses of Cultural Products? Expenses Related to Leisure Activities and Subscription to Newspapers and Magazines

An important part of the family's expenditures was devoted to cultural consumption, or the purchases of books, periodicals, theater, and cinema visits, and goods related to the numerous Kumanov's hobbies changing during the different periods of his life. That he was very keen on going to the cinema can be seen from his autobiography:

> Since 1943 I have preserved 40 tickets for the cinema and the theatre, on the backside of each of these I noted the titles, the names of the actors playing the leading parts, their nationality, and I sketched something distinctive about the title or the plot of the movie.[19]

Later in his life, he continued going to the cinema with his wife, but rarely mentioned the title of the film they saw in his consumption diary. From the 1970s onward, the entries in the diary read as follows: "cinema for Sylviya" or "cinema for Vasko" (their daughter and son). The parents gradually abandon the practice of going to the movies, but pay for their children's tickets.

In the 1960s, he mentions visits to the theater (with the titles of the plays) and a couple of symphonic orchestra concerts. The practice of going to the theater also disappears from the diary after 1978.

During the 1960s and 1970s, Kumanov used to buy materials for developing and printing photos, which indicates his hobby of the period. He also bought (or subscribed to) periodicals, dedicated to photography. His hobbies changed over the years. He was first a photographer, and then a philatelist, but gradually the items related to the practice of these passions disappear from the lists of purchases.

He conscientiously noted the titles of the books purchased. Most of the time, these were handbooks or practical guides, related to his hobbies, other advisory books on housekeeping, garden-keeping, vine-growing, titles related to medicine and health condition, books of general interest. When the family bought fiction it was only from Bulgarian and Russian authors, for example, the complete writings of Ivan Vazov, and other Bulgarian classics. He also purchased a number of volumes, entitled *History of the Bulgarian Communist Party* (since there were numerous editions from different years, I cannot tell whether he completed the series or acquired only separate volumes). Two historical titles are of particular interest—the commemorative volume *1,300 years of Bulgarian statehood* and the big *History of Bulgaria* in six volumes that were published during the 1980s on the occasion of the same commemoration. Nowadays, the ideological character of these publications is emphasized. The hidden ideology can be deciphered also in the massive distribution (or pretended popularity) of the six volumes of the *History of Bulgaria*, which was supposed to be an academic study setting high standards of research in the style and format of the book. But at the same time it became a mass publication (though not a popular reading)—it could (and still can) easily be found on the bookshelves of many a mid-range household.

The last item in Kumanov's cultural consumption I wish to highlight is his passion for periodicals. In his autobiography, he recalls that already in his school years he had a pronounced interest in reading the press. He declares that it was due to some familiarity with his father's profession—a postman in his native village—that he created this affection for the press very early in his life.

> *I would also like to share that as a result of the proximity with the postman as a profession and the contact with the mail, newspapers and magazines, very early in my school years I became a stamp-collector and afterwards a numismatist, I became addicted to the newspapers and magazines I read with great interest immediately after their arrival and delivery. I had this passion already in my childhood, when I sought and read the children's magazines and newspapers received for sale (. . .). As a result I developed a pronounced interest in daily and periodical press, and later on for decades I subscribed myself and my family for 25–30 publications.*[20]

These long lists of periodicals of about twenty-five to thirty titles can also be found in the pages of the consumption diary (usually they are listed on the last page). It is interesting to see how the titles change through the years.

In 1967, the list of subscriptions includes ten titles of newspapers, six titles of Bulgarian magazines, and another four titles of foreign magazines. The official dailies of the Communist Party (*Rabotnichesko delo*) and of the coalition partner (*Otechestven front*) are on the list, along with the professional weekly of the teacher's union (*Uchitelsko delo*), another professional weekly (*Srednoshkolsko delo*), the weekly *Narodna Kultura*, the satirical newspaper *Starshel*, sports dailies, a couple of local newspapers. The list of Bulgarian magazines is almost exclusively oriented to junior and student audience (five titles, among them *Rodna rech, Matematika, Slaveytche, Druzhinka*). At that time his daughter Sylviya was sixteen and his son Vasko was seven. The last sixth title is *Zhenata dnes*, the most popular women's magazine. The four titles of foreign magazines are from the socialist bloc: the Russian *Veselie kartinki* (children's magazine), *Fotokino* from GDR, the magazines *Roumania* and *Socialist Czechoslovakia*. The total sum paid for all the subscriptions in 1967 is 33,53 lv., which is about 25 percent of Kumanov's monthly salary at that time (133 lv.).

The family continued its subscriptions for almost the same list of titles over the next twenty years. In 1985, the number of titles rises to thirty. Even the periodicals addressing younger audience are still there, this time for the grand children of the Kumanovs, Peter and Irina. The Romanian and Czechoslovakian titles are replaced by a Russian women's magazine and the East-German *Modische Maschen* (a fashion magazine specialized in hand knitting). The total sum for all subscriptions is 143.53 lv.

Though he had the regular practice of making annual subscriptions for a long list of publications, he also bought newspapers daily, ordered separate issues of weeklies and magazines, purchased different titles at random. The item "newspapers" is almost inevitably present in his daily records. In 1967, the titles of magazines bought randomly are *Politprosveta, Ekran, Lov i Ribolov, Nasha rodina*. It is also worth mentioning that in the 1980s, there are some titles of Western magazines that appear among the randomly purchased items, such as *Le miroir du football* (at the price of 3 lv.) and the title *Autorodeo cosmodo*.

After the fall of the socialist regime in 1989, the family tried to keep up with their former habits of cultural consumption. The subscription was done monthly (because of the high inflation rate annual subscriptions were not offered in the 1990s). The list of subscribed titles is shorter—fourteen for 1994, for example. Only for the month of February of the same year, the total sum paid for a monthly subscription is equal to thirteen, 9 percent of Kumanov's monthly pension (whereas in 1967 the annual subscription was 25 percent of the monthly salary). The titles of the periodicals are completely different. Periodicals oriented to junior audience and the women's magazines are no longer there, nor are the sports journals and the magazines on photography. There are no foreign titles. Weekly and monthly periodicals of cultural and general interest, such as *Narodna kultura, ABV, Pogled, Paraleli,* which were very popular during the socialist period, are no longer present in Kumanov's list of subscriptions, either because they no longer exist or because they do not match the interests of the family. The titles are now related to health, to physical condition, and to the elderly citizens: *Domashen lekar* (Home physician), *Znahar* (Healer), *Letchitel* (Medicine Man), *Meditzina* (Medicine), *Pensioner* (Pensioner), *Treta vyrzast* (Third Age), *Bulgarski pensioner* (Bulgarian retired citizen).

Apart from the subscription, Kumanov bought the daily press almost every day, like he used to do in his younger years. In 1994 he bought *Duma*, the democratic successor of *Rabotnichesko delo*, the organ of the Bulgarian Socialist Party. Once or twice in November 1994 he bought also *Demokratsia*, the organ of the oppositional block. Though the mainstream tabloids *Trud* and *24 chasa* already existed in 1994, he bought them once or twice for the whole year (1994).

It is in 1999 that the family completely abandoned the practice of subscribing to newspapers (the last subscription is from July 1999). It might be not only for financial, but also for cultural reasons. The major part of the titles they liked and received during the previous years of their lives from the 1960s through the 1980s are no longer published or have completely changed their outlook, contents, and even political orientation. The periodicals that began appearing in the mid-1990s and later do not match the interests of the family or their age. These are mostly the Bulgarian editions of international publications such as *Cosmopolitan, National geographic, Amica, Max, Playboy*, and so forth. As for the newspapers, the organs of the political parties lost their popularity by the end of the 1990s and were replaced on the market by tabloids. Most probably, the family never got used to the new outlook and contents of the tabloid press.

If we look at the list of the Kumanov family's subscriptions from 1985, only two of the titles are still published—*Trud*, which used to be the organ of the state trade unions, but is now part of a privately owned media group and uses the tabloid format; the other title is *Narodna Kultura* (after 1990 only *Kultura)*, a weekly cultural publication using the format of a newspaper that kept its conservative and very elitist outlook and contents, but has completely changed its political orientation (it is now right of the center on the political spectrum). As a matter of fact, the family abandoned their subscription to this journal already in the late 1980s.

To sum up, Kumanov sustained his passion for reading periodicals by maintaining subscriptions to periodicals as well as by randomly purchasing various titles; both drew significant amount from the family budget, showing that he spent much of the family income on cultural consumption. In so far as conclusions can be drawn only from the titles he and his family loved, he read the officially sanctioned and praised publications. There is no evidence to the effect that he supported the regime before 1989. Neither there is evidence that he resisted it. Nevertheless, all the titles mediating the dominant discourse and ideology are in his subscription lists. It is true that he had no choice— there was simply no oppositional press. But there was the option of ignoring the main channels of ideology—the family could choose not to subscribe to the publications approved by the socialist regime and feed their passion for periodicals with titles of general interest or only with publications connected to their hobbies. Needless to say, these types of publications also imbibed the official socialist ideology, but why would he persist in subscribing to the ideological titles when he could ignore them?

When theorizing about the reception of media discourse, Stuart Hall suggested that simply ignoring a publication (or a film, or a TV program, or other type of media content) can also be read as an act of resistance: "In the study of popular culture, we should always start here: with the double stake in popular culture, the double movement of containment and resistance, which is always inevitably inside it."[21] Switching off the TV set, or not going to the movie, or not buying the newspaper is already rejecting it, therefore containment can be seen as resistance. Containment cannot be found from the evidence provided by Kumanovs' lists of subscriptions. But the opposite assumption that Kumanov supported the regime, if this assumption is based only on the record of his subscription to periodicals, is too hasty.

Other instances can be found in the other forms of cultural consumption—the titles of books he bought also clearly belong to the dominant discourse (*History of the Bulgarian Communist Party*, the literary classics, the six volumes of *History of Bulgaria*). Yet these titles were a sort of a "must have" for the ordinary Bulgarian family (probably not to read it, just to have it in the home library). They were mass publications, with or without the ideological effect that they implied. Therefore, it is not clear whether their purchase was really ideologically motivated, or just a public display of the (official) interests of the family. It could also be a mark of education. If this interpretation is correct, that is, if the ideological titles were bought simply as a display of political correctness or cultural distinction in the home library, and hence mainly simulate interest in the official discourse, then we can make no conclusion to the effect that he espoused the official ideology.

To sum up, the data from the diary are too elusive to support the conclusion that forms of "inventiveness of the week," or of creative consumption of media messages can be found in the cultural consumption of the Kumanovs. Conclusions to the effect that there were elements of resistance in the creative assimilation of the culture industry cannot be justified, but neither can we assume that Kumanov was supportive of the socialist regime, before or after the changes. The changes in the pattern of cultural consumption, as seen in the titles of newspapers and magazines through the years can be explained from the point of view of the life courses of family members: Kumanov's hobbies and interests changed with the different stages of his life; children's magazines were replaced with titles of general interest, then with publications addressing senior citizens. The family gradually abandoned reading the publications of the political parties, but never got used to the new type of tabloid press. The explanation may be that at a later stage in their lives they wouldn't be inclined to change their habits, much like their insistence to keep up with the old habit of "ordering" food at the canteens of state subsidized institutions. This is what the Kumanov family did almost all of their lives and they tried to use the same tactics after the fall of the socialist regime, this time to subvert the rules of the new capitalist system.

Instead of Conclusion: Resistance or Negotiation

My initial idea in this text was to test the applicability of Western theories of resistance in everyday life to socialist practices of consumption. In particular, I wanted to see whether a certain personal document—the consumption diary of an individual agent—can be interpreted using Michel de Certeau's theoretical model of creative consumption.

The advantage of de Certeau's model is that his notion of resistance can be very subtle: it does not imply a bipolar model of conformity/opposition to the system, but offers a more flexible vision of how the microphysics of power can be assimilated, modified, appropriated, circumvented, used for various purposes, and distorted from within. The above analysis shows that there are both instances of resistance (in de Certeau's sense) and of compliance to be found in Kumanov's consumption diary. If his cultural consumption can be read more in the key of compliance, his ways of "making do" in supplying food can be read as the inventiveness of the weak, that is, taking advantage of the gaps in the system. Evidence can be found in favor of both readings—resistance as well as compliance. In the case of our agent, he is inventive in his ways to find affordable prepared meals, but rather conformist in his cultural consumption. Whether it was about the daily diet, or about popular reading, after the fall of the regime he tries to stick to his older ways.

There is always a dialectical interplay between a set of constraints and the individual agency that can take different forms, sometimes of resistance and sometimes of compliance. Most of the time, the everyday practices are somewhere in the middle. The individual agent negotiates her/his own way, abiding by or getting around, or perverting the rules of the system. As John Fiske puts it, "I believe that under certain conditions, though may be not all the time, people can both be aware of their social interests and be capable of acting to promote them." Therefore, he calls them "socially interested agents negotiating their particular trajectories through the historical conditions into which they were born."[22] The idea of the negotiating agent can be very useful in trying to make sense of the Kumanovs' consumption practices—the making do with less, the subscription to the ideological titles and the "must have" books for the home library, the replacing of political press with titles addressing senior citizens, and the attempts to stick to his old habits of consumption after 1989.

Ordinary people in their everyday activities under socialism acted as socially interested agents, and while constantly negotiating with the social and historical conditions of their lives, they acted in ways that both maintained and perverted the system, and gradually led to its demise.

Notes

1. Grigor Slaveev Kumanov, *Kogato zamrazvat vodenitsite: Zapiski ot moya zhivot, takav kakavto beshe* [When the Watermills Freeze: Notes from my life as it was] 2007. Unpublished manuscript of autobiography, preserved at Institute for Studies of the Recent Past—Sofia.
2. *Dom, semeystvo, bit: Kniga za domakinyata* [*House, Family, Way of Living: A Handbook for the Housewife*], Sofia: Zemizdat, 1978, 34.
3. The names of the family members are changed; information about the dates of birth and their family status is taken from the autobiography, see Kumanov, *Kogato zamrazvat*.
4. The average annual salary of the employees in the sector of education for 1982 is 2093 lv. (*Statisticheski godishnik 1983*, p. 74, table 5), or approximately 175 lv. per month.

5. Michel De Certeau, *The Practice of Everyday Life*, translated by Stephen Rendall, Berkeley: University of California Press, 1984.

6. Michel Foucault, *Discipline and Punish: The Birth of the Prison*, translated by Alan Sheridan, New York: Random House, 1995.

7. De Certeau, *The Practice of Everyday Life*, 32.

8. Ibid., 166.

9. Ibid.

10. Ibid., 176.

11. Ibid., 167.

12. Ibid., xvii.

13. Ibid., 30.

14. Ibid., 31.

15. Ibid., 18.

16. *Statisticheski godishnik* na Narodna Republika Bulgaria [*Statistical Yearbook of People's Republic of Bulgaria*], Sofia: Komitet po edinna sistema za sotsialna informatsia pri ministerski savet, 1983, 90, table 24.

17. *Statistichesi godishnik*, 2008 [*Statistical Yearbook 2008*, data about 2007], Sofia: Natsionalen statisticheski institut, 2008, 124, table 11.

18. The family income corresponds to the average at the time. The average annual salary of the employees in the sector of education for 1982 was 2,093 lv. (*Statisticheski godishnik* 1983, p.74, table 5). Kumanov's annual salary for 1982 should be about 2,153 lv. (12 months × 179.46 lv., the salary for July mentioned in vol. 17 of the archive, entry from August 5, 1982) and that of his wife is about 2,172 lv. (12 × 181 lv., vol. 17, entry from August 2, 1982).

19. Kumanov, *Kogato zamrazvat*, 78.

20. Ibid., 65.

21. Stuart Hall, "Notes on deconstructing 'the popular'," in: *Cultural Theory and Popular Culture*, ed. John Storey, Harlow: Pearson & Prentice Hall, 2006, 478.

22. John Fiske, "Cultural studies and the culture of everyday life," in: *Cultural Studies*, eds. Lawrence Grossberg, Cary Nelson and Paula A. Treichler, London: Routledge, 1992, 173.

9

Housing as a Norm and as an Everyday Life Strategy in Communist Czechoslovakia (1968–89)

Hana Pelikánová

The period of recent Czech(oslovak) history following the military intervention of the Soviet army and the troops of the Warsaw Pact in 1968 up to the Velvet Revolution in 1989 is usually referred to as a "dark" era. Czechoslovak society became livelier in the brief period before the occupation (known as the Prague Spring) but all the reformist and cultural activities were suppressed later on during the twenty-year-long period of so-called normalization. Normalization brought a stricter political and economic dependence on the USSR and put an end to all attempts to reform society toward the principles of democracy. The term "normalization" was chosen to imply a return to the conditions before the reformist year 1968.

From the moment the communist regime in Czechoslovakia fell in 1989, historiography took up the difficult task of explaining the characteristics, methods, and mechanisms of a system that had been shaping the lives of millions of people for more than forty years. New interdisciplinary methods of research were gradually introduced and at present "traditional" historical research is often combined with sociological, anthropological, and psychological methods of quantitative and qualitative research.

The Czech Oral History Center at the Institute of Contemporary History of the Academy of Sciences of the Czech Republic was established for similar reasons in the year 2000. Its main aim was to execute primary research focusing on, at the time, "untraditional" sources for the interpretation of recent history—oral history sources. Recently it changed its focus from the study of political elites and dissidents' experiences to the strata of "ordinary" people and the study of everyday life in communism, especially its last two decades. A three-year project called "An Investigation of Czech Society of the 'Normalization' Era: Biographic Narrations of Workers and Intelligentsia"[1] has recently been completed and it provides extensive material in the form of 115 life-story interviews. The main aim of the project was not to confront the life views of two different social groups in an identification with their social roles, but rather to attempt a comprehensive survey of everyday life in the period of normalization. The interviews resulted in intriguing testimonies about lifestyles, life habits, and life strategies of "ordinary people" in the period of normalization. The same importance was given to the narrators' opinions, judgments, evaluations, and comparisons of the realities before and after 1989.

This chapter deals with only one specific area of this extensive research of everyday life—housing. As one of the elementary needs of every person, it appeared in all the interviews, regardless of the sex, age, or social status of the narrators. The subject of housing will be analyzed from two standpoints. The first one presents a "macro" view and deals with the legislative and political side of housing in the period of so-called normalization. It gives a concise outline of (public) housing policy, its development, and tendencies up to the Velvet Revolution in 1989. It also tackles other related issues such as the problem of housing need and housing culture, a topic closely connected to contemporary ideas about design and aesthetics. The second part of this chapter is a qualitative "micro" view on the subject based on oral history interviews. It shows the lived experience of people solving their housing issue in the period of normalization. The main goal of the chapter is to compare the norms imposed on people by the regime and the central planning and the particular life strategies developed as a result of the confrontation with these norms. It also presents a certain outline of everyday life under a communist regime in regard to its national (Czech) specifics.

Housing from a Normative Perspective

Housing as a Social Warranty in Communist Czechoslovakia

The housing and real estate market in general went through many radical changes after the rise of communism in Czechoslovakia in 1948. Due to the centralization of the economy, the ideology of egalitarianism, and planned homogenization of the population, the private sector was almost eradicated and housing was transferred to the competence of the state.

In the beginning (especially in the 1950s), this process was characterized by large-scale confiscations and the nationalization of private property and sectors of industry. Generally it was based on the idea of pauperization of small and large owners and the consequent raising of the standard of life of the lower-class, especially working-class people. It was followed by the formation of such legislative principles that would adequately put into practice the new ideology of socialist common property.

Czechoslovak real socialism was based on several leading ideas: collectivism, optimism, egalitarianism, safety, social guarantees, and state paternalism.[2] Accordingly, housing (as well as work[3]) was proclaimed and popularized as a social guarantee, that is, a social, not a private issue. Immediately after WWII, the large majority of privately owned rental housing was nationalized, as well as family villas that were afterward divided into flats.[4] The existing dwellings were later distributed among applicants.[5]

The allocation of state-owned housing stock was in the hands of the National Committees[6] during the whole communist period. National Committees were authorized to allocate dwellings in their districts to the citizens according to their housing needs and social conditions for which they kept registers of applicants.[7] The official allocation "ideology" and practice in general were designed to eliminate the "bourgeois" strata and support workers, especially those employed in the priority sectors of industry, following the Soviet example. Apartments were primarily allocated to employees in preferential sectors of industry; the rest in principle should have been distributed according to social criteria. The 1964 Housing Act on Housing Management[8] (in effect till 1991) stated that applicants were to be generally ranked according to two groups of criteria: (1) according to the urgency of the housing need of an applicant in regard to the family income and number of children and (2) according to the importance of the work position of an applicant for the interests of the national economy. Applicants were also not allowed to have permanent residence in the district in which they were applying for a flat, and the chances for allocation increased for married couples living separately or applicants living in flats with unhealthy conditions. Registers were organized according to a point system of ranking and were made public twice a year.

Scholars, housing experts, officials at local and regional levels, and in the end the interviewees themselves agree that there were no strict guidelines for the interpretation of the housing allocation rules. In fact, their lack of transparency often led to manipulation with the existing housing stock and to a prevalence of unofficial criteria of which one of the most common was party membership. Bribery and the black market were also quite common in the sector of housing. According to some experts, housing allocation therefore served primarily as a means of social and political control.[9]

As far as ownership was concerned, it developed into a specific mutation in the form of the so-called rights-of-use of state socialist property. It was transferable to children and relatives and it guaranteed its holder the right of occupancy. Since housing for extracting profit was made impossible in communist Czechoslovakia, the right of occupancy in real life in many respects equaled ownership.

Housing Typology in Communist Czechoslovakia

There were four types of housing tenure in communist Czechoslovakia: state housing, company housing, cooperative housing, and private family homes built and occupied by the owner.

The state was the main housing developer immediately after WWII (see Table 3), but housing soon became one of the key problems of the establishment. The housing deficit was most acute in the 1960s. The existing housing stock was old and inconvenient (in 1970, 20 percent of the existing inhabited housing stock was built before 1900, 39 percent in the period of 1900–48, and only 19 percent in the period of 1948–60)[10] and of a low standard (e.g., at the end of the 1960s, only 49 percent of flats in Czechoslovakia had a water supply and only every third flat was equipped with a bathroom with a toilet).[11] From a demographic point of view, the rise of housing demand can also be connected to a remarkable baby boom in the 1970s.[12] Housing was also characterized by high construction costs and low and heavily subsidized rents (in accordance with the ideology of general affordability).[13]

Looking at the situation from the tenants' point of view, we can see that obtaining a flat was a difficult and sometimes even an adventurous task. Waiting lists became extremely long,[14] especially in the normalization period due to a general shortage of flats. The regime was therefore compelled to introduce new developers to solve the housing issue.

The first implemented alternative was company housing, which formally belonged to the state-owned housing stock. The allocation of housing by companies was not usually connected with long waiting lists or with problems known from the municipal and cooperative sectors, although companies also kept registers. The main purpose of company investments in housing was to eliminate or at least restrict labor fluctuation. Because of general housing scarcity in the normalization period, company housing was quite an efficient method to convince workers not to change jobs. Moreover, employers often offered interest-free loans if the employee signed a contract to stay with the company for a certain period of time. As with state housing, the right-to-use decree guaranteed an unlimited right of occupancy, which was transferable to children or relatives. Low rents remained the same during almost the entire period of normalization. Companies were a strong provider of housing during the 1970s, but in the 1980s they were surpassed by cooperative schemes (see Table 3).

Table 3 Dwellings Completed by Developer A, 1948–89[a]

Period	Total	Communal (state) (percent)	Cooperative (percent)	Company and kolkhoz (percent)	Owner-occ. family houses (percent)
1945–50	110.245	72.6	0	0	27.4
1951–56	196.114	73.4	0	0	26.6
1956–60	314.031	57.5	3.2	2.0	37.3
1961–65	408.561	36.8	27.7	6.2	29.3
1966–70	439.185	18.0	48.5	8.5	24.9
1971–75	615.199	20.4	30.7	21.7	27.2
1976–80	648.218	23.0	30.5	17.8	28.7
1981–85	485.000	19.3	43.5	3.6	32.8

[a]*Source*: Johan Jeroen De Deken, *Social Policy in Postwar Czechoslovakia. The Development of Old-Age Pensions and Housing Policies during the Period 1945–1989*. Florence: European University Institute, 1994, 112. On the other hand, obtaining housing was quite affordable. No input expenses connected with allocated dwelling by the state were necessary. Moreover, during normalization, the state offered generous low interest loans to certain strata of the population, for example, young families and newly-weds were entitled to some types of non-irrevocable loans.

Cooperative housing became an important option in the 1960s and further on in the normalization period as well. Together with owner-occupied houses, it represented the non-state housing sector. Cooperative building production was funded by membership fees, state subsidies, and bank loans and it was introduced primarily to speed up construction through the use of the financial resources of the citizens.[15] At the beginning of the 1970s, the number of cooperative members rapidly increased, which resulted in establishing a new form of cooperative house construction where a part of the financial contribution was substituted by personal labor (the so-called do-it-yourself scheme).[16] For the members it usually meant working at the construction site during the weekends and in their free time for several years. It involved a number of additional problems connected with obtaining building material, machinery, and equipment. Moreover, cooperative housing was more expensive because members had to cover all the operating costs themselves. However, in the 1960–90 period, cooperatives were the most dominant developers (see Table 3) with 19 percent of the entire 1991 housing stock.[17]

Owner-occupied houses remained the second most important form of tenure during normalization. Building a private home was possible, but due to general scarcity, it was difficult to acquire material, labor, and machinery. This situation often led to bribery and the mobilization of informal networks, used both for obtaining material and for services. Family houses were left only for personal use and were limited to a maximum size of five rooms or 120 sqm.[18] The building of private houses was typical of smaller settlements and villages. The construction rate also rose in the 1960s due to state subsidies in this sector. This category also includes secondary homes (cottages and weekend houses) that were very popular with a considerable part of the Czechoslovak population (according to a 1980 census, 10.5 percent of all households owned a second dwelling), also because they were quite affordable.

Housing in the So-called Normalization Period

As was already mentioned, the housing shortage in Czechoslovakia reached its peak during the 1960s. The situation in the capital became almost unbearable due to rapid urbanization and overcrowded (mostly standardized two-room) flats became a "normality" for many citizens.

The state reacted to the housing need with a program of extensive construction of mainly high-rise buildings and corresponding housing estates (*sídliště*) and this remained at the core of the state housing policy during the whole period of normalization. Ambitious government plans for dealing with the housing shortage were enabled by new building technologies—industrialized prefabs or the so-called *panels*, that is, building elements corresponding to the walls in the rooms of the future flats. This soon became the main building method in Czechoslovakia, as well as in most other communist countries.

The construction rate in Prague, and in Czechoslovakia as a whole, reached impressive heights during the 1970s. Almost 20 percent of the present housing stock was built in that period.[19] In 1975, the rate of newly constructed dwellings reached almost 100,000, and most of them are in prefab housing estates. Currently, there are more than one million flats in the Czech Republic in prefab housing estates and every seventh housing estate can be found in the capital.[20]

Housing estates (*paneláky*) built by this method were located mostly on city outskirts or vacant land. They offered an immediate solution to the demand for housing but were of inadequate quality and poorly

Figure 4 An Example of a Panel Housing Estate in Prague, Northern City—Prosek, After Revitalization (2008)

Photo by the author.

Figure 5 A Close Up of the Same Panel Housing Estate

Photo by the author.

maintained. According to some experts, the life expectancy of a prefab flat is a mere generation[21] and at present many such buildings are in need of large and costly reconstructions (Figures 4 and 5). On the other hand, low rents, higher living standards, and also the mere availability of flats were at the time the main reasons for their "popularity."

The panel estates were not only of low quality (e.g., the lack of any sort of heating insulation is worth noting), but also marked by the uniformity of the exteriors (due to so-called crane architecture), which, in combination with the often monstrous dimensions of the housing estates, formed unique panoramas in almost every Czech city and town. At the beginning, the inhabitants had to struggle with some serious problems with the plans, especially due to the lack of employment opportunities in the area and very poor local infrastructure. Nowadays, panel housing estates are a common topic of intellectual and media debates and there are many attempts at their "humanization," which, in a way, reflects the general opinion about socialist housing estates.

On the other hand, the distributive state housing policy during the socialist period never led to any problems of social stratification in prefab housing estates. Since apartments were allocated to families regardless of their income, panel houses (and rental houses in general) were often inhabited by a rich social mix, which is still preserved and this is one of the main factors preventing their "ghettoization" as a lower quality housing stock.

Not only were housing construction and the allocation of dwellings directed centrally by the state; the system oversaw trends in architecture, design, and fashion as well. In the beginning, the communist regime was represented through a specific movement in art and literature—socialist realism, popularly called *sorela*. The main emphasis in *sorela* was placed on the achievements and glory of real socialism.

It can be said that during the period of normalization, Czechoslovak architecture and design were focused on the mass construction of housing estates and the standardized production of consumer items. Uniformity, strict standardization and radical industrialization were the results of both limited funds and the ideology of technological planning and progress. The overall scarcity and centralized production of utilities consequently also led to the uniformity of the interiors, which could be best represented by the widespread use of sectional furniture[22] appropriately named *Universal.*

There were several institutions appointed by the state to oversee these matters of which the most important were the Experimental Institute of Construction and Architecture, which dealt with research of architecture and urbanism,[23] and the Institute for Housing and Clothing Culture.[24]

Housing as an Everyday Life Strategy

"Workers and Intelligentsia" Project

In more than 115 life-story interviews conducted during our project, we encountered a wide range of narratives connected with housing. The field research focused on two strata of Czechoslovak society—manual workers and the "working" intelligentsia, that is, citizens who were productive during the normalization period. The two groups of narrators were initially chosen to compare the lived experience of a social group favored by the regime and one that was placed in the awkward position of balancing on the edge of becoming "bourgeois."

The interviews produced extensive material (approximately six thousand transcribed pages) on everyday life during Czechoslovak communism across two generations (our narrators were born in the period of 1930–60). Life-story interviews consisted of two sessions, the first was open and biographical, the second semi-structured where interviewers focused their attention on several themes connected with both the private and the public life of the narrators—work, family, politics, and free time.

Housing was covered in all of these interviews. The lived experiences could be divided according to two criteria, generational and geographical. Some of our interviewees experienced the postwar housing situation, including the process of nationalization of property, both in the cities and in the countryside. Others were allocated a dwelling that was confiscated after the expulsion of the Sudeten German population. Many of them had experience with the "under-occupancy" regulation or with building private houses, but the majority underwent some kind of process of allocation of apartments. The interviews also differ geographically since the housing conditions in Czechoslovakia were rather different in the capital, in smaller towns, in villages, and according to the location of various sectors of industry. The narratives dealt with all four existing types of housing tenure.

In the following section, I will take a closer look at the life stories of people who were remembering the strategies they had to apply with regard to housing during the last two decades of the communist regime in Czechoslovakia. For the majority of them, these were their first dwellings.

Housing as a Creative Circumvention of Norms

When speaking about housing, the majority of our narrators emphasized that it was a complicated issue that took them many years to solve. Considering the contemporary standards, the most common first step of young couples in need of housing was to apply for a flat at the district's National Committee or to join a cooperative in their place of residence following the advice of parents or relatives. The chances for obtaining a dwelling rose when both partners were members of cooperatives. A certain percent of our narrators also considered themselves to have been "privileged" from the very beginning as they had the opportunity to take over a part of their parents' home.

The second most common strategy was connected with the narrators' chances of employment. As reflected in the interviews, the general shortage of housing had a considerable influence on work mobility. More often than not, an apartment was considered *a conditio sine qua non* when applying for a job. Some of our interviewees accepted a job position only with an employer who offered housing, others intentionally applied for work in regions with better possibilities for obtaining a dwelling (e.g., in the regions with a higher concentration of heavy industry and higher pollution). This strategy was obviously used more by manual workers than by the intelligentsia.

> *HP: So you gave up your previous job . . .*
> *JJ: Yes. . . . The work was interesting, but everyone there wanted a flat. And they couldn't resolve that. . . . They [at the second employer's] solved everything in two hours, you came, gave them your ID, the document from the last employer including the document about your army service. I signed the contract and in about a week I could collect my recruitment benefit and they immediately gave me the decree for the apartment with the information when it would become available, because it was still under construction.*[25]

However, as soon as interviewees obtained "optimal" housing with regard to the contemporary circumstances, their mobility rapidly decreased. Once settled, they did not tend to move, especially those living in family houses. The reasons were not only long waiting periods, time-consuming and costly house constructions, bank loans, and general difficulties with the housing allocation process, but also the institute of the so-called labor force stabilization. Housing was used by companies as an instrument of restriction of work fluctuation. To be allocated a company flat was more than often conditioned by signing a long-term contract (approx. ten years) with the employer.

Moreover, housing law itself was restrictive and it forbade being included on a register of applicants seeking to find a more "suitable" dwelling in the same district (i.e., raising the standard of one's housing for any other reason than the social one). Many of our interviewees (more frequently workers) therefore lived in one place all their lives and also worked for one company until they retired.

Dwellings were usually financed through loans that were offered both by banks and by employers. The loans for newly-weds[26] were particularly popular and the narrators usually used them to furnish their apartments. The possibility of taking out loans and other types of subsidies also served as a motivation when choosing employment and a place of residence. The narrators evaluate this situation both as a privilege and as an anachronism from their current point of view. Subsidies and loans were easily accessible and affordable. In combination with the fact that a job was both an obligation and a right of an employee, taking up loans was not experienced as a stressful commitment and did not bring about feelings of uncertainty for one's future. This is of course a result of the comparison with the current situation: the narrators often considered themselves to be privileged in this respect when reflecting on the problems their children are having with housing: *to them nobody would ever give a flat as they did to us.*[27]

One of the most aggravating circumstances of the communist housing system in Czechoslovakia for young couples was the fact that the allocation of a dwelling was a long process. Narrators frequently report having obtained their own flat as late as a few years after the birth of their children, many years after they had decided to register. Many of them had to bridge this period by living at their parents' houses, living in inadequate conditions (one room for the whole family) or even living separately.

> *When we returned to Prague, we didn't have a place to live, so we had to live at our parents' house. First we lived at my wife's parents, then, when my grandmother died, we lived in her room at my parents' house. In 1987 our second daughter was born and then we lived separately, the older daughter [born in 1980] and I at my parents', and my wife with the younger child at her parents' house. It wasn't so far away, so*

it didn't have that much effect on our lives. And then I finally got a co-operative flat which I had to help build. . . . So, in 1988 we moved to our very first flat.[28]

The family life of this interviewee (and many others) was additionally complicated by the do-it-yourself cooperative scheme in which a part of the expenses for building of a house was covered by engaging cooperative members in the process of construction. It often resulted in the absence of the father of the family from home after work and during weekends. The construction work usually took several years:

I was working at the construction site every Saturday and Sunday, starting from 7 a.m., finishing at about 5 p.m., and this was very unpleasant. I didn't want to, but I had to go. And as I wasn't qualified, I mean, if I had been a brick layer or a plumber I could have done some qualified work at the building site, but I wasn't, so I did only the so-called ancillary jobs. And in the contract it was written that I needed to work off 6,500 crowns which was transferred into hours. I was counted 2,5 crowns for an hour so that was 100 hours for 250 crowns and more than 2,000 hours in total! In the end we had been building that house for five or six years before we could move in.[29]

Construction in general was a very demanding and time-consuming process that complicated the family lives of our narrators. Many of them decided to build a family house, sometimes relying on state subsidies. However, building meant a long struggle that began at the local National Committee, which allocated (or granted permission to sell) building sites and issued building permits. Another great complication was the scarcity of building material and building services. Private building companies did not exist and people were dependent on their own ability and the help of their family or relatives: *And it is quite difficult to build by yourself, even only nailing down a board, you need to find a way to fix it at the other end . . .*[30]

Some items of the building material (mortar, cement, lime, etc.) were produced at home, which prolonged the construction process. Others (bricks, pavers, etc.) required long waiting lists or standing in queues during periods when building material shops announced the availability of goods (people talk about twenty-four-hour long queues as no rare occurrence). Machinery was often borrowed from friends. Building know-how was obtained through manuals and more experienced friends as well. In light of these facts, building was not an easy task. The words of one narrator could be used to character-ize the feelings of everyone who started the construction of a family home and talked about it in this project: *I had nothing, no money, no know-how, only my enthusiasm that kept me going.*[31]

Building a house involved working during the afternoons and week-ends, that is, spending all one's free time at the building site. Families would move in as soon as a room was ready and continued to work on the unfinished parts of the house. Interviewees therefore often refer to construction as drudgery (especially women who had to coordinate minor construction jobs, the household, family, and their own jobs), as periods in their lives they would gladly forget: *I spent the best years of my life in the worst possible way, building a house . . .*[32]

When the house was finished, the problem with interior decoration (furniture, flooring, lighting, pavers, etc.) emerged, as materials were scarce or very often didn't match the taste of the owners. The narra-tors again talk about long queues for equipment or ordering it from distant cities. Moreover, any "above-standard" goods could usually be obtained only through acquaintances and on the black market. One interviewee made a generalization about this situation of overall scarcity: *During communism you didn't buy things; you were scraping them together.*[33]

Many Czech households were therefore similar in appearance in the interior as well. The common strategy of the narrators to combat both the scarcity of materials and the uniformity of appearance was through the development of handicrafts. Men usually assembled the furniture by hand, built shelves, and so on, and women were in charge not only of the embellishment of the household (knitting, crochet) but often sewed much of the household items of everyday use as well, including clothes.

As far as living in prefab estates is concerned, it was more typical for larger cities, especially the capital. It was also common for towns with industrial sectors. The narrators who lived in *panelák* flats usu-ally considered it to be an improvement of their standard of life, due to the bathrooms, central heating, and hot water. The housing estates, especially in smaller towns, were often inhabited by people of the same age, working at the same factory, and were therefore remembered positively by the narrators as a friendly and pleasant environment.

Many of our interviewees were also in possession of a secondary home—a very popular Czech cottage or a weekend house. To many of them they served as the only form of recreation and "escape," as they often called it, both from the urban environment (especially if they had children) and from the work routine. On the other hand, cottages also required a lot of physical maintenance, but many people (particularly those living in the cities) welcomed it as a good form of relaxation. In most cases, the narrators also built the cottages themselves, sometimes together with a family house. Some of them stressed the fact that the fresh fruit and vegetables they produced at their cottages helped their household budgets considerably. Small gardens served the same purpose. A strip of land with a small shed in the vicinity of one's flat was a good compromise to having a cottage. These gardens, usually located on the outskirts of cities, are often being bought out by large private developers these days as building sites for new residential projects.

Housing as a Means of Social and Political Control

When we analyze stories about housing, we often come across decisions that "had to be made." Judged from their present point of view, some narrators admit having made certain "compromises" in order to improve their chances to obtain a dwelling. One of the most common was entering the Communist Party (CP).[34]

Some of the interviewees, especially manual workers employed in the industrial sector, mention that the unofficial policy of their companies was to allocate dwellings primarily to members of the CP and that they were reminded of this fact every time they sought to apply:

> JS: *When you got married, did you live here right from the beginning?*
> EP: *No, no. When we got married, we didn't have an apartment, because my husband wasn't a party member. So they promised it to us but also conditioned it by membership and that didn't happen.*[35]

Another interviewee and his wife stated that they entered the party intentionally in order to "accelerate" their housing application after three refusals:

> JE: *They were constructing apartments here a lot at that time. . . . We lived in one room with my parents and applied for an apartment because we wanted to live alone. And that was an endless process. One, two applications, everyone was getting an apartment except for us and every time we saw who actually got a flat, we were really so mad. They were the friends and lovers of those directors. So finally*

they came to see me and asked if I wanted to become a member. They said, comrade, you are young, you are promising, you have applied three times for an apartment already. Come and join us! So my wife and I, in the end, we joined, we signed. We weren't communists, but we were among them and that was an advantage.

MV: Did you have any duties or was it just the apartment?
JE: No! I didn't join to do politics, I really only wanted an apartment. I am telling you the truth. If I hadn't done that, I wouldn't have gotten the apartment till today.[36]

In light of many other life strategies gathered in this project, it can be seen that housing was often used as a "recruitment instrument" of the party:

JS: What did they try to persuade you with to enter the party?"
EP: Well, with all the advantages. Company flats, recreation possibilities, etc. I never had any of those, but I didn't mind.

JS: Do you think they were successful in persuading other people?
EP: Yes, many, many of them. Many of them got a company flat which was basically for free! They got it for being employed! This is unthinkable today. And my family had to build our apartment. Nobody ever gave us anything.[37]

Of course, not all of our interviewees evaluated their joining the party as a compromise, but many of them explicitly stated that membership helped them considerably in solving their housing problem. Also the mere possibility of being offered a company flat was judged by some narrators (especially workers) as a positive aspect of the contemporary housing policy. One of the narrators even stated it was one of the most important positive aspects of the communist regime as a whole:

JS: So you consider this to be a positive side of socialism? (speaking about housing)
MP: Definitely. Because at least they gave you the possibility to obtain a company flat. Everyone who was a bit diligent and capable was respected by the company and was offered a flat, so they signed the contract with the company for ten years and immediately had an apartment.[38]

On the other hand, narrators from the intelligentsia group usually judged the general principles of housing allocation and policy as "humiliating." A university teacher experienced the whole process of obtaining housing as a moral and economic pressure, because each little "favor," as she called it, of the government had its own price, as in her case the participation in the construction of a public relaxation center in exchange for a building permit.[39]

The state control over the activities of the citizens can also be seen in various institutions founded to serve this purpose. As far as housing was concerned, one of them was the position of the so-called housing confidants, officially in the position of concierge. Housing confidants together with the members of the so-called street committees (an organ of the local branch of the Communist Party) were in charge of handling the reports about applicants for housing to the local National Committees. This "political control at every entrance door" had a considerable effect on the success rate of individual applications. Obviously, it was based on an evaluation of the behavior of the applicant and his/her loyalty to the regime. Similar evaluations were also issued by employers.

Even after the allocation of a state or company dwelling, narrators mentioned the necessity of politically correct behavior, as it was possible to annul the right-to-use decree for the reasons of "general interest of the state." Therefore, a number of our interviewees stated that because of all this, and in some cases, when all other solutions had failed (allocation of a dwelling from the state, company, etc.), they decided to start constructing a family house. It was a solution for those not willing to enter the party or accept other conditions of the state that they considered to be compromising.

The narrators also mentioned that it was not easy to make changes having once obtained a dwelling. An official real estate market did not exist. Flats, houses, and building sites were under the control of the local National Committees and so their "blessing" had to be obtained for any change. In real life this often disabled or considerably complicated the possibility to make free decisions, for example, the choice of a building site or of a particular plot of land, as official registers and waiting lists were kept. People therefore often participated in semiofficial exchanges. The contacts for exchanges of real estate were usually obtained through advertisements in local newspapers, shopping centers, and so on.

Conclusion

For many of our interviewees, their housing situation was an important issue during the so-called normalization period in Czechoslovakia. The strategies individuals and families used in order to obtain a dwelling depended on numerous factors such as profession, age, family background, place of residence, and so on. Based on the interviews, we can conclude that the communist housing system and politics lead toward strong dependence on the state. Paternalism and the overall imposed control postponed the independence of young couples and complicated the creation of individual household units at the very start of family life. The life stories confirm that the allocation of dwellings and the criteria for it can be seen not only as a form of political control, but also as a means of socialization. Bureaucracy made people dependent on arbitrary decisions of state officials but it also put forward certain criteria and preferences (e.g., party membership, marital status, a clean "work and ideology record,") that accelerated the allocation process. Thus, patterns of "normality" were established that contributed to socializing Czechoslovak citizens in the desired direction. On the other hand, it can be seen from our narrators' life stories that the social criteria were often taken into account by the system and this is generally evaluated positively as a social "guarantee."

The housing policies in socialist Czechoslovakia had another interesting impact on the life strategies of its population in connection with housing. The environment of limited possibilities led people toward creativity. Many narrators present their housing situation in the normalization period as a creative struggle in which they had to depend entirely on their own abilities. This in turn led to a form of individualism where no "favors" were expected, people had to rely on themselves and to develop new skills required for construction, decoration, and so forth. However, there were also many downsides to this particular individualism, such as restricted mobility and the tendency to become isolated in dwellings earned after many years and with many difficulties.[40] A form of this isolation was also the well-known phenomenon of Czech cottages and weekend houses (popular interpretation being that people used to take refuge in their private "worlds" there). They were directly related not only to housing, but also to the lack of cultural alternatives and the restrictions on traveling abroad typical of Czechoslovak society in the normalization period.

Notes

1. Financed by the Grant Agency of the Czech Republic under the number (GA ČR) 409/06/0878. Slovakia was not included in the field research.
2. CIVÍN, Jan: Československý komunistický režim v letech 1985–1989. http://www.cepsr.com/clanek.php?ID=244 [uploaded 20/10/2008].
3. Work was proclaimed a duty after the end of WWII. At first it was a part of the postwar construction resolutions. The Communist regime proclaimed work to be a right but it also transformed it into the social duty of every citizen according to the Soviet example. The regime postulated penalties for those who did not comply to this rule and transformed this originally ethical issue into a legislative one.
4. For example, after WWII, the concepts of "under-occupied" and "over-crowded" housing were introduced, which determined 12 sqm as the normal occupational space for a person in a household and were often used to make people give up (a part) of their house.
5. The new elites, the so-called *nomenklatura*, usually occupied real estate at prestigious addresses. A certain percentage of the state housing stock was also reserved for the military forces and the employees of the Ministry of Internal Affairs.
6. Czechoslovak organ of local government.
7. National Committees also provided building land needed for construction, approved any sort of private family house construction, and handled the confiscations from "capitalists and collaborators" after WWII.
8. *Zákon č. 41/1964 Sb.*
9. Christian Donner, *Housing Policies in Central Eastern Europe*. Vienna: Christian Donner, 2006, 37.
10. Lenka Kalinová, *Sociální reforma a sociální realita v Československu v šedesátých letech* [*Social Reforms and Social Realities in Czechoslovakia*], Praha: VŠE, 1999, 72.
11. Cyril Říha, "V čem je panelák kamarádem?," in: *Husákovo 3+1*. [Husák's 3+1], eds. Lada Hubátová-Vacková and Cyril Říha, Praha: VŠUP, 2007, 20.
12. One generation later, the situation is being repeated since the generation of so-called Husák's babies (Gustáv Husák was the president of Czechoslovakia in the period 1975–89) born during the 1970s, are currently in need of housing that causes a major housing demand in the Czech Republic at the present moment (2009).
13. Rents for the normalization period were stipulated by the 1964 Housing Act on Housing Management, which remained in effect until 1991 despite the price and wage increases. Rents therefore usually covered only half of the actual operating costs (Donner, *Housing Policies*, p. 37).
14. The 1968 sources mention ten to twelve years of waiting, while in the 1970s twenty years of waiting was no exception.
15. De Deken, *Social Policy*, 109.
16. *Svépomocná družstva.*
17. Donner, *Housing Policies*, 72.
18. Ibid., 37.

19. Říha, "V čem je panelák," 20.
20. Ibid., 18.
21. Ibid., 22.
22. Sectional furniture was a type of component furniture massively produced and used in households during the period of normalization. It was easy to assemble and dismantle and made creative solutions possible depending on the needs of the household (birth of a child, etc.).
23. *Výzkumný ústav výstavby a architektury.*
24. *Ústav bytové a oděvní kultury.*
25. JJ (male), born in 1947, electrician, now retired.
26. On the other hand, certain strata of society (such as single adults or divorced people) had very low priority with the planners.
27. JŠ (male), born in 1950, electrician. Interviewees' "housing vocabulary" often included words like "obtain" or "get" rather than "purchase," and "give" rather than "sell" or "let."
28. PM (male), born in 1953, surgeon.
29. Ibid.
30. JŠ (male), born in 1950, electrician.
31. SV (male), born in 1945, technician.
32. IB (female), born in 1948, photographer, now retired.
33. JŠ (male), born in 1950, electrician.
34. Another condition that was considerably "raising" applicants' chances of being allocated an apartment was their marital status. Some of our narrators got married very soon after they had met their life partners precisely due to this motivation: *I married basically because I met my husband who had been told he couldn't get a company flat if he wasn't married. They told him to first get married and then hand in the application so we got married.* MP (female), born in 1953, cook.
35. EP (female), born in 1949, manual worker in the automobile industry.
36. JE (male), born in 1948, manual worker in a factory producing sewing machines.
37. EP (female), born in 1949, manual worker in the automobile industry.
38. MP (female), born in 1953, cook.
39. Participation in the so-called Akce Z (voluntary work done by citizens or employees for the embellishment of the environment) was often requested in exchange for such and similar "favors" of the state.
40. We could mention another one, which is more of an aesthetic nature. "Scraping things up" led to the necessity to collect and not throw away anything that could be used creatively in the process of building and adaptation of the dwellings, which in effect turned many of Czechoslovak backyards, basements, and attics into storage areas of possible building material, visible still to this day.

10

The Indifferent, the Obedient, and the Adjusted: Three Women's Narratives about Socialism in Croatia

Sanja Potkonjak

> *There is alchemy that turns the bad things that happened*
> *to us into good things*
> *(Jacques Derrida, in Safaa Fathy,* Derrida's Elsewhere, *1999)*

The thought Jacques Derrida expressed in the biographical movie *Derrida's Elsewhere*[1] can be seen as something like an epigraph to this chapter. In fact, what Derrida said on that occasion, reconciling himself with the most unpleasant events in his own life, was that speech, writing, and "voicing" represented the beginning of convalescence and of a healing of wounds. They would work as a kind of self-healing mechanism that turned bad things into good, negative experience into positive. Derrida referred to this psychological phenomenon as "the optimism of memory." In a way, it implied a paradox, namely, that survival was sustained by both forgetting and remembering.

Based on this idea, my project draws upon the performative acts of women who, through "vocalizing" their histories, have allowed new texts to be narrated and taboos to be disclosed and, subsequently, negotiated with facts glorified into truths by victorious history.

Driving through the busy streets of Zagreb, Croatia, with Bojan, a friend of mine, I told him about the article I was writing on how Tito's culture survived and how I was engaged in research on Tito's cult a year ago. He was pleased and smiled at me. I lost his trust years ago

195

because of my unequivocally cynical attitude toward socialism. My newborn interest in that period pleased him in a certain way.

There were three of us, friends from the immediate neighborhood, growing up together in the late eighties and the beginning of the nineties, when socialism was obviously entering its last phase and the outburst of war was just a matter of time. People were restless, and we were no exception. Bojan was one of those friends. He reminded me, on this occasion, how rigorous I had been at that time, using some naive philosophy to explain to my friends an apparent and obvious fact—that socialism no longer had a future and that it was an illusion we were all supporting in one way or another. We used to quarrel a lot when we were together.

Once, I got a birthday present: a drawing Bojan handed to me (Figure 6). I can imagine him sitting at his father's table copying the image of Yugoslavia, a map of the whole country with no internal borders marking the republics that constituted it, a symbol of the unity Yugoslavia supposedly guaranteed, with a star placed somewhere in the middle of the drawing, and a heart intermingled with the star, which he drew just for me. I see him absorbed and entertained with teaching me a lesson I was distrustful of. Above the illustration, he put Tito's famous slogan "Protect brotherhood and unity like the apple of your eye," and painstakingly went through books to find images of monuments that were meaningful to every Yugoslav in order to draw a symbolic representation of the suffering of the population that Yugoslavia was built upon. Using the words of the Yugoslav anthem as cornerstones of Yugoslavia's earthly appearance on the drawing, he placed the mythical land between the Slovenian Mountain of Triglav, Serbia's Đerdap Canyon, and the Croatian Adriatic Sea. At the heart of Yugoslavia he placed his father's birthplace—Kozara, a region heroic in itself and poetically celebrated in many partisan epics, as I recalled.[2] There was a quiz organized for me on that occasion. In front of the group of loving friends I had to pass an exam, a rite of socialist passage, to confirm whether I was a "traitor" or one of them. I had to name all the monuments and the events that they commemorated. The monuments represented the "seven wonders" of Yugoslav socialism. Everybody was familiar with them and everyone was expected to be introduced to these "memory places." It would have been considered a scandal to disregard them. In short, I failed the quiz. The only monument I could locate in my personal narrative of socialism was that of "Jasenovac"—the most significant in "socialist

Figure 6 Bojan's Drawing: A Map of Yugoslavia with Its Symbols

Author's archive.

vernacular"—erected to commemorate the Jewish, Serbian, Roma, and Croatian communist victims of the interwar fascist government in Croatia. However, the fact that I had failed the quiz, characteristic of my disobedient nature, did not jeopardize my belonging to the group and I remained one of them. In a way, the quiz showed me and them that I had never been properly introduced to the socialist symbolic narrative and to its emblematic common images. Whether this was the fault of the schooling system, my parents, or of my own laziness—in a word, I was a failure. Still, there was hope, as my friends told me. I accepted the facts and promised that I would learn all the symbols by heart. I did not keep the promise. Nevertheless, something prevented me from throwing away the piece of paper I had received on that occasion. Only now, when thinking about it, am I aware of what my friends had put into the drawing, however banal it may seem: a fear of the coming changes, and a need for coherence, structure, and rules, which were provided by the system we lived in. All this was "frozen" in the drawing. Instead of telling me what bothered them, they drew what they believed should not be torn apart. They felt I should not desecrate the memories of our childhood, not even by speaking critically of socialism.

It all came to mind again when I started to think about this chapter. I had to excavate my piles of books and papers to find the drawing. This piece of paper had survived frequent moves and occasional selective fits when the past was on the losing side, and personal artifacts were weighed on the scales of present-day significance and thrown away as bothersome reminders or meaningless chunks of personal prehistory. This drawing lived to tell the tale of my personal relationship to a version of socialism—the intelligibility of the political project I had never interiorized while I lived in it, to borrow Levi-Strauss' phrase. Only after everything had vanished did I start to give meaning to it, to realize that the experience of socialism had marked me for a lifetime. The temporality or worldliness of it had been preserved. I started to struggle against the new and imposed reality I was living in, not allowing my own history to become a myth detached from materiality, unintelligibly obscure, frightening, and unknown. With the eye of a witness, I recollected my past experience and rehabilitated it in a personal history. My new personal narrative was to help sustain individuality and construct selfhood in a struggle with the disciplining "truth" we were beginning to take into consideration as democracy in Croatia demarcated the new culture.

This chapter has a single task. It is a family history as well as an extremely personal insight into three women's views on socialism. It simultaneously looks at the idiosyncrasies of personal female memories as against collective (male) history. For this purpose, I have decided to present my own, my mother's, and my grandmother's life experiences. This text, as every historical account, comes too late to change anything. It traces particular memory curves over which I linger. It is the mystique of the past that I want to undo. In addition, the text explores personal conflicts generated by the oblivion imposed by societal transition and that triggered the process of renegotiation of what life under socialism was. Lastly, with the aim of understanding how and why the everyday life I lived in socialism has become stigmatized, I try to establish the markers of socialism relevant to my family universe, if any. The story is gendered simply because I have chosen to present socialism through the scope of a single family history narrated by women who somehow overruled men in the family. What I hope this chapter will reveal is that society's normalizing mechanisms and private life may have—but equally may not have—gone hand in hand.

Did socialism ever foster individuality and how? Contrary to proclaimed and superimposed socialist uniformity, there was an urge to construct the self beyond the matrix, beyond the frightening "Borg"[3] of socialism that supposedly was all around us, producing a collective experience of reality. There was an urge to construct oneself to sustain an intelligible singularity of personhood. The rigid discipline that we tend to link with socialism, its normalizing superpower, was to some degree disowned by the existence of a parallel world of tacit hierarchy, with implicit social segregation, poetics of individuation, and disruptive voices of political opposition, established as utopia became a lived practice.

Where Has Their Story Gone?

By the time I started writing this text, I was no longer exempt from knowing that there were many competing personal and historical accounts where there had once stood a single universal history. I wondered if reflexivity and reciprocity and the introduction of the personal to open up space for alternative voices while abandoning the hierarchical relationship between the "subject" and the "object" of research were to be productive in any respect. I needed to start where "history and fiction meet," in a meta-academic space, which Mirna Velčić called a "radical autobiography."[4] While history is to no lesser degree a part of my focus, the fixation on the fictitious—where "fictitious" stands for the personal and for the particular endeavor of dethroning history and creating an account of a highly unverifiable and perhaps mythical personal nature—provided me with a powerful tool for handling the tensions between the personally meaningful and the historically corroborated. Embracing the "purposeful" history[5] may feel like opting for a personal myth against the frame of a universal myth, since personal historical narratives are no less prone to mystification. Needless to say, they are an attempt to escape the rigor of the political system, which long ago established what was cognizable and what was experiential. On the other hand, the personal history as a personal and self-delusive myth communicates the need for constructing oneself beyond the mirror image that is already substantiated, always given and taken *a priori*, in the apodictic historical image of the "proper" socialist citizen.

The urge to individualize historical myths came along with the perception that historiography has failed to acknowledge individual experience within socialist cultures. On the other hand, literary accounts such as those of Milan Kundera[6] or Alexander Solzhenitsyn[7] set up a critical model of writing for many East European followers. These records, both fictional and documentary essay crossovers, provided images of individual lives confined within the limits of a political system. Family stories and personal narrative, otherwise hidden from the gaze of the state, became the central phantasm of such writing. In this mythology of the personal, a family framework was set up to uncover the contradictions within the political system, perceived through the lens of a particular generation, family, or individual (see, e.g., Ćosić, who already wrote such an account in 1970).[8] This genre of geopolitical fiction echoed what was unthinkable to be said in public disputes, scientific analyses, or in top-level politics. In other words, while the phenomenology of socialist life entered literature so as to produce the picture of a world not closed to socialist utopia, and while fiction became an alternative form of political speech—a literal subversion, mimicked in fictitious events and persons—there appeared an idea that totalizing experience could be dethroned by the power reclaimed by an individual.

During the years immediately following the political changes in Eastern Europe in the early 1990s, a number of writers drew on their dissident experience of socialism. In this literary genre, Slavenka Drakulić[9] provided a real inventory of socialist imagery and alternative facts and figures, sometimes carrying the joke too far in her endeavor to explore and uncover daily life in socialism with its fascination with food, hygiene, lack of privacy, and mechanisms of state control, depicting her own life and that of her female friends with whom she had shared experiences.

In the case of Dubravka Ugrešić, her writing is concerned with what we perceived as selfhood in socialism after its collapse. In the title of her book, *The Culture of Lies*[10] Ugrešić, who is a postsocialist expatriate, summoned the paradoxes of democracy in her homeland after 1990. She opposed the totalitarian project reified in the new postsocialist truths, rhetorically fixated on the evils of socialism to the point that they annihilated the right of those who lived in socialism to remember themselves and their lives in any other register than that of shame. The experience of Ugrešić, who was forced into political exile by an intolerant public opinion in Croatia and the "democratic" crowd, could obviously not be connected to nascent democracy. Her writing has shown that postsocialism triggered the very same disciplinary mechanisms that could be influenced by individual voice and personal experience. Therefore the autobiographical writing she insists on produces the same outcomes as political fiction in socialism. Paradoxically, the "democratic" outcome was the exclusion of personal experience and the exile of the writer. How then not to be provoked into embracing a personal perspective?

But what is a personal history? Mockery, a revenge of the subjugated, a "real" history that turns general tropes and doubts into the history of a particular agent, actor, or subject? A personal history renegotiates and repositions the subject of history, bringing the subject face to face with the actor of history. Rooted in the idea of political struggle and transferred into a scientific struggle over the power of representation, personal history conveys the "absences."[11]

Beginning with the "absences" and acknowledging the urge to make a history personal, I decided to take recourse to the politics of dissident writing that aims to individualize the truth. So I started by talking with members of my family—my grandmother and my mother—and in the long conversations, which, as it turned out, preceded the interviews, I bombarded them with questions and discussed the idea of writing a chapter on socialism, all in order to persuade the women in my family to talk about themselves, "women in socialism." This job turned my everyday life into an investigation. Every visit my mother paid me grew into an interview. We would watch a documentary on socialism, and

I would ask her to comment on it, provoking and encouraging her to talk about the past. My grandmother was agitated by the recording device I had grown so accustomed to bringing with me on a regular basis that I did not even notice its presence might be intrusive. I never knew when my family members might start talking about something I felt should be recorded. I was amused and intrigued by this self-imposed mission of producing personal "documents" of the past, though other family members started to remark upon my unhealthy interest in socialism, now that it was "finally over."

"Every beginning contains an element of memory,"[12] and as I am not making an exception here, I must begin with my grandmother and my mother who, unlike me, lived a large part of their lives in socialism. This autobiographical text commences with our family's social, cultural, and political experience. It is also partly an attempt to understand things beyond official socialism.

When I try to evoke memories of socialism, I think in colors. The color of this period is red. The whole period is red. And as experience has taught me, this color has become fatigued, worn out, has left the desirable repertoire of political iconography. To "be red" has long gone out of fashion although there are people walking the streets of our towns for whom red is not only the color of their blood. Behind gray suits and tired old faces, once in a while, a youthful idea turns red.

Obviously, something has changed in our perception of socialism and particularly in our self-perception since the fall of socialism. Referring to these changes, Dubravka Ugrešić[13] has rightly pointed out that the "changes" brought about by the war and the new political system, that of democracy and accompanying capitalism, stand as "generator[s] of confusion." Hence, I want to take into account the trajectory of a personal identity, feeling the need to ground myself and my history in family narratives.

The Indifferent

In my attempt to evoke my so-called red childhood in socialism, I had no difficulties in describing everyday life. I met with difficulties when I had to determine my position in regard to the political ideology of socialism. I think I grew up without clear political guidelines. I was born in the 1970s, in a period when socialism in Yugoslavia was going through its second great political crisis,[14] and the revolution was in the process of "eating up its children," as I learned only in the years following the fall of the communist governments in Southeast Europe and the breakdown of Yugoslavia into its constituent parts. Lacking any clear political structures and cultural references to socialism, the communist imaginary of my private perception of socialism was left quite empty. Essentially, I knew nothing about Yugoslav communism, nor about communism in its North Korean, Albanian, or Romanian versions, nor about the repressions to which friends I met later in life had been exposed in the neighboring socialist countries. I learned these things only some ten years after the breakdown. Before that, I was immersed in the media and consumer products of the West, spending my childhood in a diluted and anemic variant of socialism, which had lost its strength, credibility, and charisma. The distinctiveness of a uniform socialist mass culture was diminishing. Socialism no longer denoted a political system sensitive to social issues and justice, but was showing first signs of a quasi-capitalist society whose leading slogan even sounded cynically: "Manage your own business, comrade, and you'll do just fine." At least, this was the guiding principle in my family. In any case, it seems to me that I had lived my life—apart from the youth "Pioneer" ceremony, which, together with the symbolism and thrills intrinsic to any rite of passage, was a socialist one—more or less independently of socialism with a capital, revolutionary "S." I did not connect socialism to the Day of Youth celebration, which I used to await and watch regularly on TV, enjoying the mass performance of exercises for Tito. Nor did I connect it to the Yugoslav performances at the Eurovision Song Contest, nor to the selection of Miss Yugoslavia at the national pageant—all the "typical" cultural manifestations of socialism in the era in which I was growing up. These manifestations of popular culture were just a girlish fad, and since I knew no better, they were just fine.

The first time I traveled abroad was in the fourth grade of primary school when I represented my class in an exchange program that sent Croatian children to Austria. I was mesmerized by what I saw there. At that time, back home, there was an influential British TV series called "Blake's 7," which was broadcast regularly on national TV. Children playing in the school yard would impersonate the characters from the series. We ate "Milka" chocolate at home, and sometimes "Euroblok," a chocolate substitute with a minimum of cocoa added, produced in Yugoslavia. My brother had the newest high-tech toys bought in the West, and I read children's books purchased for me in London. Memories of Humpty-Dumpty, who "sat on the wall" and Mother Goose who "lay golden eggs" still linger in my mind.

From this small-scale perspective, I did not perceive that I was living in socialism. To try to recast these years as a socialist childhood would be an attempt to establish a lie. I was struck more than once with the irrelevance of my memories when I spoke about them with my friends, those who had supposedly shared those years with me. These memories and the way I expressed them never seemed to mean to them what they meant to me. Needless to say, they could hardly recollect the events I was talking about, giving no importance to them in spite of my belief that they were formative and instructive for our lives. The meaning was all mine and had probably been attached to the facts later, but it provided a sense of separateness that pushed me into believing that my friends, I, and other people I knew had very narrow and individual images of the system we had lived in.

On the other hand, I was a child of socialism. In spite of the fact that I had been daydreaming most of the time, some socialist "phenomena" did impact on my life. I experienced socialism as a form of externally imposed humiliation. The most unpleasant things I remember from early childhood were the rationing measures that forced people to infinitely queue in front of shops to buy detergent and coffee or bananas. They certainly—I mean the bananas—could make a difference. When, for example, my family forced me to give a present to my teacher on Women's Day, as was the custom, exotic fruit (pineapple and bananas) would make a difference. The symbolic nature of the gift was replaced by a "real" gift of supplies, and having plenty of supplies generated an aura of prestige. Stores were short of hairspray, and women who wanted a fashionable hairstyle, like my mother, had to buy it in Italy. Under the slogan of egalitarianism, some state institutions worked out strategies of keeping us all the same and these strategies significantly influenced consumer habits in my immediate surroundings. Outwitting the system became the general survival tactic. The rule stated, "One person may purchase only one package of a product." Family reserves were strategically piled up in expectation of a new crisis—my aunt was miraculously skillful in this task. A system of information developed on which store would stock a certain product when and those members of the family with any kind of connection to commerce were highly respected. The paradox of socialism: tradesmen became our best friends and shopping our prime fascination. Shopping was not only the topic of the day but also a way of survival. Society was to be homogenized in an anti-consumer anesthesia against the common enemy—Western capitalism and consumerism—and words like "stabilization," "economic restriction," and "energy crisis" entered lightless homes and my mind. I was brought up in a schizophrenic atmosphere to become cynical about myself. My friends envied me for having things from abroad, and my family was always cautious about my showing off. I was warned not to stick out. But the class structure of socialism had already become evident and I was caught up somewhere in the middle, neither quite like my friends who were less fortunate, nor like those I thought of as exceptionally fortunate. With the fractures, inner divisions, and inequalities everyone could see, it was unclear where socialism really existed. Not in my neighborhood, for sure. Working-class people—if one excludes my parents whose "life skills" had made them a rather peculiar kind of working class—were hardly traceable. National heroes—old ladies who regularly visited my school to saturate children's minds with the sufferings they had undergone in the partisan movement in order for us to be able to enjoy freedom and prosperity in a society of equals, university professors, economists, party officials, and other party beneficiaries—all of them populated our private socialist paradise. It was not that I felt special all the time, but my schoolmates seemed to feel like that about me, think-ing of my family as private entrepreneurs. Living in a house made me different from those who lived in the community housing projects— children would point out the differences our parents preferred not to notice. In my view, I was painfully aware of the differences. My father did not allow me to go to a summer school in the UK as many of his friends' children did. "This would not be appropriate, even wise, as we are just working folk," were his words. The Russian car he used to drive "suited our position"; he was careful not to be singled out and judged for the property he gained. He was full of cautious proverbs and restrictive moves, and was often annoyed with us children who wanted more than he could provide and were never satisfied with what we had. My brother and I were greedy children, self-trained in the smart social skills we saw in our neighborhood: drama group, young botanists, private classes in French, English, skiing, tennis, and ice-skating, Western clothes, and Western toys. My mother supported all the fancy fantasies we had with words like, "A child has to try out what he or she is good at, they have only one childhood, it's mere luck that we are not needy and that we can afford to support them." This commodity-driven childhood made me believe I could do and have anything if I wanted it strongly enough and worked for it hard enough, free of political restraints.

The Obedient

A testimony of another kind, concerning the years immediately after World War II and the lives of alleged collaborators and victims of forced labor, was given by my grandmother, Dobrila. She was born in 1925 in a small village in Central Dalmatia, where she has lived all her life. She belonged to the first generation of socialist women in my family. After primary school, she did not receive any other education. During World War II, she was a teenage girl.[15]

I recall her telling us how her mother used to hide her and her sisters in the attic of their house so that the Italian army officers who lodged in their home would not find the girls and harass them. Over the years, partly on the basis of her own experience, she forged a clear opinion about socialism, although she would express it only in undertones and only when asked directly. She repeated the following statement bitterly in a telephone conversation I had with her about this chapter, as well as in an earlier interview in 2003: "Socialism brought some advantages to the poor and the miserable, the others learned to live with it." This was a cautious phrasing of an alternative definition of socialism my grandmother offered me and maybe even a criticism as well. She put a life of hiding, self-delusion but also of reconciliation into a brief sentence wrapping up more than forty years of her life.

After the end of World War II, when people were divided into those who had won and those who had lost, my grandmother was unlucky. Her family was unable to receive aid since during the war they had made the wrong political choices and decisions. Recalling the first years of World War II, my grandmother pointed out the existence of two categories of people, describing the way the rural community had lived divided into partisans and those who were not: "One became a partisan. Those who didn't [join the partisans] became the authorities." Her father had been seen as such. The authorities were designated from a single standpoint, as comes across in my grandmother's story. For the partisans, "whoever did not join them was an enemy." A middle ground did not exist, "You had to belong, to take sides." In a world divided into two conflicting forces, you either belonged to the "evil side" (fascists, occupation army, Italians, Germans) or you belonged to the "good guys" (partisans). After the war, as a consequence of her father's alliance with the occupying army—after all, they had boarded in his house—he was treated like a traitor. "He was not in favor of the (new) government; he was not for communism . . ."

A visit I paid to my grandmother recently made me believe I had got it all wrong. Her father had been absent from home during the greater part of the war. When the Italian army had first arrived in the village, his property had been confiscated and boarded up, the horses and wagons were taken to the nearby town, and he himself had been forced to serve as an internee and compelled to work in an Italian military garrison. The family received instructions to hide and keep a low profile in the house, while the children were instructed not to take anything from the army officers who moved in. The family was left on its own without the father to take care of them. The children behaved as they were told. They refused food offered to them by the Italian cook. An event my grandmother remembers vividly and laughs about even now when she recalls those years indicates very subtly what kind of rebellion was left to the children. Once, when they were offered some leftovers by a soldier lodging in the house—"an enemy in the likeness of a compassionate friend"—they turned the offer down. The youngest brother, a child himself but "the man of the house," kicked the plate. The soldier had expected gratitude, and his pity for the hungry children turned into rage making him curse them for their stubbornness. His angry words, "piccolo, non mangi pasta, mangi fighi" (*little one, if you don't want to eat pasta [you will] eat figs*—the only food provided abundantly by nature), were repeated in the family whenever someone was too stubborn to take into account his or her evident and immediate interests.

The political decision to house "occupying forces" made by my grandmother's father influenced the family's status after the war and generated a kind of social isolation. Although it is unclear from my family's "history" to what extent they directly paid for the mistaken political decisions taken by the paterfamilias, in the years that followed the constitution of Yugoslavia as a federative and people's republic, male members of the family began to emigrate to other continents, while Dobrila, the eldest daughter, together with her father, experienced the "minor discomfort" of being convicted and sent to a labor camp. No boy from the family was left in the village, only the girls remained— those who should have been spared the rage of the victors.

The family, once well off, now shared poverty as the common fate of the population in the postwar era. During the interview, my grandmother paid great attention to this sort of problem. The girls of the family, facing utmost poverty and lacking both food and clothes, sought help as many others did, from the "new authorities." When describing such situations, my grandmother retains bitterness in her voice to this day:

> The partisan women wouldn't give us anything, just some rags. My sisters and I were the children of the wrong man. An enemy of the partisans. We weren't guilty of anything. Our father had to provide room for the Italians. Our house was the largest in the village and we had enough space. It was logical that the Italian commander would settle there.

Silk clothes brought from America as well as silverware disappeared from the house. I found remnants of the latter a few years ago in the very same attic my grandmother and her sisters used to hide in during the war.

After the war, Dobrila was the only girl from her village to end up in a labor camp on the island of Brač.[16] She was sentenced to work in the quarry at Pučišća because, together with her younger sister, she had been caught collecting firewood in the municipal forest. When the verdict was delivered, she refused to sign a statement that she no longer remembers. Her interpretation of this event has lost its clarity, and what remains is expressed in fragments, incoherently and always bitterly pointing to the circumstances of the trial and her conviction:

> I was punished because they thought that dad did not support communism, wasn't for communism. and so for that I was taken there. There were many of us [before the court]. Everyone was "freed"; only I was [convicted]. Because they [the court] found ... that I should sign ... to extract from me that I had been collecting [wood], and I wouldn't sign and then I was taken there [to the labor camp].

The others, those who signed the papers, were freed of the charges. This signature, in her mind, represented something of a betrayal, a false and forced statement, a humiliating imperative to buy off her freedom. Together with another villager she was taken to the island of Brač in 1948 to serve her sentence.

> We were met by the police and taken to a building. A big building, and beds all around ... a barracks, we called it the storehouse.

Dobrila served three months for stealing communal property—firewood. She remembers that the guards were good to her because she worked hard and did not fall behind the men, although at the time she was still a girl, small and weak.

On Brač, she shared her fate with three other women sentenced to forced labor. They were from the surrounding area: from Vranjic near Split, and from Imotski, while the origin of an elderly woman was not known. The women were housed in a separate building. The place was not enclosed by barbed wire, she recalled, as the island was a barrier itself.

The convicts' working day began in the morning:

> . . . work was at six. It had to be . . . we walked to a bay, there, in the
> quarry; as it was called, "in the cove," where stone was cut. And I
> was [sent] there for eight days. Then he [the guard] orders me to pre-
> pare a bucket of sand and make some cement. And what was that
> for me . . . and he's watching . . . what I'm doing. And so I received a
> commendation . . .

My grandmother believed that the hard work had exculpated her and that the days of physical work in the quarry were over. From then on, she "was in charge of taking food and tea" to the internees. As they "went to work in the quarry every day . . . they would leave their socks with me, to wash them . . . and if they needed to be repaired and so on . . ." The other three women also helped in the kitchen, serving inmates who worked at the quarry, and helped with the laundry.

At the time of conviction, Dobrila was legally an adult and held responsible. Her father proposed to the court authorities that he would serve the sentence instead of her, but this was out of question. In the meantime, he was also sentenced to forced labor in the town of Skradin—for concealing farm produce liable for submission to a government commission. He was able to visit his daughter only once, the only time that the camp authorities allowed him to see her. For her part, Dobrila managed to write only one letter home during the time she served in the camp. Like the girls, the boys in the family had problems too:

> They could not find work in the "zadruga" [cooperative]. Work was
> only for the winners. They had to leave. There were four of them. The
> eldest was born in 1936. And then they fled with their boats to the
> Italian side [of the Adriatic]. Two of them ran away; one concluded

> *a marriage of convenience and the girl drew him down there [to Australia]. The youngest brother stayed in Croatia.*

A few years later, Dobrila married a fisherman, partisan and Stalinist: my grandfather. She had her children baptized in secret in the church of a nearby village when the oldest was thirteen and the youngest nine years old. By that time, she had decided to start working, although this seemed wrong and foolish in her husband's opinion. She could not stand poverty. The only job she could get was in the construction industry: after all, the "country was building itself." Flourishing socialism demanded new tourist resorts and hotels, and workforce was needed. In the following years, she earned her first pay and today she proudly declares that she never gave any of it to her husband. The first thing she bought was a wooden door that she needed for her home. She transported the door on her back, walking a few kilometers from the town where she worked all the way home with the wooden door attached to her back. Also she bought "everything the children needed . . . clothes, food" providing even the pocket money for her youngest when he went to school in the country's capital. She kept her personal views quiet and was an obedient socialist citizen.

The Adjusted

My grandmother had five children, the oldest of whom was a daughter, my mother Nada-Antica, born in 1950. She left her village a few years after she finished primary school, since her father did not approve of girls continuing their education. After a year or two of pointlessly persuading her father to let her go to school, she became weaker in her demands but grew increasingly disobedient. The first time her teacher persuaded her to proceed to high school, her father had grinned at the "offer." Nada-Antica backed down and tried to limit her wishes. She proposed an alternative—a trade school. Her father rejected her request. She retreated further, pleading for a typists' school—appropriate for women, she argued—in order to soften up her father. Since he refused to appreciate the idea of women working, she tried a trick. To talk her father into letting her attend any kind of school, she presented the typists' skill as a welcome and money-earning ability the new system would need. Instead of letting her go to school, however, her father arranged a marriage. The women of the family gathered secretly, and my grandmother arranged for my mother to run away to the capital— far beyond the reach of an angry father. The money my grandmother earned from her job in construction was well spent. A network of aunts and women from the neighborhood organized the trip for my mother, then an 18-year-old girl. This is how Nada-Antica moved to the country's capital, stayed with her father's aunt in full secrecy, started to work in a restaurant owned by a friend of the family, and enrolled in an evening school for adults—a trade school. In 1970, she got married. A year later, she gave birth to her first child—me.

After her retirement, my mother lives in Dalmatia for the greater part of the year. She also agreed to "talk about socialism and how it affected our family." I talked to her at length on the phone; I missed her not being within immediate reach, a confident and comforting ear. The bond we had established and the admiration I had for her strength, all this had made her an important figure in my life. I used to think of myself as a good listener. However, it seems that I was wrong for I never discovered so many family stories prior to my work on this text. In a telephone conversation, which lasted for more than an hour, I faced the fact for the first time in my life that my mother had completed the party school in Kumrovec.[17] It is not that I had no previous knowledge about this part of my family's history. There were family pictures from that period, "souvenirs from Kumrovec," "Mum in a "civil protection" unit,"[18] mother's "party books," notebooks that were dragged around the house, and which my brother and I used to go through without any fear of the contents and without understanding. Ideology had not been part of my (socialist) upbringing. Therefore, my mother's socialist past was a discovery and motivated me to try and understand the difference she made between socialism as an ideology and her everyday life.

In contrast to what one may expect of a former socialist novice like my mother, she could not recall when she had finished the party school. I decided to visit the Croatian State Archive in the hope of digging up some piece of official information on my mother, such as an unsentimental note on her attendance at the party school or perhaps a personal file that would bring her past to life and closer to me. I found out that she was a member of the first generation of students starting their studies at the "Josip Broz Tito" Political School of the Alliance of Communists of Yugoslavia, around 1975–76.[19] My mother's testimony regarding the party school in Kumrovec is "an insider's testimony" and refers to the period of intensive ideologization of society, as I learned when researching the subject.[20] Again, I found her narrative vague, fragmented, devoid of political passion, and strikingly unsophisticated as well as stripped of the importance I had intended to give to the newly discovered facts of her life. She claimed:

> I was in Kumrovec, in the party school. I couldn't follow those lectures. I had little knowledge about these things. Now he [the instructor] spoke about Nietzsche. I simply knew too little to be able to follow.

In her dispassionate narrative, I could not discern the loyalty to the system I had expected, nor the reasons why she had joined the school. How could she have adhered to the political school during those years when any oppositional opinion was prosecuted? This behavior contrasted with everything she had stood for in our family life. Before I started to digest this idea, she continued:

> Every company had to propose a young person for the party school. I wasn't an "omladinac" [a member of the party youth organization] but I was a young person. As such I had to go. I wasn't up to it. You know what it's like to sit among fifty people, and no one understands a thing. You have to have some previous knowledge. I remember a lecture. There was some joint lecture in the municipal building. On the final evening you were supposed to say something . . . a woman made a comment. The rest of us were quiet. So, I remember these uncomfortable situations. It was a school, the "Party School," the youth, members of the party went.

Somewhere in the middle of her testimony, I asked her whether she had been a party member.

> Well naturally, I was a member of the party. I asked your dad what to do. Because a friend from Zaton[21] nominated me. He said he had nominated me. He asked, "Will you become a member of the party?" I came home. I asked "dad" [my father], and he said "well, go . . . ." It was clear to me that if I wanted to advance I had to be a member of the party.

My mother went to the party school for about half a year. I was a small child then, which allowed her the privilege of traveling every day from Zagreb to Kumrovec after work and back to her family in the evening. Mother could not remember exactly when she went to school there, but it was definitely after 1970 when she got her first job. It seemed to her that more men than women attended the school at that time. Everything was very exhausting. After finishing the school, she received a diploma certifying that she "had completed the course." I was confused—"the course," she said, had been a duty, an obligation, there had been no eagerness about it, it was something "she had had to do," a compromise she had made in order to obtain a better position. If I wanted to think about this moment without feeling disappointment, I should deal with it the way she did. It was nothing more than an "adjustment." The art of survival. The socialist propaganda industry and its totalitarian projects were tricked by the time that passed since the revolution. The new socialists seemed to be just tuning in, uttering empty words, doing as the others did, following them, not sticking out, "chameleonizing" to the environment and to a socialist way of life. No socialist education could guarantee socialist practices and views. A stainless, clean memory of what I had expected to be revealed as "real lived" socialism had vanished from my mother's recollections. Nowadays, she implicitly embraces socialism for its social orientation, principle of equality, educational rights, and rights for women.

Following the political changes in the 1990s, her narrative of socialism changed. "Everyone lived about the same, since what we all needed was about the same and the state provided this minimum of sameness," she used to say. Agitated, she condemns the social inequality and poverty she sees today looking at the majority of her fellow citizens.

Somehow, she either did not need or learned not to need more joy, consumer products, life, and experience of wealth when she was living in socialism, as her children did. She adjusted well. The miniature moves she made at home, in the privacy of her family, were but her way of maternally protecting her family from the outside world. Instead of helping her children "adjust," she willingly "provided" for them the illusion of a politically free space to grow up in, a fantasy of a "better tomorrow." To separate the public from the private (person) was her mandate, to raise her children in ignorance (of politics) was her rebellion.

Concluding Remarks: Unwrapping the Biographical

Bringing the socialist legacy back to mind has prompted lively scholarly activity.[22] Crucial to this scholarship has been a strategy that has "extracted" a phenomenology of socialism from mainstream history and pointed to the paths everyday socialism faced in its decline and transition to democracy and capitalism. Predictably, following the decay of the political core of the socialist state, collectivism and uniformity, the voice of the individual has been promoted as the most pertinent means of obtaining an insight into the world of socialist "outcasts." This has invigorated the supremacy of the individual against state-mediated truths. Yet these narratives have been permeated by the total rejection of discourses differing from that of sharp criticism.

To assert that criticism appeared only after the collapse of socialism would not do justice to those "voices" that had already appeared by the late 1980s. At that time, criticism of socialism on the academic as well as on the everyday level became an exclusive form of democratization of the language and political culture of speech, influenced mostly by the weakening of political structure and collective identification with socialism.[23] Public opinion from that moment on was filled with testimonies of dissidence, experiences of victimization, and resistance. Homogeneous collective memory in postsocialist countries has been saturated with personal testimonies up to the point that theory has fought back, calling this confessional trend nothing but a "memory industry," a "craze," or a "boom."[24] On the other hand, feminist historians embracing the strategy of personal narrative have pointed to the empowering effect of testimonies, life stories, and oral history when it comes to voicing women's experiences.[25]

Living with/in hegemony, never reaching the limits but exploring them was a way of existence for ordinary citizens. The system parodied itself, as Alexei Yurchak put it. Speaking of ideological discourse in late Soviet socialism, he distinguished the "meaningful" from the "formulaic." Katherine Verdery[26] conveyed the same notion in her thesis that socialism "functioned" on two separate levels: that of the state and that of the "people"—the "others" in their own state—invoking the paradox of a two-world scheme, the state and its shade, in which people handled socialism in their own ways.

My family story, whose elements contain traces of parody, has made me incapable of analyzing and idealizing the sociability of socialism through "structural nostalgia," and of cherishing an unconditional optimism where the past is concerned. More likely I should conclude that my tranquilizing experience of socialism, the peaceful childhood I enjoyed, made me more prone to see and claim the parodical nature of socialism. The comparison with the experience of previous generations—the "adjustment" my mother made "outside the domestic domain," impersonating a socialist novice in order to "succeed," and my grandmother's performance of the obedient citizen in order to avoid persecution—has helped me go back to finally gain that knowledge. With the help of Bojan's drawing, which evoked in me what I wanted to forget, as well as the retrospective and healing nature of "dissident writing," I felt that it might be possible to overcome the alienation of inexistent personal narrative.

Notes

1. *Derrida's Elsewhere*, documentary film (1999). Director and scriptwriter: Safaa Fathy. Production: Laurent Levole, Isabelle Pragier for Gloria films, La septe/ARTE, Egypt and France.
2. This image of an imposed male genealogy disturbed me, as I had never, or at least prior to this occasion, seen myself in a mythical matrilineal genealogy as daughter of my mother and granddaughter of my grandmother, looking back at my ancestors as if they provided meaning to my existence. My family background was somewhat dispersed. I was not from the heart of Yugoslavia, and I had never invoked an epic ancestry to show my affection, as my friend did. I took it as a slight provocation, due to the obvious "ancestry talk" linked with an established male genealogy. It appeared to take away an illusion of independence and put me in a historical debt to a narrative, an epic domain of history, making me less of an agent of my life than I was willing to accept.
3. Here I borrow an image from popular culture: the idea of a cybernetic collective named "Borg" introduced by the *Star Track* television series. The collective abducts humans and de-individualizes them to annihilate personal agency and provide collective obedience to the ideas of "Borg." The mind-invading strategies of "Borg" and forced obedience turn people into robotic creatures that are unable to think autonomously.
4. Mirna Velčić, *Otisak priče. Intertekstualno proučavanje autobiografije.* Zagreb: August Cesarec, 1991, 127.
5. Ibid.
6. Milan Kundera, *Knjiga smijeha i zaborava* [*The Book of Laughter and Forgetting*], Zagreb: Meandar, 2001.
7. Aleksandar Solženjicin, *Arhipelag gulag. 1918–1956.* Belgrade: Pokušaj književnog istraživanja. I–II. Rad, 1980.
8. Bora Ćosić, *Uloga moje porodice u svetskoj revoluciji* [My Family's Role in the World Revolution], Belgrade: Prosveta, 1970.
9. Slavenka Drakulić, *Sabrani eseji* [*Collected Essays*], Zageb: Profil International, 2005.
10. Dubravka Ugrešić, *The Culture of Lies.* London: Phoenix, 1998.
11. Michel-Rolph Trouillot, *Silencing the Past. Power and the Production of History.* Boston: Beacon Press, 1995.
12. Paul Connerton, *Kako društva pamte* [*How Societies Remember*], Belgrade: Samizdat B92, 2002, 15.
13. Ugrešić, *The Culture of Lies*, 79.
14. According to Croatian historians Radule Knežević and Slaven Ravlić, the decline of socialism became apparent in the early 1970s. Therefore, the Yugoslav Communist Party started a process of re-ideologization. Marxism was once again envisioned as the foundation of education. Political education was promoted by the opening of a political school in Kumrovec (Tito's

birthplace), and left radicalism was on the rise (Radule Knežević, Slaven Ravlić (ed.), *Hrvatska politologija 1962–2002: Preteče, razvojna razdoblja i rezultati* [*Croatian Political Science: Precursors, Development and Results*], Zagreb: Fakultet političkih znanosti, 2002, 27).

15. In WWII, the region where my grandmother lived was marked by the fact that her village belonged to Italy. The relationship between the Independent State of Croatia (NDH), Germany, and Italy in the World War II was characterized by a type of informal government of the newly established Croatian state by the latter two forces. The Independent State of Croatia was actually a German–Italian protectorate. Therefore, "due to the development of the bilateral relationships between the Third Reich and Italy, the Third Reich had logically (. . .) conveyed political influence in NDH to its ally, respecting Italy's attempt to establish a personal union with the NDH. Specific monetary and customs conditions were applied to Dalmatia, one of the annexed regions. The NDH was obliged to exploit natural resources and supply the Italian Army in the demarcation zones, but in doing so, it failed to adequately regulate the status of the population of the annexed regions—their nationality, citizenship and rights as a national minority within the Italian state" (Ivo Goldstein, *Hrvatska 1918–2008*. Zagreb: EPH Liber, 2008, 249, author's translation). The Rome agreements, signed by Italian representatives in 1941, defined the regions of interest to Italy in parts of Croatia that did not belong to the NDH. According to the agreements, "Italy gained rights over almost the entire Croatian coastline (. . .). The largest towns and ports—Split, Šibenik, Trogir and Sušak—became Italian (. . .). (Ibid., 237).
   As far as the immediate post-WWII political situation is concerned, contemporary Croatian history has provided accounts of communist repression. Alternative histories, testimonies, and documents relating to the destinies of the defeated, collaborators, "enemies of the people," and others who were in any respect unwelcome in the newly established political system on the basis of their political, cultural, social, or national background, have been provided only recently (Vladimir Geiger (ed.), *Radni logor Valpovo 1945–1946. Dokumenti*. Osijek: Njemačka narodnosna zajednica, 1999; Vladimir Geiger, "Logorska sudbina Njemica u Hrvatskoj (Jugoslaviji) nakon Drugog svjetskog rata," in: *Zbornik Mire Kolar-Dimitrijević: zbornik radova povodom 70. Rođendana* [*Collection in Honour of Mire Kolar-Dimitrievič on the Occasion of his 70th Birthday*], ed. Damir Agičić, Zagreb: FF Press, 2003, 441–48; Anna Maria Grünfelder, *Zaboravljene žrtve nacionalsocializma i fašizma i robovske radnice* [*Forgotten Victims of National Socialism and Fascism, and Forced Labourers*], Zagreb: Kruh i ruže, Ženska infoteka, 2004, http://www.zinfo.hr/hrvatski/izdavastvo/kruhiruze/kir23/23grunfelder. htm, accessed on July 12, 2005).

16. Recently, research has been conducted on the labor camps and their internees in Croatia during the first year of socialist government. The most influential reports/histories have been compiled by Vladimir Gaiger and Anna Maria Grünfelder (see endnote 15). No research has yet explored the labor camps in Dalmatia.

17. See endnote 3 for the rationale behind the opening of the political school, SKJ "Josip Broz Tito," in the town of Kumrovec. Knežević and Ravlić consider the period from 1962 up to 1974 as the formative years of the establishment of political science in Croatia. Apart from the launch of intensive re-education for party members, young officials, and future leaders in Kumrovec, the period was also marked by the introduction of mandatory Marxism courses at high schools and universities (Knežević, Ravlić, *Hrvatska politologija*, 27). In my mother's opinion, the students at the Kumrovec School were young party members with the prospect of joining union or political life in the future. The school provided them with knowledge about the origin of the Yugoslav Socialist Party, its function, and its role in society. "The school showed us how to act, work, and behave as a young party member," she explained.

18. "*Civilna zaštita*" [civil protection, defense] was a mass organization of civilians for the protection of communities and material goods in time of crises or military attack. According to estimates, around 250,000 people were involved in civilian protection units in Yugoslavia in the 1970s, http://www.duzs.hr/page.aspx?PageID=156.

19. Information from the Croatian State Archives in Zagreb indicates that archival material concerning political parties and stored under the category "Other" contains material from the political school in Kumrovec. A provisional listing of the archival material was made in 2000 following an acquisition dated 1992. The collection contains 455 folders. Apart from documents relating to the first year of the school's operation, the archive is closed to the public due to a thirty-year moratorium (Croatian State Archives, provisional listing of the material of the Political School of the Alliance of Communists of Yugoslavia "Josip Broz Tito").

20. Zaton is a village close to my mother's birthplace. Her immediate boss in the company she worked for came from there. Their shared solidarity resulted from the fact that they came from the same region and thought they should look out for each other.

21. See Knežević, Ravlić, *Hrvatska politologija*.

22. Recently Katherine Verdery, *Šta je bio socijalizam i šta dolazi posle njega?* [*What Was Socialism and What Comes Next*], Belgrade: Edicija Reč, 2005; Alexei Yurchak, "Soviet Hegemony of Form: Everything Was Forever, Until It Was No More," *Comparative Studies in Society and History*, vol. 45 (3), 2003, 480–509; Chris M. Hann, (ed.) *Postsocialism. Ideas, Ideologies and Practices in Eurasia*. London and New York: Routledge, 2002.

23. Renata Salecl, *Protiv ravnodušnosti* [*Against Indifference*] Arkzin, Društvo za teorijsku psihoanalizu, Udruga što, kako i za koga, Zagreb, Sarajevo, 2002, 30.

24. David Berliner, "The Abuses of Memory: Reflections on the Memory Boom in Anthropology," *Anthropological Quarterly*, vol. 78 (1), 2005, 197–211.

25. For example, Krassimira Daskalova in her book *Voices of Their Own. Oral History Interviews of Women*. Sofia: Polis, 2004, publishes the memories of Bulgarian women in socialism; the authors of *Women's Oral History* (2002) embrace testimony and oral history as a female emancipatory strategy,

turning testimony into a form of vital resistance to deadpan and intrusive "great" history: Dolores Delgado Bernal, "Grassroots Leadership Reconceptualized: Chicana Oral Histories and the 1968 East Los Angeles School Blowouts," in: *Women's Oral History. The Frontiers Reader*, eds. Susan Armitage, Patricia Hart, Karen Weathermon. Lincoln and London: University of Nebraska press, 2002, 229. See also Andrea Pető, "Women's Life Stories. Feminist Genealogies in Hungary," in: *Gender Relations in South Eastern Europe: Historical Perspectives on Womanhood and Manhood in 19th and 20th Century*, eds. Miroslav Jovanović and Slobodan Naumović. Belgrade and Graz: Udruženje za društvenu istoriju—iedje 4, 2002, 211–12.

26. Verdery, *Šta je bio socijalizam.*

The Authors

Simina Bădică is a researcher and curator at the Romanian Peasant Museum in Bucharest, where she is in charge of collecting and exhibiting artifacts pertaining to the communist past. She is currently completing her PhD at Central European University, Budapest, on representations of communism in Romanian museums. Her publications are on everyday life, museums, and memory issues in communism and post-communism.

Nadezhda Galabova holds a PhD in History and Theory of Culture awarded in 2009. Her dissertation is on "Socialism and its foreign language: The English Language School in the cultural field of socialist Bulgaria (1950–1989)." Her main fields of interest are oral history, history of everyday life, socialism.

Valentina Gueorguieva, PhD, is an assistant professor at the Department for History and Theory of Culture, St. Kliment Ohridski University of Sofia. Her interests are in the field of everyday life and cultural consumption during socialism, the field of digital media and their use in everyday cultural practices including youth cultures and socialist legacy online.

Ana Hofman is a postdoctoral fellow at the Centre for Interdisciplinary Research at the Scientific Research Centre of Slovenian Academy of Sciences and Arts, Ljubljana, Slovenia. Her research interests include gender politics and music in socialist and postsocialist societies; music in border and conflict areas; music and memory; applied ethnomusicology. She also teaches at the Faculty of Humanities, University of Nova Gorica, and is the director of the Centre for Balkan Music Research in Belgrade, Serbia.

Daniela Koleva is an associate professor at the Department for History and Theory of Culture, St. Kliment Ohridski University of

Sofia. Her research interests are in the field of oral history and anthropology of socialism and the postsocialist transformations, public and personal memory, biographical research, gender, ethnic and religious identities. She has published widely on these topics in international peer-reviewed journals and collective volumes, in addition to two monographs in Bulgarian and a few edited volumes in Bulgarian and English.

Hana Pelikánová is a PhD candidate in Anthropology at the Faculty of Humanities, Charles University, Prague. Her thesis focuses on housing in Czechoslovakia and especially on everyday life in socialist prefabricated housing estates studied on the basis of interviews with long-term inhabitants. Her research interests include also methods of auto/biographical research, memory study, and contemporary history in former communist countries. Currently she teaches Methods of qualitative research and Biographical research at Faculty of Humanities, Charles University.

Tanja Petrović, PhD, is a research fellow at the Scientific Research Center in Ljubljana and assistant professor at the University of Nova Gorica. Her main academic interests lie at the intersection of linguistic, social, and cultural phenomena with emphasis on ideologies and remembering. Her publications include books, articles, and chapters in edited volumes on linguistic and cultural identities and processes in the former Yugoslavia.

Sanja Potkonjak is a senior research assistant in the Department of Ethnology and Cultural Anthropology, Faculty of Humanities and Social Sciences, University of Zagreb, Croatia. Together with Željka Jelavić and Helena Rožman she co-edited the collection *One Border. Two ethnologies?* (Croatian Ethnological Society, 2009). Her current research is focused on postsocialism, public places, and the transformation of socialist aesthetics.

Ewelina Szpak took her MA degree in History at Jagiellonian University in 2004. Her thesis was published as *Między osiedlem I zagrodą. Życie codzienne mieszkańców PGR-ów. (Between a housing estate and a homestead. Everyday life of the residents of PGRs Polish socialist state farms)*, Warsaw, 2005. She specializes in social and cultural history of twentieth-century Poland as well as oral and microhistory. She is a co-author of the oral history manual *Elementarz. Historia mówiona* [Primer. Oral history], Warsaw 2008. She obtained her PhD in 2010 with a thesis on the changes of Polish rural mentality during communism.

Eszter Zsófia Tóth holds a PhD in Hungarian history. She teaches at ELTE University of Arts in Budapest and has a position at the Hungarian National Archive. Her research interests are in the field of Hungarian social history after World War II, oral history, methodological questions, and gender.

Nina Vodopivec is a research fellow at the Institute for Contemporary History in Ljubljana. She holds a PhD in Social Anthropology. In 2007, she published a book *Labirinti postsocializma: socialni spomin tekstilnih delavk in delavcev* (The Labyrinths of Postsocialism: The social memory of textile workers). Her research is focused on industrial workers in socialism and postsocialism, anthropology of postsocialism, organization of labor, meanings of work, memory, and gender studies, particularly in the area of Central/Eastern Europe.

Index